The
SUPREME COURT
and Confessions
of Guilt

The
SUPREME COURT
and Confessions
of Guilt

OTIS H. STEPHENS, JR.

THE UNIVERSITY OF TENNESSEE PRESS
KNOXVILLE

Library of Congress Cataloging in Publication Data

Stephens, Otis H   1936–
    The Supreme Court and confessions of guilt.
    1. Confession (Law)—United States. 2. United
States. Supreme Court. I. Title.
KF9664.S7   345'.73'06   73–8777
ISBN 0–87049–147–4

For Linda

Foreword

A CONTINUING PROBLEM in a free society is the search for a proper balance between the need for order and security and the rights afforded criminal suspects and defendants. Perhaps there can never be a final solution since so much depends on public attitudes, various philosophies of political leaders and judges, and the relative effectiveness of administrative controls of police and prosecution officials.

Each decade since the 1920s has witnessed an increasing concern with the interrogation practices of police and prosecutors. Perhaps the Wickersham reports of the early 1930s mark the watershed. Before that time the American public showed little, if any, concern for the way accused persons were treated; after the reports, more Americans were willing to believe that standards of law enforcement agencies should be raised and that stories of police use of strong-arm tactics and psychological pressure were not myths.

The story which Otis H. Stephens, Jr., unfolds in his valuable study of *The Supreme Court and Confessions of Guilt* is a revealing example of how the supposedly least representative branch of our complex polity, the Supreme Court, tried to draw the balance between order and rights in one specific area. His chronicle shows how the Court's early tentative interventions increased in frequency and intensity with each decade, culminating finally in the controversial decision in *Miranda* v. *Arizona* (1966), where the Court tried to lay down rules for the governance of in-custody interrogations.

It is understandable that this judicial attempt to restrain the police at a time when politicians and the public were expressing anguish over rising crime rates would produce severe criticism and proposals to curtail judicial power. The commentary, pro- and con-Court, on this issue has been voluminous. Unfortunately, much of it is highly technical criticism of specific decisions, and frequently appears in journals of limited circulation. Other discussion is highly polemical, often reflecting the particular bias of the writer arising from his role or status in the legal order. Professor Stephens' balanced and illuminating study avoids the pitfalls of partisanship. It elevates the controversy to the high level it deserves, and, while scholarly in its approach, depicts lucidly the expanding role of the Supreme Court in seeking a more humane and just balance between freedom and order.

Denver, Colorado

WILLIAM M. BEANEY
Professor of Law
College of Law
University of Denver

Acknowledgments

THE WRITING OF THIS BOOK has been greatly facilitated by the individual and collective efforts of many persons. The work was supported at important stages by two grants from the Faculty Research Fund of The University of Tennessee. Initial development of the project owes much to the encouragement of the late Carl Brent Swisher who offered extensive and penetrating comments on parts of chapters two, three, and five drawn from the doctoral dissertation that I wrote under his direction at Johns Hopkins University. Professor Albert B. Saye of the University of Georgia has offered valuable suggestions at every stage of the research and writing.

Professor Jack E. Holmes of Arizona State University made helpful observations on the organization and presentation of survey data summarized in chapter seven. Robert L. Flanders of Macon, Georgia, and J. Lewis Cannon of Auburn University worked closely with me in formulating and administering the questionnaire used for interviewing police detectives. Roger G. Brown of Knoxville, Tennessee, ably assisted by conducting several of the interviews. Attorney Howell W. Ragsdale of Atlanta, Georgia, helped me in arranging interviews with trial judges and lawyers.

A number of friends have provided useful appraisals and suggestions at various stages of the project. In particular I wish to express my appreciation to Professor Robert D. Ward of the Department of History at Georgia Southern College, Professor Joseph G. Cook of The University of Tennessee College of Law, and my colleagues in the Department of Political Science, The University of Tennessee, Knoxville, for their comments and expressions of interest.

Several graduate students in political science at The University of Tennessee have ably assisted me by reviewing portions of the manuscript. Stanley A. Cook, Ronald E. Dean, and William A. Summerford have been especially helpful in this regard. I also wish to thank Miss Jannice Grissom, my undergraduate student assistant, for her extensive work during the final stages of revision. Professor Eleanor Goehring and Miss Angela Stramiello, staff members of The University of Tennessee Graduate and Law Libraries, respectively, greatly facilitated my research by providing ready access to a variety of reference materials.

I also wish to express my appreciation to Mrs. Harriet Lee Hitch who prepared the index, and to Mrs. Kate K. Leake, Mrs. Phyllis J. Price, and Mrs. Irene F. Fansler, who completed the typescript.

Without the steadfast encouragement and comprehensive assistance of my wife, this book could not have been written. My debt to her is incalculable.

Knoxville, Tennessee   Otis H. Stephens, Jr.
November, 1972

Contents

Tables

The
SUPREME COURT
and Confessions
of Guilt

Introduction

AN OPEN SOCIETY is characterized by continuing conflict between legitimate claims of individual rights and public order. This conflict is clearly reflected in the dual responsibilities of law enforcement officers to apprehend and prosecute criminals but in so doing to follow prescribed patterns of procedure designed to protect private individuals against arbitrary treatment by governmental officials. In the United States such responsibilities rest on statutory and constitutional authority and are subject to extensive judicial interpretation. Courts, in effect, make constant adjustments in the dual responsibilities of law enforcement, and, inevitably, some of these efforts arouse bitter resentment.

The most difficult questions here, as in many other areas of public policy, make their way eventually to the United States Supreme Court. Accordingly, although only a tiny fraction of disputes over official conduct ever reaches this tribunal, its decisions receive a lion's share of attention, much of it taking the form of resounding criticism or praise. During the 1960s in particular the Court greatly expanded constitutional requirements governing the administration of criminal justice in general and the investigatory activities of police in particular. This enlargement of procedural safeguards was grounded solidly in provisions of the Bill of Rights, notably the Fourth Amendment restriction on unreasonable search and seizure, the Fifth Amendment immunity against compulsory self-incrimination, and the Sixth Amendment right to the assistance of counsel, each of which by 1964 was fully applicable to the states through the Fourteenth Amendment. Sharp clashes between the competing claims of public order and individual rights were, of course, portrayed in many cases decided long before the recent period of judicial activity in this area. To note only a few examples, the exclusionary rule implementing constitutional restrictions on search and seizure in federal cases dates from 1914.[1] A Court majority recognized as early as 1923 the applicability of a "fair trial" standard to state prosecutions as a basic requirement of the Due Process Clause of the Fourteenth Amendment,[2] and in 1932 extended this requirement to include the guarantee of the assistance of counsel to indigent defendants in capital cases.[3] Four years later the Court had occasion to apply this standard in excluding coerced confessions from evidence in a state trial.[4]

For the most part the Court's early attention centered on spectacular instances of arbitrariness and abuse—the warrantless ransacking of private property for incriminating evidence, use of physical force to obtain confessions of guilt, or detention and trial under the immediate threat of a lynch mob. Since the 1930s the Court has given increasing attention to methods of law enforcement that permit, and in some situations encourage, serious, if less drastic, procedural violations. This shift of emphasis from individual case situations to law enforcement methods has followed a meandering course over the past three decades and, in the 1970s, is far from complete. The Court has continued to rely, although less exclusively, on the due process approach with its accent on the discrete circumstances of individual cases. But by the mid-1960s a majority of the justices seemed to attach greater importance to the conditions that produced procedural violations than to the violations themselves. Thus in 1966, Chief Justice Earl Warren, writing for the Court in *Miranda* v. *Arizona*, could assert that "the very fact of custodial interrogation exacts a heavy toll on individual liberty and trades on the weakness of individuals."[5] Although stopping short of an outright denunciation of private police ques-

---

[1] *Weeks* v. *United States*, 232 U. S. 383.

[2] *Moore* v. *Dempsey*, 261 U. S. 86. For an earlier endorsement of the "fair trial" standard, see the dissenting opinion of Justice Oliver Wendell Holmes, joined by Justice Charles Evans Hughes, in *Frank* v. *Mangum*, 237 U. S. 309, 347 (1915). An excellent summary and analysis of the background of this decision is provided by Clement Charlton Moesley, "The Case of Leo M. Frank, 1913–1915," *Georgia Historical Quarterly* 51 (Mar. 1967), 42–62.

[3] *Powell* v. *Alabama*, 287 U. S. 45, 69.

[4] *Brown* v. *Mississippi*, 297 U. S. 278 (1936).

[5] 384 U. S. 436, 455–56.

tioning in general, the Court here prescribed elaborate rules designed to eliminate the opportunity for resort to coercive tactics. Ironically, these enlarged restrictions on the police came during a time of national alarm over the growth of violent crime and disorder in many American cities—a mood reflected vividly in the "law and order" issue of the 1968 presidential campaign and, indirectly, in the subsequent selection of new Supreme Court personnel, beginning with the appointment of Warren E. Burger as Chief Justice Warren's successor. By the early 1970s a new Court majority was beginning to take a highly sceptical view of judicial restrictions on routine police procedures, thus reemphasizing the uncertainty that has long characterized judicial policy-making in the interrogation field.

Most critics of police administration in the United States have attributed procedural violations among law enforcement officers to the ardor with which they perform their duties and to the lack of education or technical proficiency in sophisticated methods of crime detection.[6] These observers agree that the educational and technical standards of the police have, however, risen significantly since the 1920s, the decade in which major attention was first directed to the widespread presence of illegal methods of law enforcement throughout the United States. On the other hand, sharp disagreement exists as to the amount of illegal police conduct in recent years.[7] It seems clear that the forms of illegality,

[6] See United States Commission on Civil Rights, Bk. Five, *Justice*, 1961; Alan Barth, *The Price of Liberty*, (New York: Viking, 1961), 67. Cf. J. Edgar Hoover, "Civil Liberties and Law Enforcement: The Role of the F. B. I.," *Iowa Law Review* 37 (Winter 1951), 175–95. It is likely, however, that this explanation of the causes of police misconduct is far from complete. Professor Jerome H. Skolnick has questioned the widely held conception of the problem's solution as simply a matter of "changing the quality of people, rather than the philosophies of policing." He argues convincingly that police conduct "may be related in a fundamental way to the character and goals of the institution itself—the duties police are called upon to perform, associated with the assumptions of the system of legal justice—and that it may not be men who are good or bad, so much as the premises and design of the system in which they find themselves." *Justice Without Trial: Law Enforcement in a Democratic Society*, (New York: Wiley, 1966), 4, 5.

[7] In a 1967 study one critic of police malpractice in the United States acknowledged that, although police brutality was once "an institutional pattern and most of the officers on a given force used totally unnecessary violence, open brutality is now an infrequent, isolated occurrence, the result of an individual officer's lack of restraint." Ed Cray, *Big Blue Line: Police Power vs. Human Rights* (New York:

whatever their extent, have, for the most part, become less extreme. The use of overt physical violence has largely given way to the employment of more subtle kinds of pressure. "Psychological persuasion" has replaced the rubber hose in the interrogation room, and sensitive techniques of surveillance have in part replaced strong-arm tactics in the realm of search and seizure. Yet despite these changes of tone and technique, police malpractice has persisted. It is not surprising that a Supreme Court, increasingly committed during the fifties and sixties to the ideals of individual freedom and equality, would find ample opportunity to raise and sharpen the formal requirements of criminal procedure at all levels of law enforcement.

Growing Supreme Court involvement in this area naturally aroused bitter resentment in law enforcement circles—resentment that often took the form of a sharp counterattack in which the Court was labeled a collective coddler of criminals. Strong opposition was also voiced by many private individuals and groups. Recent congressional efforts to overrule interrogation and lineup identification requirements in federal law enforcement, for example, received strong popular support, despite their doubtful constitutionality.[8] While in recent years criticism may have overshadowed applause, Court performance in expanding procedural safeguards has drawn praise, not only from organized defenders of civil rights and liberties, but also from many legal scholars and other members of the academic community.

For the most part, however, political scientists, law professors, and other students of the Court have sought to avoid the extremes of controversy by systematically analyzing decisions, placing them in historical and philosophical perspective, or identifying patterns of intra-Court cleavage.[9] Several studies have also given attention

---

Coward-McCann, 1967), 10. For a somewhat more sceptical assessment, see H. Frank Way, Jr., *Liberty in the Balance: Current Issues in Civil Liberties* (New York: McGraw Hill, 1964), Ch. 5.

[8] Act of June 19, 1968, Public Law No. 90–351, Title II, Sec. 3501A, 82 Stat. 210. For an indication of the intensity of controversy in this area, see U. S., Congress, Senate, *Controlling Crime Through More Effective Law Enforcement*, Hearings before the Subcommittee on Criminal Laws and Procedures of the Committee on the Judiciary, 90 Cong., 1 sess., 1967, pp. 4, 259, 1173.

[9] To cite a few examples of these forms of analysis, see David Fellman, *The De-*

to the policy implications of major decisions both for the administration of criminal justice and for the many roles of the Court
within the American political system.[10] This book pursues these
objectives by examining the Court's development of standards
controlling the admissibility of confessions, admissions, and related forms of evidence obtained by police interrogation. Emphasis is placed on the rationale and impact of the *Miranda* ruling,
and the apparent effect of the ensuing public reaction upon the
Court's criminal justice priorities in the early 1970s. Origins and
early enlargement of judicial requirements in the confession field
are analyzed in detail and are placed within the broader setting of
Supreme Court activity in the realm of criminal procedure.

Prior to the mid-1960s decisions on the admissibility of confessions fell into two broad categories: (1) federal cases resting either
on the Fifth Amendment restriction against self-incrimination
or the Court's extraconstitutional supervisory authority over the
administration of criminal justice in federal courts; (2) state
cases governed by the Due Process Clause of the Fourteenth
Amendment. Separate and fairly extensive sets of requirements
were articulated for each of these categories. Decisions enlarging the right to counsel in state cases and applying the Self-
incrimination Clause to the state via the Fourteenth Amendment

---

fendant's Rights (New York: Rinehart, 1958); Jacob W. Landynski, *Search and
Seizure and the Supreme Court: A Study in Constitutional Interpretation* (Balti-
more: Johns Hopkins, 1966); Walter F. Murphy, *Wiretapping on Trial: A Case
Study in the Judicial Process* (New York: Random, 1965); Anthony Lewis, *Gid-
eon's Trumpet* (New York: Random, 1964); Fred P. Graham, *The Self-Inflicted
Wound* (New York: Macmillan, 1970); B. James George, ed., *A New Look at
Confessions: Escobedo—the Second Round* (Ann Arbor: Institute of Continuing
Legal Education, 1967); Walter V. Schaefer, *The Suspect and Society: Criminal
Procedure and Converging Constitutional Doctrines*, 1966 Rosenthal Lectures,
Northwestern University School of Law (Evanston: Northwestern Univ. Press,
1967); Lawrence Herman, "The Supreme Court and Restrictions on Police Inter-
rogation," *Ohio State Law Journal* 25 (Fall 1964), 449–500; Arthur E. Suther-
land, "Crime and Confession," *Harvard Law Review* 79 (Nov. 1965), 21–41.

[10] This focus is represented by: Richard J. Medalie, Leonard Zeitz, and Paul
Alexander, "Custodial Police Interrogation in Our Nation's Capital: The Attempt
to Implement *Miranda*," *Michigan Law Review* 66 (May 1968), 1347–1422. See
generally Theodore L. Becker, ed., *The Impact of Supreme Court Decisions* (New
York: Oxford Univ. Press, 1969), and Stephen L. Wasby, *The Impact of the
United States Supreme Court—Some Perspectives* (Homewood, Illinois: Dorsey
Press, 1970).

paved the way for abandonment of these distinctions.[11] By 1966 virtually all differences between state and federal standards of confession admissibility were erased.[12]

Early chapters of this book will trace and analyze the numerous and sometimes conflicting lines of development that merged in the *Miranda* decision. Substantive analysis of Court opinions is supplemented by the identification of voting blocs characteristic of many of these decisions. Later chapters examine the Warren Court's enlargement of police interrogation requirements, congressional response to this activity, and empirical studies designed to assess the impact of these requirements on certain law enforcement agencies. In addition to a general review of published findings respecting the impact of recent interrogation requirements, systematic surveys of police departments in two southern cities were conducted as a part of this study. The results of these surveys are reported and evaluated in chapter seven.

As in any work of this kind, a number of assumptions and attitudes about the Supreme Court—its capacity to resolve basic conflicts, its interaction with other agencies of government and with public opinion—strongly influence analysis and evaluation. In the interest of clarity, these views are stated as fully as possible at the outset: I assume that most of the decisions examined in the following pages are statements of public policy as well as authoritative interpretations of the basic law and see no necessary conflict or clear division between these categories. I assume that since the Court has extensive control over its own docket, it can and does choose, within broad limits, the kinds of cases it wishes to decide. The Court must, of course, pay attention to the circumstances of particular cases, but it is decidedly not the passive judicial agency described by some of its observers. I assume further that the justices of the Supreme Court inevitably make law through the process of deciding cases that require constitutional, statutory, and other types of formal interpretation. This law-making function may be peripheral to the central task of legal interpretation, but it has

---

[11] See especially *Gideon* v. *Wainwright*, 372 U. S. 335 (1963); *Malloy* v. *Hogan*, 378 U. S. 1 (1964); *Murphy* v. *Waterfront Commission*, 378 U. S. 52 (1964).
[12] See *Miranda* v. *Arizona*, 384 U. S. 436.

major implications of a political character. I assume that the Supreme Court participates in the political process; that this participation is an integral part of its broad role in formulating public policy at all levels of government; but that its political participation is conditioned by an elaborate legal framework in which rule and precedent play a crucial part. Thus I do not subscribe to the view that the Court's involvement in the political process is indistinguishable from that of the Congress or the President. I assume the existence of distinct legal and political elements in the judicial process and believe that their interaction gives a unique quality to the performance of appellate courts in general and the Supreme Court in particular. Finally, I assume that Supreme Court decisions in the field of confessions and police interrogation admirably represent the ideals of an open society, but that as formulations of public policy they have limited practical effectiveness. While implementation is not the only criterion by which to evaluate the influence and importance of a Supreme Court decision, this factor deserves more systematic attention than students of the Court have traditionally accorded it.

2

Background of Legal Restraint

SUPREME COURT REVIEW of state and federal convictions based in whole or in part on coerced confessions was initially directed, for the most part, toward condemnation of "third degree" practices of the police. The "third degree" has been defined as "the employment of methods which inflict suffering, physical or mental, upon a person in order to obtain information about a crime."[1] The Court's attention has shifted in recent years to milder forms of police pressure, but the element of psychological coercion, real or potential, remains of central importance. The "information" thus sought by the police has traditionally been in the form of a confession or admission of guilt from the person under interrogation or the naming of another person as the guilty party. An individual forced to make a confession, either through physical compulsion or psychological pressure, has a number of at least theoretical grounds for seeking judicial protection. He may, for example, bring a suit for damages against the police officers who forced his confession. This civil remedy has, however, proved inadequate and impractical. In the first place, the victims of police malpractice have traditionally been the underdogs of society—the uneducated, the poor, and the uninfluential. Such individuals are rarely able to bring civil actions against police officers. Secondly, the contentions of a suspect are almost certain to be difficult to substantiate, since in most instances law enforcement officers firmly and persuasively deny that force has been used to obtain incriminating statements. They are often able to make such denials confidently, because the "third degree" and milder forms of persuasion are usually admin-

[1] National Commission on Law Observance and Enforcement, *Report on Lawlessness in Law Enforcement* (Washington, D. C.: United States Government Printing Office, 1931), 2.

istered in private, witnessed only by the police themselves. A third limitation on the feasibility of damage suits is the uncertainty of compensation even if a judgment is obtained in the plaintiff's favor. Police salaries are notoriously low, and officers are thus likely to be unable to pay the amounts assessed by the courts. As for compensation from the employing government, no uniform rule exists at state and local levels making the units of government financially liable for the misconduct of public officials in performing their duties.[2]

Another possible remedy available to the suspect is judicial release by means of the writ of habeas corpus. The granting of this writ can free him from illegal detention, but obviously the remedy is available only if it is known that the suspect is in the custody of the police. Since illegal detention may be secret and incommunicado in nature, the suspect's family, friends, or lawyer may not have such knowledge. The victim of this kind of arbitrary treatment is not likely to be one of the leading figures of organized crime with constant access to skilled legal counsel and may be acquainted with no attorney at all. Furthermore, if the intent of the police is secret detention and questioning, the formal requirements of warning and waiver prior to interrogation, as set forth by the Supreme Court, are, as a practical matter, irrelevant. The writ of habeas corpus therefore provides, at best, only a marginal remedy for this kind of police abuse of procedural rights.

A third possible remedy is provided by federal civil rights statutes, under which the Department of Justice may bring criminal action against state or local law enforcement officials for mistreating a suspect.[3] A few such prosecutions have occurred in recent years, though only one of these cases involving admitted extortion of a confession has reached the Supreme Court.[4] Despite sharply increased federal funds in support of local law enforcement, the

---

[2] For a discussion of this and related difficulties in obtaining redress for malpractice, see Ed Cray, *Big Blue Line*, Ch. 11. See also Delmar Karlen *et al., Anglo-American Criminal Justice* (New York: Oxford Univ. Press, 1967), Ch. 1.

[3] See 18 U. S. C. 241–42 (1964).

[4] *Williams* v. *United States*, 341 U. S. 97 (1951). Cf. *Screws* v. *United States*, 325 U. S. 91 (1945).

artment of Justice has not thus far undertaken a vigorous cam-
ɟn against police misconduct.[5] Accordingly, the criminal sus-
ct cannot rely very heavily upon the assistance of the federal
government in his challenge of illegal methods of law enforcement
at city and county levels where such practices are most frequent.

The most common legal sanction against undue police pressure
in the questioning of suspects has been the challenge of the admissibility of evidence thus obtained. Often this evidence is in the
form of a signed confession, but it may consist of a variety of other
statements, exculpatory or inculpatory. It may also include derivative evidence (a murder weapon, for example) obtained as a result of statements made by the suspect. The Supreme Court has
been far more explicit in developing uniform requirements governing the admissibility of confessions and related statements than in
determining the status of derivative evidence.[6] Doubt remains, in
fact, about whether even the far-reaching requirements of *Miranda* v. *Arizona* apply to this form of evidence.[7] While this study
deals almost exclusively with what the Court has done in develop-

[5] Title I of the Omnibus Crime Control and Safe Streets Act of 1968 (82 Stat.
210) authorized the appropriation of $100,111,000 in fiscal 1969 and $300,000,000
in fiscal 1970 for improvement of state and local police agencies and law enforcement methods. For summary and analysis of this legislation, see *Crime and Justice
in America*. 2d ed. (Washington, D. C.: Congressional Quarterly Service, Dec.
1968), 32–34, 44.

[6] For a discussion of the derivative evidence problem, see B. James George, ed.,
A New Look at Confessions, Pt. 3. See also annotation, 12 L. Ed. 2d 1340, 1341
(1964).

[7] As Professor George, among others, has pointed out, one sentence in Chief
Justice Warren's majority opinion in *Miranda* might support the existence of a
derivative evidence rule: "But unless and until such warning and waiver are demonstrated by the prosecution at trial, no evidence obtained as a result of interrogation
can be used against 'the defendant' " (384 U. S., at 479). George argued, however,
that Warren's opinion is inconclusive on this point. "If the Court wants a derivative evidence rule it should say so explicitly in a case that directly presents the
question on its facts." B. James George, ed., *A New Look at Confessions*, 122, 124.
Professor Yale Kamisar, another recognized authority in this field, insisted that a
derivative evidence rule was clearly implicit in the *Miranda* decision and pointed
out that the dissenting justices obviously assumed its presence. He argued that if the
decision "is to make any sense," if it "is to be taken seriously," and if it is "to be
afforded a real chance of deterring objectionable and impermissible police interrogation practices, then the stolen property and the murder weapon and other physical
evidence obtained as a result of these inadmissible statements must be thrown out."
Ibid., at 150.

ing standards of admissibility in the field of confessions and police interrogation, one should keep in mind the existence of such interrelated areas, largely untouched by its decisions.

In addition to its development of safeguards against coerced confessions, the Supreme Court has also endorsed the evidentiary rule requiring corroboration of any extrajudicial confession, admission, or other statement made by the defendant and later introduced as evidence of guilt. Two variations of this rule have emerged: one stressing corroboration of the truth or reliability of the confession; the other requiring independent proof "tending to establish the corpus delicti, that is, the fact that the crime charged has been committed."[8] While most American courts have tended to favor the latter variation, nothing approaching unanimity has been reached, and confusion seems to have been produced by failure to differentiate clearly between these two formulations of the rule.[9] This ambivalence has been reflected in Supreme Court decisions. For example, in *Smith* v. *United States,* the Court regarded corroboration sufficient, in a case of income tax fraud, if it merely buttressed the truth of the defendant's admissions. Justice Tom C. Clark pointed out that the rule was grounded "in a long history of judicial experience with confessions and in the realization that sound law enforcement requires police investigations which extend beyond the words of the accused."[10] But in the later case of *Wong Sun* v. *United States,* Justice William J. Brennan, Jr., writing for the majority, stated that: "Where the crime involves physical damage to person or property, the prosecution must generally show that the injury for which the accused confesses responsibility did in fact occur and that some person was criminally culpable."[11] Despite this apparent equiv-

---

[8] Charles T. McCormick, *Handbook of the Law of Evidence.* 1st ed. (St. Paul: West Publishing Company, 1954), Sec. 110.

[9] For general background, see John H. Wigmore, A *Treatise on the Anglo-American System of Evidence in Trials at Common Law,* 3d ed., vol. 7 (Boston: Little, 1940), secs. 2070–71. For more recent developments, see *ibid.* (Supp. 1970); and Edward W. Cleary, *McCormick's Handbook of the Law of Evidence,* 2d ed. (St. Paul: West Publishing Company, 1972), sec. 158.

[10] 348 U. S. 147, 153 (1954).

[11] 371 U. S. 471, 489 n. 15 (1963).

ocation, the Court's endorsement of the corroboration rule underscores the sceptical view that it has long taken toward the out-of-court confession as a basis of criminal conviction.

Over the years the Supreme Court has reviewed numerous challenges of confessions on a variety of grounds. These include (1) evidentiary rules originating in English common law; (2) constitutional requirements implicit in the guarantee against self-incrimination, the right to the assistance of counsel, and the broad concept of due process of law; and (3) the Court's extraconstitutional supervisory power over the administration of criminal justice in the federal courts. In state prosecutions prior to the mid-1960s, such contentions centered around the broad requirements of the Due Process Clause of the Fourteenth Amendment. Emphasis was placed on the "voluntariness" of a challenged statement, the alleged circumstances of coercion, and the supposed ability of the suspect to withstand police pressure. In determining the admissibility of a confession, the Supreme Court generally confines itself to an examination of the undisputed "facts" regarding the detention and interrogation of the accused. Since the defendant's allegations are almost always disputed in whole or in part, he encounters great difficulty in obtaining a favorable decision. If he is successful, however, the Court reverses his conviction and prohibits further use of the challenged confession as evidence of guilt. It is then squarely up to the prosecutor to estimate whether enough admissible evidence remains to justify the time and expense of a new trial. Although this cumbersome procedure affords a greater degree of protection to the accused than other legal remedies, it does not provide an adequate barrier against the use of coercive interrogation methods. The introduction of illegally obtained evidence may go unchallenged in hundreds of trials, irrespective of Supreme Court rulings condemning police misconduct. Moreover, the high proportion of guilty pleas effectively blocks many potential challenges of law enforcement irregularities. On the other hand police malpractice may lead to the reversal of a conviction, despite overwhelming evidence pointing to the defendant's guilt.

In light of these limitations the role of the Supreme Court in the field of confessions and police interrogation should not be accorded an exaggerated degree of significance. Nevertheless, there is danger in moving too far in the opposite direction. Supreme Court decisions may not revolutionize law enforcement practices, but some of them appear to have had an appreciable impact. For example, the Court since the mid-1930s has spoken with unanimity in condemning extreme forms of the "third degree," [12] and we may reasonably assume that its pronouncements have added much weight to the widespread criticism of this form of police brutality.[13] Interviews with prosecutors, defense attorneys, police magistrates, and trial judges in connection with this study support this conclusion.[14] Those interviewed generally agreed that these unanimous decisions, taken together, have established a precise constitutional standard by which state and federal courts have been clearly guided. Moreover, it was generally agreed that these decisions were instrumental in directing critical public attention to the more extreme forms of "third degree" methods of interrogation, long practiced but previously taken for granted in this country.

[12] See *Brown* v. *Mississippi,* 297 U. S. 278 (1936); *Chambers* v. *Florida,* 309 U. S. 227 (1940); *Ward* v. *Texas,* 316 U. S. 547 (1942); *Beecher* v. *Alabama,* 389 U. S. 35 (1967); *Brooks* v. *Florida,* 389 U. S. 413 (1967). In the *Beecher* and *Brooks* cases, Justice Black concurred in the reversal of convictions but did not join the *per curiam* opinions of the Court. Justice Brennan, supported by Chief Justice Warren and Justice Douglas, filed a concurring opinion in the *Beecher* case. These justices did not, however, take exception to the Court's sharp denunciation of the extreme forms of police brutality revealed by the records in these cases.

[13] Criticism of the general problem should not, however, be equated with automatic adherence to the Court's decisions. For a discussion of the limited influence of the Supreme Court's confession rulings on state courts during the pre-*Escobedo-Miranda* period, see H. Frank Way, Jr., "The Supreme Court and State Coerced Confessions," *Journal of Public Law* 12, no. 1 (1963), 53–67.

[14] Interviews in which this question was discussed were conducted during the years 1961–67. The officials interviewed invariably raised much sharper objections to Supreme Court decisions restricting search and seizure or the formal interrogation process itself than to decisions condemning the use of overt physical or psychological coercion. It was generally conceded that the latter rulings contributed to a marked decline in the incidence of traditional "third degree" methods as an accompaniment to questioning. Interview with Judge Emory Niles, Baltimore Supreme Bench, Baltimore, Maryland, Dec. 8, 1961; interview with Harold A. Boney, agent, Federal Bureau of Investigation, Statesboro, Georgia, Aug. 19, 1964; interview with Lewis R. Slaton, Fulton County solicitor-general, Atlanta, Georgia, Feb. 13, 1967; interview with Assistant Chief Joe C. Fowler, Knoxville Police Department, Knoxville, Tennessee, Dec. 6, 1967.

On the other hand, the bulk of empirical research on the impact of recent police interrogation decisions indicates that little important change in law enforcement practices can be attributed to the Court's pronouncements.[15] The Court has failed repeatedly to reach anything approaching full agreement in cases characterized by forms of police pressure less drastic than physical force or overt threats. Private interrogation, conducted intermittently and unaccompanied by violence and other forms of intimidation, has been regarded by a number of justices as a necessary component of criminal investigation. Until the mid-1960s this point of view was endorsed by a Court majority; and since that time it has had the support of no fewer than three members of the Court.[16] Intra-Court disagreement has also arisen over the point separating legitimate interrogation from unconstitutional coercion. Some justices (frequently a majority) have maintained that this distinction should be made largely on the basis of the individual suspect's supposed ability to withstand the pressure of police questioning. Other members of the Court have insisted on condemning as "inherently coercive" sessions of interrogation that exceed a given number of hours or occur in the absence of formal warnings of the right to remain silent and the right to the presence of an attorney.[17]

[15] See, for example, Medalie, Zeitz, and Alexander, "Custodial Police Interrogation in Our Nation's Capital," 1347–1422; Richard H. Seeburger and R. Stanton Wettick, Jr., "*Miranda* in Pittsburgh—A Statistical Study," *University of Pittsburgh Law Review* 29 (Oct. 1967), 1–26; "Interrogations in New Haven: The Impact of *Miranda*," *Yale Law Journal* 76 (July 1967), 1521–1648. These studies add support to an observation made several years earlier: "One is led to the reluctant conclusion that the occasional exclusion of an allegedly coerced confession at the trial, or the occasional reversal of a conviction for failure of such exclusion, by an appellate court, including the Supreme Court . . . can have but a peripheral effect on police methods." Lewis Mayers, *The American Legal System*, 2d ed. (New York: Harper, 1964), 50.

[16] Justices Clark, Harlan, Stewart, and White dissented from the Court's extension of interrogation requirements in *Escobedo* v. *Illinois*, 378 U. S. 478 (1964) and *Miranda* v. *Arizona*, 384 U. S. 436 (1966). Justice Clark's successor, Justice Thurgood Marshall, joined the *Miranda* majority, see *Orozco* v. *Texas*, 394 U. S. 324 (1969). Harlan, Stewart, and White continued to express opposition to the new rationale, although in the *Orozco* case Harlan concurred with the majority "purely out of respect for *stare decisis* . . . ." 394 U. S., at 328. Compare the dissenting opinion of Justice White, supported by Justices Harlan and Stewart, in *Mathis* v. *United States*, 391 U. S. 1, 5–8 (1968).

[17] The phrase "inherently coercive" was first used in this context by Justice Black in his majority opinion in *Ashcraft* v. *Tennessee*, 322 U. S. 143, 154 (1944).

This group, constituting a majority during the last seven years of the Warren era, did not attempt to weigh the effect of such questioning on the defendant himself in determining a confession's admissibility.

Current Supreme Court restrictions on the admissibility of confessions bear little resemblance, either in scope or in purpose, to the original English common-law rule excluding involuntary confessions. Yet that rule, as adopted by American courts, served as the earliest basis for Supreme Court decisions in this field. Furthermore, its influence continued long after the Court began to invoke constitutional provisions in condemning coerced confessions. The common-law rule was designed primarily to guard against the introduction of unreliable evidence. It was based on the assumption that a criminal suspect subjected to threats or other forms of intimidation might make a false confession to save himself from further coercion. The common-law rule was thus aimed not at objectionable interrogation practices per se, but at the protection of the defendant against an erroneous conviction. The Supreme Court, on the other hand, has been more concerned with the basic fairness of proceedings against the individual, irrespective of the authenticity of any statement resulting from interrogation. Historically, this shift of emphasis toward standards of fairness, with emphasis on interrogation practices, and away from the "trustworthiness" of confessions, followed an erratic course. For many years the Court vascillated between the dual objectives of formulating policy for law enforcement officials in the realm of interrogation and enunciating evidentiary requirements in particular cases. One result was that, while it seldom recognized the traditional rule against involuntary confessions, it did not formally repudiate this rationale of "trustworthiness" until 1961.[18] In analyzing Supreme Court performance, distinctions between the original confessions rule and modern standards governing police interrogation should be kept clearly in mind. Accordingly, some attention must be given to the origins of the English common-law rule against "involuntary" confessions and its subsequent adoption by courts in the United States. The following summary traces

[18] *Rogers v. Richmond*, 365 U. S. 534.

major developments in broad outline. The details of the rule's gradual emergence in the eighteenth century, the conflicting rationales underlying it, and its indirect connection with the right against self-incrimination, are covered in far greater depth elsewhere.[19] My purpose here is not to duplicate this effort, but rather to provide essential background for an understanding of the role of the United States Supreme Court in developing standards of confession admissibility and police interrogation.

In England and in other western European countries during much of the medieval period, little significance seems to have been accorded to criminal confessions. The guilt or innocence of one suspected of crime was not determined by an elaborate "theory of proof" or in accordance with detailed rules of evidence. Reliance was placed on the outcome of a test of physical strength, prowess, or endurance.[20] Procedures such as "trial by ordeal," "trial by water," and "trial by battle" were thus commonly employed. With the revival of the study of Roman law in England and on the Continent in the twelfth century, however, such practices gradually fell into disuse. Standards of evidence rose appreciably and were accompanied by growing emphasis on the importance of confessions of guilt. Consequently, the use of torture—ample precedent for which could be found in Roman law—became widespread as a means of extracting confessions.[21]

In England, where development of the common law and the jury system minimized the continuing influence of Roman law, torture was perhaps less widely employed than in such countries as France and Spain, where the Roman legal tradition remained strong. Nevertheless, torture was employed in the prosecution of a number of common-law offenses until the beginning of the seventeenth century and in connection with political offenses un-

---

[19] See John H. Wigmore, *Evidence*, vol. 3, secs. 817–19; Charles T. McCormick, *Handbook of the Law of Evidence*, Sec. 75. A more recent treatment of this subject is found in Leonard Levy's scholarly study *Origins of the Fifth Amendment*, (New York: Oxford Univ. Press, 1968), 326–29, 375.

[20] See A. Lawrence Lowell, "The Judicial Use of Torture," *Harvard Law Review* 11 (Nov. and Dec. 1897), 220, 222–28.

[21] *Ibid.*, 220 ff.

til the abolition of the Court of the Star Chamber in 1641.[22] Long after torture was made illegal, however, confessions continued to be extorted, sometimes by physical force, but more often by threats, promises of leniency, and other forms of psychological pressure.

During the reign of Charles I, 1625–49, the right against self-incrimination emerged in English common law, largely in response to repressive measures taken, in the name of the law, against some of the king's most persistent critics.[23] The protection which this immunity afforded to defendants apparently extended only to judicial proceedings and not to questioning prior to the filing of formal charges.[24] The common-law rule against involuntary confessions did not appear until the eighteenth century, although the precise date of its first application remains in doubt.[25] Nevertheless, as one authority has aptly pointed out, "the kinship of the two rules is too apparent for denial. It is significant that the shadow of the rack and the thumb screw was part of the background from which each rule emerged."[26]

English trial judges were placing restrictions on the admissibility of confessions prior to the mid-eighteenth century. It appears, however, that the formal rule of exclusion was first stated in 1783:

> A free and voluntary confession is deserving of the highest credit, because it is presumed to flow from the strongest sense of guilt,

[22] *Ibid.*, 294 ff.

[23] See generally Levy, *Origins of the Fifth Amendment*, 266–332. See also E. M. Morgan, "The Privilege Against Self-Incrimination," *Minnesota Law Review* 34 (Dec. 1949), 1–45, at 9–10.

[24] "Up to the middle of the seventeenth century torture was used to extort confessions, and there was no serious contention that such extorted confessions were inadmissible against the victim. Even Coke, the great advocate of the applicability of the privilege against self-incrimination to proceedings in the common law courts seems never to have regarded it as having any application to extorted confessions or to proceedings before the committing magistrates." Morgan, "The Privilege Against Self-Incrimination," 18.

[25] For a discussion of the origins of the rule and its earliest recognition by English legal commentators, see Levy, *Origins of the Fifth Amendment*, 327–28; Wigmore, *Evidence*, vol. 3, sec. 818; Morgan, "The Privilege Against Self-Incrimination," 17–18.

[26] Charles T. McCormick, "The Scope of Privilege in the Law of Evidence," *Texas Law Review* 16 (June 1938), 447–70, at 453, reprinted in McCormick, *Handbook of the Law of Evidence*, sec. 75, at 155.

and therefore it is admitted as proof of the crime to which it refers; but a confession forced from the mind by the flattery of hope, or by the torture of fear, comes in so questionable a shape when it is to be considered as the evidence of guilt, that no credit ought to be given to it; and therefore it is rejected.[27]

It is noteworthy that English judges of the eighteenth century accorded importance to the defendant's state of mind at the time of his confession. They showed a keen awareness of what has since come to be termed "psychological coercion."[28] Implicit in the rule was the assumption that judges could somehow determine whether a confession, made during a preliminary examination outside the courtroom, was in fact voluntary or involuntary. On that dubious assumption—fully shared by many American judges down to the present, though long ago abandoned by the English—has turned much of the confusion surrounding proper standards of confession admissibility. Criticism leveled at the *Miranda* decision resulted in large part from its repudiation of the voluntariness test as the principal criterion governing the use of confessions.[29]

Although the common-law rule prohibiting the admission of involuntary confessions into evidence was designed to protect the defendant against an erroneous conviction, there is some indication that it was influenced by the reform movement in criminal law administration beginning in the mid-eighteenth century. John H. Wigmore, in his famous treatise on the law of evidence, concluded that the limitation upon the use of confessions "was generated as a natural reaction from the harshness and unjust severity prevailing in penal administration up to that time."[30] Broadly speaking, the rule reflected the same high regard for human dig-

[27] *The King* v. *Warickshall*, 1 Leach 263–64, 168 Eng. Rep. 234–35 (K. B. 1783).
[28] The United States Supreme Court first came to grips with the question of psychological coercion in *Ziang Sung Wan* v. *United States*, 266 U. S. 1 (1924), a case originating in Washington, D. C. The first such decision based on a case arising from a state court was *Chambers* v. *Florida*, 309 U. S. 227 (1940).
[29] See, for example, Raymond L. Spring, "The Nebulous Nexus: *Escobedo, Miranda* and the New Fifth Amendment," *Washburn Law Journal* 6 (Spring 1967), 428–47, at 442–46.
[30] Wigmore, *Evidence*, vol. 3, sec. 815. For a discussion of English criminal law reform in the eighteenth century, see Leon Radzinowicz, *A History of English Criminal Law* (New York: Macmillan, 1948), 399–493.

nity and individuality that led to the immunity against compulsory self-incrimination. The confessions rule simply protected one aspect of that immunity not explicitly covered but ultimately inseparable from the guarantee that one shall not be compelled to be a witness against himself. Insistence on a rigid compartmentalization of the confessions and self-incrimination rules, championed in doctrinaire fashion by Wigmore, among others, may account in large part for the development of these rules (in the United States though not in England) along separate lines until the mid-1960s.[31]

Influenced in part by the general movement of reform in criminal law, English judges during the nineteenth century looked with mounting suspicion upon confessions of guilt as reliable pieces of evidence. A Parliamentary Act of 1848 converted the preliminary interrogation of a suspect into a judicial proceeding "in which the right [against self-incrimination] was fully respected."[32] Thus the English incorporated the comparatively modern practice of police interrogation into the judicial process, bringing it within the scope of a common-law rule developed long before the emergence of the first police department. By contrast, police interrogation in the United States has remained largely outside the judicial process. Only in recent years have some important judicial safeguards been extended piecemeal to the police station.[33] Since 1912 the Judges' Rules have been developed in England to guard against unfair methods of police interrogation. Unlike the United States Supreme Court's Exclusionary Rules, the English Judges' Rules are, in effect, simply administrative guidelines for interrogation procedure. Their violation, even if clear-cut, does not automatically result in the exclusion of evidence thus produced. Although suppression is likely in this instance, the decision of whether to admit or bar such evidence remains within the discretion of the trial judge. The traditional requirement of voluntariness thus contin-

---

[31] For a trenchant criticism of Wigmore's position, see Levy, *Origins of the Fifth Amendment*, 495–97 n. 43.

[32] *Ibid.*, 329.

[33] See *Escobedo v. Illinois*, 378 U. S. 478 (1964); *Miranda v. Arizona*, 384 U. S. 436 (1966); *Orozco v. Texas*, 394 U. S. 324 (1969). Even those protections explicitly recognized in these and related decisions (notably the assistance of counsel and the right to remain silent) may be waived "voluntarily" by an uncounseled suspect.

ues to be the only absolute prerequisite to the admissibility of a confession obtained by the police. The Judges' Rules have nevertheless been highly influential, particularly as a prototype for judicial formulation of interrogation policy in Commonwealth countries and in the United States. On the other hand, the rules have been criticized for their alleged vagueness and the uncertainty of their deterrent value. As revised in 1964, the Judges' Rules provide, among other things, that: "As soon as a police officer has evidence which would afford reasonable grounds for suspecting that a person has committed an offense, he shall caution that person or cause him to be cautioned before putting to him any questions, or further questions, relating to that offense." The "caution" reads as follows: "You are not obliged to say anything unless you wish to do so but what you say may be put into writing and given in evidence."[34] Freedom from compulsory self-incrimination is thus accorded much practical importance in the English police station. But, to repeat, its violation does not automatically render any resulting statement inadmissible at trial. English courts recognize the broad principle that, whether or not he is in custody, a person may communicate with his attorney at any stage of a criminal investigation. This principle, which is independent of the Judges' Rules, is more limited than the Supreme Court's endorsement of a right to counsel, either retained or appointed, and its further requirement that before introducing his statement, the police must demonstrate that a suspect who submitted to private questioning "knowingly and intelligently" waived this right.[35] Any comparison of English and American standards of interrogation should take account of these substantial differences.

English colonies in America readily followed the lead of the mother country in establishing restrictions against torture and

[34] For the full text of the revised Judges' Rules, see The Judges' Rules and Administrative Directions to the Police, *Home Office Circular No. 31*, 1964, reprinted in *Criminal Law Review* (Mar. 1964), 165–73. For additional background, see Patrick Devlin, *The Criminal Prosecution in England* (New Haven: Yale Univ. Press, 1958), Ch. 2. For a recent indication of the sharply limited sanctions imposed by the Judges' Rules and of the current trend toward their further weakening, see "Case and Comment," *Criminal Law Review* (Jan. 1972), 31–34.

[35] *Miranda v. Arizona*, 384 U. S. 436 (1966).

compulsory self-incrimination in the seventeenth century.[36] Undoubtedly restrictions on the use of out-of-court confessions were applied by colonial judges by the mid-eighteenth century.[37] The common-law rule of 1783 was explicitly recognized in the newly independent United States as early as 1792 in the Pennsylvania case of *Commonwealth* v. *Dillon*.[38] Within a short time state courts throughout the country had endorsed this restriction. Until the comparatively recent entry of the federal Supreme Court into state confession cases via the Due Process Clause of the Fourteenth Amendment, state courts continued to rely almost exclusively on the original common-law rationale of trustworthiness in determining the admissibility of confessions of guilt.

Until the passage of the Fourteenth Amendment in 1868, Supreme Court review of criminal procedure was confined to federal prosecutions. These were few in number by comparison with the volume of state litigation, and the Court had little occasion to interpret procedural guarantees of the Bill of Rights. Even after the passage of the Fourteenth Amendment, the Court showed little inclination to disturb trial-court procedure, state or federal, beyond placing a few restrictions on overt manifestations of racial discrimination in this context.[39] Thus it was not until 1884 that the Court invoked the well-established common-law rule against involuntary confessions. Justice John M. Harlan (the elder) was the Court's spokesman in this case, which arose from the Utah Territory. Under review was a murder conviction and death sentence, challenged on several grounds, including the admissibility of the defendant's confession. Applying the rule in its original form, and without reference to any constitutional guarantee, Harlan, for a unanimous Court, concluded that the confession was

[36] Morgan, "The Privilege Against Self-Incrimination," 18–23; R. Carter Pittman, "The Colonial and Constitutional History of the Privilege Against Self-Incrimination in America," *Virginia Law Review* 21 (May 1935), 763–89, at 766–69, 775–83. Levy, *Origins of the Fifth Amendment*, Ch. 12.

[37] Levy, *Origins of the Fifth Amendment*, 375.

[38] 4 Dallas 116.

[39] The Court's narrow view of the scope of the Fourteenth Amendment in state criminal proceedings was reflected in such cases as *Hurtado* v. *California*, 110 U. S. 516 (1884); *Maxwell* v. *Dow*, 176 U. S. 581 (1900); and *Twining* v. *New Jersey*, 211 U. S. 78 (1908).

voluntary.[40] In three decisions handed down during 1895 and 1896, the Supreme Court likewise applied the common-law rule in affirming convictions based in part on challenged confessions.[41] In the last of this initial series of confession cases, however, Chief Justice Melville Fuller, writing for a unanimous Court, went somewhat beyond a restatement of the traditional rule of voluntariness. A voluntary statement, he maintained, was not rendered inadmissible merely by failure to provide the suspect with a lawyer during questioning, or to advise him that he need not answer and that any statement he did make might be used against him. The Chief Justice asserted that even the threat of "mobbing" the suspect the night before he made the statements in question did not of itself render these statements inadmissible.[42] It is doubtful from the language of Fuller's opinion whether his references uniformly applied to confessions, admissions, and denials made by the suspect. The challenged evidence was in the form of a denial of guilt, but the Court was equivocal and vague in distinguishing between requirements governing this evidence and standards applicable to confessions. Even so, the Court's great reluctance to reject statements made under questionable circumstances stands in sharp contrast to its rigid scrutiny of the circumstances of potential coercion in most of the confession cases reviewed since this decision.

In December of the following year (1897), the Court abruptly departed from its permissive approach to confession admissibility and its exclusive reliance on the common-law rule of "trustworthiness." By a six-three vote in *Bram* v. *United States*,[43] the Court, speaking through Justice Edward D. White, reversed a murder conviction, holding that statements of the accused introduced in evidence as confession of guilt were made involuntarily. The majority, however, did not base its judgment on the standard of "trustworthiness." Rather, it relied explicitly on the Self-incrimination Clause of the Fifth Amendment. Disregarding the independent origins of the confessions rule, White asserted that

[40] *Hopt* v. *Utah Territory*, 110 U. S. 574 (1884).
[41] *Sparf and Hansen* v. *United States*, 156 U. S. 51 (1895); *Pierce* v. *United States*, 160 U. S. 355 (1896); *Wilson* v. *United States*, 162 U. S. 613 (1896).
[42] *Wilson* v. *United States*, 162 U. S. 613, 624.
[43] 168 U. S. 532 (1897).

the principle from which the self-incrimination restriction sprang "was in its essence comprehensive enough to exclude all manifestations of compulsion, whether arising from torture or from moral causes . . . ."[44] The language of the Fifth Amendment was "but a crystallization of the doctrine as to confessions, well settled when the Amendment was adopted . . . ."[45] Because of the doubtful historical connection between the right against self-incrimination and the confessions rule, this decision was sharply criticized by a number of legal scholars.[46] Justice White's new rationale was not, however, questioned by the three dissenting justices.[47]

It appears, however, that the Court soon began to have second thoughts about the *Bram* rationale, influenced perhaps by criticism of its questionable history. As early as 1902, the justices began to avoid specific reliance on the Fifth Amendment in declaring confessions inadmissible.[48] In 1908 the Court rejected the contention that the right against self-incrimination was applicable to the states through the Due Process Clause of the Fourteenth Amendment.[49] Accordingly, the elaborate development of standards governing the admissibility of confessions in state courts followed a course altogether different from that suggested by the *Bram* decision. Not until the "incorporation" of the Fifth Amendment immunity into the Fourteenth Amendment in 1964 was the Self-incrimination Clause linked unequivocally to the require-

[44] *Ibid.*, at 547.
[45] *Ibid.*, at 543.
[46] See, for example, Wigmore, *Evidence*, vol. 3, sec. 823.
[47] Justice David J. Brewer's brief opinion, joined by Chief Justice Fuller and Justice Henry B. Brown, was restricted to the conclusion that the challenged statements were voluntary and therefore properly admitted into evidence. 168 U. S., at 569.
[48] For example, in *Hardy v. United States*, 186 U. S. 224 (1902), the Court affirmed a murder conviction, rejecting the petitioner's contention that certain admittedly voluntary statements had been obtained in violation of statutory requirements and were thus inadmissible. Observing that "statements . . . obtained by coercion or threat or promise . . ." were subject to challenge, Justice Brewer for a unanimous Court cited *Bram v. United States*, but made no reference to the Fifth Amendment right against self-incrimination, 186 U. S., at 229. In *Powers v. United States*, 223 U. S. 303 (1912), the Court, through Justice Day, held that the Fifth Amendment guarantee was not violated by the admission into evidence of voluntary statements made at the preliminary hearing, even though the accused was not warned that what he said might be used against him. Cf. *Kent v. Porto [sic] Rico*, 207 U. S. 113, 117 (1907).
[49] *Twining v. New Jersey*, 211 U. S. 78 (1908).

ments of confession admissibility in state courts.[50] And not until the *Miranda* decision in 1966 was this constitutional provision once more accorded full recognition in confession cases at the federal level.[51]

The Court's abandonment of the *Bram* rationale in the early 1900s did not take the form of a direct repudiation of that precedent. It was characterized by an apparent recognition of the continuing relevance of the common-law test, emphasizing the unreliability of a coerced confession. More important in the Court's shift of emphasis, however, was its increasing concern with the basic fairness of proceedings against the defendant. This concern was reflected in several fields of criminal adjudication besides that of confession admissibility.[52] Gradually, the emerging standard was absorbed into the concept of due process of law. More and more the Court turned its attention to standards of conduct followed by public officials in enforcing the law. Justice Louis D. Brandeis, speaking in dissent in a 1921 decision outside the field of confessions, eloquently stated the essence of this new approach:

> At the foundation of our civil liberty lies the principle which denies to government officials an exceptional position before the law, and which subjects them to the same rules of conduct that are commands to the citizen .... Respect for law will not be advanced by resort, in its enforcement, to means which shock the common man's sense of decency and fair play.[53]

The development of this standard of "decency and fair play" was reflected in the growth of the "fair trial" doctrine as a basic element of due process as guaranteed by the Fourteenth Amendment. The Supreme Court's employment of this doctrine in its subsequent review of state convictions based in large part on allegedly coerced confessions provides the central theme of the following chapter. It is significant to note at this point, however, that

[50] *Malloy* v. *Hogan*, 378 U. S. 1 (1964). But cf. *Gallegos* v. *Colorado*, 370 U. S. 49 (1962).
[51] *Miranda* v. *Arizona*, 384 U. S. 436.
[52] See, for example, *Silverthorne Lumber Company* v. *United States*, 251 U. S. 385 (1920); *Moore* v. *Dempsey*, 261 U. S. 86 (1923); *Tumey* v. *Ohio*, 273 U. S. 510 (1927).
[53] *Burdeau* v. *McDowell*, 256 U. S. 465, 477 (1921).

the new emphasis in judicial thinking was clearly reflected in two significant decisions of the 1920s involving the use of challenged confessions and admissions in federal cases. The first of these decisions turned on the admissibility in a federal deportation proceeding of certain voluntary admissions made by the accused while in the custody of state authorities. It was alleged, among other things, that the absence of counsel during the preliminary hearing and the failure of state officers to apprise the defendant of his right to remain silent violated those constitutional guarantees "embraced within the conception of due process of law." Justice Brandeis, speaking for a unanimous Court, rejected this allegation, and in so doing invoked the broad standard of fairness previously discussed. "In the absence of a rule forbidding interrogation, or requiring the presence of counsel," he said, "mere examination ... does not render the hearing unfair." [54] Read in the light of subsequent enlargement of the right to counsel and the immunity against self-incrimination, this opinion suggests the dimensions of the modern revolution in criminal procedure. Brandeis pointed out that the rule against involuntary confessions had no specific application in this case but clearly implied that even if it had been relevant, the standard of fairness would have remained the ultimate criterion of judgment.

In a 1924 case the Court reviewed a federal conviction for murder in which the question of a confession's admissibility was of central importance. *Ziang Sung Wan v. United States*[55] involved the undenied use of extreme psychological police pressure on a physically ill defendant. Justice Brandeis, again for a unanimous Court, set forth in some detail the circumstances of coercion, emphasizing such factors as Ziang's incommunicado detention in a hotel room for more than one week, relentless police questioning during this period and later at the station house, refusal to allow the suspect to sleep, and the continuance of his illness throughout this ordeal. The confession thus wrung from the defendant was held to have been improperly admitted into evidence. In reversing Ziang's conviction, Justice Brandeis invoked no provision of the

[54] *United States ex rel Bilokumsky v. Tod*, 263 U. S. 149, 156, (1923).
[55] 266 U. S. 1.

federal Constitution. On the other hand, he conspicuously omitted reference to the common-law rule involving the determination of a confession's authenticity. Implicit in his account of the facts of coercion was the unmistakable emphasis upon a concept of basic fairness and human decency. Without explicitly rejecting either the common-law rule or Justice White's self-incrimination rationale as expressed in the *Bram* case, Brandeis moved far toward the formal endorsement of a due process standard independent of both these tests of admissibility. In light of the Court's subsequent role in establishing state confession standards under the Due Process Clause of the Fourteenth Amendment, this development in the *Ziang* case was highly significant. The Court reviewed no other federal conviction in the field of confessions until the early 1940s. By that time the due process approach to state confession cases was well established and widely assumed to apply equally to federal prosecutions under the Fifth Amendment. This broad rationale was not restricted to formal confessions but was applied to such frequent by-products as pleas of guilty. Thus in reviewing a federal conviction in 1942, the Court concluded that such a plea, "coerced by a federal law enforcement officer [was] no more consistent with due process than a conviction supported by a coerced confession."[56]

The Court's failure to develop clear constitutional standards governing federal confession cases during this period stands in sharp contrast with its enlargement of the scope of rights and immunities under the Fourth Amendment.[57] After announcement of the *Weeks* Exclusionary Rule in 1914, the Court undertook the piecemeal explication of requirements governing search and seizure, wiretapping, and related practices in the realm of federal law enforcement, guided for the most part by the same general notions of decency and fairness identified with due process of law and applicable, at least in theory, to all phases of the criminal process. Not until 1943 did the Court lay down an exclusionary rule ap-

---

[56] *Waley* v. *Johnston*, 316 U. S. 101, 104.
[57] Compare *Weeks* v. *United States*, 232 U. S. 383 (1914); *Silverthorne Lumber Company* v. *United States*, 251 U. S. 385 (1920). A striking exception to the Court's expansion of procedural rights in this area came in the famous wiretapping case, *Olmstead* v. *United States*, 277 U. S. 438 (1928).

28

plicable to the use of confessions in federal trials. This rule, moreover, was aimed not at the determination of voluntariness or coercion per se, but at the exclusion of confessions obtained in violation of statutory requirements of prompt arraignment. It rested on no constitutional provision but on the Court's broad supervisory power over the administration of criminal justice in the federal courts. Thus the objectives and rationale of the restriction had little to do with the common-law rule on confessions or, for that matter, with the due process standard by which the admissibility of state confessions was then measured. The divergent growth of state and federal requirements of confession admissibility is analyzed in the next two chapters. Before turning to these developments, the Supreme Court's confession standards, as drawn and redrawn since the 1930s, should be placed in the broader context of judicial emphasis on a variety of individual rights and liberties.

The pace of Supreme Court activity in the field of confessions quickened sharply after the "judicial revolution" of 1937, although important developments were well under way by that time. This activity was an integral part of the growing pattern of judicial involvement not only in matters of criminal procedure but also in the domains of freedom of expression and race relations. The Court's earliest state confession rulings were, in fact, repudiations of the extremes of racism which it condemned just as unequivocally in other contexts.[58] Growing restrictions on police interrogation represented only one aspect of a larger effort to check arbitrary methods of law enforcement—methods used against the nonconformist street orator or member of an unpopular religious cult no less than against the suspect whose confession was needed for conviction.[59] Evolving confession standards reflected the Court's effort to minimize the extremes of legal inequality imposed not only by membership in an exploited racial minority but

[58] See *Moore v. Dempsey*, 261 U. S. 86 (1923); *Powell v. Alabama*, 287 U. S. 45 (1932); *Norris v. Alabama*, 294 U. S. 587 (1935); *Patterson v. Alabama*, 294 U. S. 600 (1935); *Missouri ex rel Gaines v. Canada*, 305 U. S. 337 (1938); *Mitchell v. United States*, 313 U. S. 80 (1941).

[59] Compare *Kunz v. New York*, 340 U. S. 290 (1951); *Cantwell v. Connecticut*, 310 U. S. 296 (1940).

also by poverty, lack of education, and similar disabling factors. This emphasis was likewise apparent in other phases of criminal procedure and, less directly, in the recognition of new dimensions of human dignity.[60] In short, Supreme Court performance in the field of confessions and police interrogation has, since the 1930s, reflected its general commitment to the enlargement of individual rights. The Court has seldom been fully united in this commitment, and its general expansion of constitutional safeguards has followed an erratic course. In this respect also the confession decisions provide a fairly accurate index of judicial mood and emphasis. As the following chapters will reveal, activity in this area has displayed much of the same internal friction and periodic change of direction characteristic of the Court from the chief justiceship of Charles Evans Hughes to the close of the Warren era and beyond.

[60] See generally Jerome Hall, "Police and Law in a Democratic Society," *Indiana Law Journal* 28 (Winter 1953), 133–77; Benjamin M. Ziegler, *Desegregation and the Supreme Court* (New York: Heath, 1953).

3

State Coerced Confessions and the "Fair Trial" Doctrine

As WE HAVE SEEN, the Supreme Court seldom invoked explicit provisions of the federal Constitution in reviewing early federal confession cases. Its one important departure from this tendency —reliance on the Self-incrimination Clause of the Fifth Amendment in *Bram v. United States*[1]—was not followed by further development of constitutional standards applicable to federal criminal prosecutions. Instead the Court began to suggest in the 1920s that basic standards of fairness, implicit in the concept of due process of law, were applicable to the use of confessions as evidence of guilt. Not until its first review of a state confession case in 1936, however, did the Court clearly identify this rationale with a provision of the federal Constitution. That decision, *Brown v. Mississippi*,[2] extended the "fair trial" doctrine to confessions extracted by physical torture and declared them inadmissible under the Due Process Clause of the Fourteenth Amendment. Almost thirty years earlier, in *Twining v. New Jersey*,[3] the Court had rejected the contention that the right against self-incrimination was applicable to the states through the Fourteenth Amendment. Despite occasional attempts by a few justices to link state confession standards to this right,[4] it was not until after the *Twining* decision was overruled in 1964 that this position was endorsed by a Court

[1] 168 U. S. 532 (1897).
[2] 297 U. S. 278.
[3] 211 U. S. 78 (1908).
[4] See, for example, Justice Murphy's dissenting opinion, joined by Justice Black, in *Lyons v. Oklahoma*, 322 U. S. 596, 605–606 (1944); and the dissenting opinion of Justice Black in *Stein v. New York*, 346 U. S. 156, 197–98 (1953). See also Justice Douglas' concurring opinion in *Reck v. Pate*, 367 U. S. 433, 448 (1961).

majority.[5] Thus in the intervening period (1936–64), the Court relied exclusively on the due process requirement of the Fourteenth Amendment in developing constitutional requirements applicable to state confession cases.

The numerous cases decided under this rationale were characterized by a variety of differences in the forms of coercion employed, the circumstances under which such pressure was applied, and the supposed ability of a suspect to withstand a given technique of persuasion. From the earliest of this long line of cases, in which extreme physical brutality was used to wrench confessions from helpless and fear-ridden defendants, through a number of later cases revealing the use of far more subtle forms of coercion against hardened and experienced suspects, the Court struggled with the task of defining the scope of constitutional limitations upon the conduct of state law enforcement officials. This sequence of cases, stretching across more than one-quarter of a century and demonstrating the intricate process of judicial refinement, qualification, and readjustment, will be analyzed in some detail. The first major phase of development, in which the Court emphasized the broad and often indefinite requirements of a fair trial, is examined in this chapter.

Despite the expanding activity of federal law enforcement agencies, most criminal cases are decided in state courts. Moreover, the standards of local law enforcement units, within state jurisdiction, have long been regarded as generally lower than their federal counterparts.[6] Accordingly, the Supreme Court's comparatively late inclusion of a confession requirement within the Due

[5] *Escobedo* v. *Illinois*, 378 U. S. 478 (1964); *Miranda* v. *Arizona*, 384 U. S. 436 (1966).

[6] This is not to suggest, however, that state and local law enforcement agencies are uniformly inferior to such agencies at the federal level. Exceptions may be enumerated, and basic differences between the roles of the F.B.I. and a typical city police department may be cited. Nevertheless, to the extent that generalization about complex social phenomena is valid, the distinction between state and federal law enforcement standards seems justified. For general background, see *The Challenge of Crime in a Free Society*, A Report by the President's Commission on Law Enforcement and Administration of Justice, 1967, Ch. 4; Richard C. Donnelly, "Police Authority and Practices," *Annals of the Academy of Political and Social*

Process Clause of the Fourteenth Amendment raises some interesting questions. In considering these questions, it should be remembered that state criminal proceedings came under the surveillance of the Supreme Court very gradually after the adoption of the Fourteenth Amendment and did not begin to receive its careful attention until well into the twentieth century. It is true that the Court as early as 1880 invalidated as a violation of the Equal Protection Clause a West Virginia statute excluding Negroes from jury service,[7] but this case by no means indicated a trend toward more frequent review of state convictions. More important than the Equal Protection Clause in this area, the Court recognized that the Due Process Clause of the Fourteenth Amendment imposed upon it a measure of responsibility with respect to state criminal proceedings, but it interpreted this new authority quite narrowly. Prior to the 1920s it would overturn a state conviction only if it found that the state courts lacked jurisdiction, that "corrective process" was not available at the state level, or that the basic due process requirements of adequate notice and impartial hearing had been disregarded.[8]

Implicit in the requirements of notice and hearing was the "fair trial" doctrine, gradually developed by the Supreme Court during the twenties and thirties. It is clear that at least two members of the Court, Justices Holmes and Hughes, accepted the "fair trial" standard as early as 1915;[9] but not until the 1923 decision of *Moore v. Dempsey*[10] did it receive the endorsement of a Court majority. In this case the Court, speaking through Justice Holmes, reversed the convictions of five Negro defendants on the ground that their mob-dominated trial in an Arkansas court was simply one phase of an entire proceeding pointedly described as a "mask" under which "counsel, jury and judge were swept to the fatal end

---

Science 339 (Jan. 1962), 90–110; Roscoe Pound, *Criminal Justice in America*, (New York: Henry Holt, 1930), Ch. 5; National Commission on Law Observance and Enforcement, *Report on Police* (Washington, D. C.: United States Government Printing Office, 1931).

[7] *Strauder v. West Virginia*, 100 U. S. 303.

[8] *Frank v. Mangum*, 237 U. S. 309 (1915).

[9] *Ibid.*, at 347.

[10] 261 U. S. 86.

by an irresistible wave of public passion . . . ."[11] Although the coerced-confession issue was not a factor in this case, the threat of force was used to subvert the standards of fairness and justice. Because the threat or actual use of force was of central importance in early state confession cases, the relevance of *Moore* v. *Dempsey* was direct and substantial.

In a 1926 decision, arising from attempts to enforce federal and state prohibition laws, Justice Willis Van Devanter restated and amplified a basic conception of due process of law articulated by Justice Stanley Matthews some forty years earlier.[12] Because his statement was subsequently accorded importance in the Court's review of state criminal convictions, it may be regarded as an expression of the constitutional theory upon which the "fair trial" doctrine rested.

> The due process of law clause in the Fourteenth Amendment does not take up the statutes of the several States and make them the test of what it requires; nor does it enable this Court to revise the decisions of the State courts on questions of State law. What it does require is that State action, whether through one agency or another, shall be consistent with the fundamental principles of liberty and justice which lie at the base of all our civil and political institutions and not infrequently are designated as "law of the land."[13]

By applying this broad standard to state convictions, the Court could look beyond the formal requirements of procedure to such basic and often controlling factors as: public interest or excitement produced by a case; the corresponding atmosphere surrounding the trial; the defendant's vulnerability as determined by his age, education, economic status, race, and general standing in the community. Increasingly, the Court adopted the view that these and similar considerations were more crucial in determining violations of Fourteenth Amendment due process than particular modes of procedure specified in state constitutions or statutes. Even the clear violation of state law by those entrusted with its en-

[11] *Ibid.*, at 91.
[12] *Hurtado* v. *California*, 110 U. S. 516, (1884).
[13] *Hebert* v. *Louisiana*, 272 U. S. 312, 316–17.

forcement came to be regarded as less important in determining the constitutional fairness of a trial than the "spirit" in which the whole proceeding was conducted.[14]

In the first of the famous Scottsboro cases, *Powell* v. *Alabama*,[15] the Court raised no objection to the state's criminal procedure respecting the appointment of counsel in capital cases. Nor did it fully "incorporate" into the Due Process Clause the sweeping right-to-counsel provision of the Sixth Amendment. Rather, it carefully considered circumstances surrounding the arrest, detention, and trial of the nine young Negro defendants, noting in particular the intense public hostility displayed toward them and the unmistakable overtones of racial prejudice characterizing this hostility. It took into account the defendants' youth, "ignorance," and illiteracy, as well as their out-of-state residence and denial of any opportunity amid their new and unfamiliar surroundings to contact relatives or friends for help. A final factor to which the Court alluded was the great haste in which the proceedings were conducted and the casual manner in which defense counsel was belatedly appointed. In light of these considerations, Justice George Sutherland concluded for the majority that it was the duty of the trial judge to appoint counsel for the defendants, and that this duty was not fulfilled by appointment "at such a time or under such circumstances as to preclude the giving of *effective* aid in the preparation and trial of the case."[16] The decision turned on the adequacy and effectiveness of the trial judge's provision for counsel, not on technical aspects of the procedure that he followed. This decision broadened the scope of the "fair trial" doctrine and laid much of the foundation for the Court's review of state confession cases.

In 1935, just one year before its decision in *Brown* v. *Mississippi*, the Court further broadened this doctrine by ruling that a criminal

[14] See *Lisenba* v. *California*, 314 U. S. 219 (1941); discussed infra, 56–62.
[15] 287 U. S. 45 (1932).
[16] *Ibid.*, at 71. Italics added. For a detailed discussion of the *Powell* decision, its antecedents and aftermath, see William M. Beaney, *The Right to Counsel in American Courts* (Ann Arbor: Univ. of Michigan Press, 1955), Ch. 5. A fascinating, scholarly account of this case in broad social and historical perspective is provided by Dan T. Carter in *Scottsboro, A Tragedy of the American South* (Baton Rouge: Louisiana State Univ. Press, 1969).

conviction based solely on testimony known by the state to be perjured violated the Due Process Clause of the Fourteenth Amendment.[17] One statement in the Court's *per curiam* opinion indicates that the justices were mindful of the relationship of the confession problem to those already embraced by the "fair trial" doctrine. Referring to the deliberate introduction of "tainted" testimony, it observed that "such a contrivance by a state to procure the conviction and imprisonment of a defendant is as inconsistent with the rudimentary demands of justice as is the obtaining of a like result by intimidation."[18]

The preceding paragraphs have briefly summarized the chronological development of a standard ultimately accepted by a unanimous Supreme Court as the basis for deciding state confession cases. But a judicial rationale, such as the "fair trial" doctrine, does not grow in a vacuum. It is shaped by intense conflict and tension within society and reflects broad human values, not the least of which is a sense of fair play. Its inclusion within the basic law is dependent upon a variety of factors ranging from the issues of the case under review to personal values held by justices and the perceived capacity of the judicial process to limit social inequities. The evolution of a constitutional doctrine cannot be adequately analyzed without some reference to the latter—the extralegal factors influencing judicial formulation of public policy.

While it is impossible to reconstruct in full detail the complex interplay of circumstances, pressures, and attitudes that influenced the Court's movement into the state confession field, several factors are clearly discernible. Most obvious of all perhaps is the close connection between the growth of the "fair trial" doctrine and increasing concern for protection of the rights of the Negro minority in the South. It is noteworthy that *Brown* v. *Mississippi* and the six confession cases following directly upon it involved Negro defendants.[19] The active role of the National Association for the

[17] *Mooney* v. *Holohan*, 293 U. S. 103.
[18] *Ibid.*, at 112.
[19] In chronological order these cases are: *Chambers* v. *Florida*, 309 U. S. 227 (1940); *Canty* v. *Alabama*, 309 U. S. 629 (1940); *White* v. *Texas*, 309 U. S. 631 (1940) (denial of motion for rehearing, 310 U. S. 530); *Lomax* v. *Texas*, 313

Advancement of Colored People was of central importance. Beginning with its Supreme Court victory in the "Grandfather Clause" case of 1915,[20] this organization spearheaded the battle against various forms of racial discrimination.[21] It was instrumental in bringing before the Supreme Court most of the cases reviewed by that tribunal involving violations of the rights of Negro defendants prior to and including the early confession decisions.[22] Without organized support such as that provided by the NAACP it is very unlikely that Negro victims of the "third degree" would have been able to petition the Supreme Court for review of their convictions.

Police brutality in the interrogation process has, of course, never been confined to one particular region of the country or perpetrated against only a single group of its citizens.[23] On the contrary, state appellate courts outside the South had occasion, especially during the 1920s, to review convictions based in whole or in part on confessions secured by extreme forms of physical and psychological torture. Although some of these acts of brutality were directed against Negroes, many of them were aimed at other racial minorities and at white persons of various ethnic backgrounds.[24] The *National Commission on Law Observance and Enforcement*, reporting in 1931 on conditions during the preceding decade, found "third degree" practices of the police widespread in the United States.[25] Nor were the highest courts in various southern

---

U. S. 544 (1941); *Vernon v. Alabama*, 313 U. S. 547 (1941); *Ward v. Texas*, 316 U. S. 547 (1942).

[20] *Guinn v. United States*, 238 U. S. 247.

[21] See generally Mary White Ovington, *The Walls Came Tumbling Down* (New York: Henry Holt, 1948), Chs. 4 and 5.

[22] For an excellent analysis of the role of the NAACP in challenging racial discrimination in private housing, see Clement E. Vose, *Caucasians Only* (Berkeley: Univ. of California Press, 1959).

[23] National Commission on Law Observance and Enforcement, *Report on Lawlessness in Law Enforcement*, 153, 155.

[24] See Notes, "Third Degree," *Harvard Law Review* 43 (Feb. 1930), 617–23, and cases cited therein. Note in particular the following: *People v. Dorn*, (N. Y.) 159 A. 379 (1927); *People v. Berardi*, (Ill.) 151 N. E. 555 (1926); *People v. Weiner*, (N. Y.) 161 N. E. 441 (1928); *Lang v. State* (Wis.), 189 N. W. 558 (1922); *State v. King* (Neb.), 187 N. W. 934 (1922); *People v. Lipsczinska* (Mich.), 180 N. W. 617 (1920).

[25] *Report on Lawlessness in Law Enforcement*, at 153.

states altogether unwilling to condemn the use of such police methods against the Negro minority.[26]

Recognition of these qualifying factors, however, does not justify the conclusion that the lot of the southern Negro was no worse than that of other citizens with respect to "strong arm" methods of the police. The available evidence clearly indicates that such conduct was more widely and frequently employed against this minority than against any other group in the country, and that such abuses were not appreciably curbed by statutes or judicial pronouncements.[27] As previously noted, the victims of police malpractice, both during the interrogation process and during other phases of detention, have traditionally been the uneducated, the unpopular, the uninfluential members of society. They have usually come from the lowest economic and social levels of the community and have been in no position to protest their treatment without assistance from some outside source. Of all minority groups in the United States during the period with which we are dealing, southern Negroes came closest to filling these categories. It would thus be surprising if they did not appear in a substantial majority of the confession cases.

Although state courts had long recognized the common-law rule against the admissibility of "involuntary" confessions, it was not until the decade between 1910 and 1920 that its application showed a marked increase.[28] By the 1920s many state appellate tribunals were reviewing substantial numbers of coerced confession cases, reflecting a growing concern with the issue and in turn helping to draw attention to it. There is no indication, however, that increasing judicial activity in this area was produced by a sudden and dramatic growth in the incidence of police brutality in the procurement of confessions. The "third degree" (in practice if

---

[26] See *Harvard Law Review* 43 (Feb. 1930), 617–23, especially the following: *State v. Bing*, (S. C.), 106 S. E. 573 (1921); *Williams v. State* (Tex.), 225 S. W. 177 (1920); *Rowe v. State* (Fla.), 123 So. 523 (1929); *State v. Murphy*, (La.), 97 So. 397 (1923); *Whip v. State* (Miss.), 109 So. 697 (1926); *Rollins v. State* (Ala.), 92 So. 35 (1922).

[27] For discussion, see Edwin R. Keedy, "The Third Degree and Legal Interrogation of Suspects," *University of Pennsylvania Law Review* 85 (June 1937), 761–77.

[28] See Notes, "Coerced Confessions," *Virginia Law Review* 8 (May 1922), 527–30.

not in name) can be clearly traced to early colonial days in this country and to a more remote period in English history.[29] Unfortunately, though by no means surprisingly, there seems never to have been anything approaching a golden age of police administration in the United States. Prior to the time with which we are dealing, there was, however, a very long period of public apathy or, at best, grim resignation respecting the well established institution of the "third degree." Because techniques of physical and psychological coercion were seldom visible, either through newspaper coverage or direct observation, it is reasonable to conclude that many otherwise informed and responsible people were virtually unaware of the problem.[30]

During the early years of this century increasing interest was shown in a variety of social, economic, and political reforms. The expanding complexity of society in a rapidly changing technological age contributed to the growth of a sense of public responsibility and a corresponding decline in acceptance of traditional values of individualism, from a practical if not a philosophical standpoint. This general transition no doubt influenced and stimulated the attention increasingly directed to the matter of police misconduct. The highly publicized "crime wave" of the 1920s probably added impetus to the growing concern; and the trend toward urbanization, as well as passage of the Eighteenth Amendment, both of which influenced the growth of organized crime, called for more careful appraisal of the methods of police administration. In view of these factors (and they are far from a complete enumeration) it is easy enough to understand the great concern over the problem of the "third degree" widely expressed in legal and judicial circles by the end of the 1920s.[31]

In 1930, Emanuel H. Lavine, a police reporter for a New York City newspaper, published a popularized and sensationalistic account of specific instances in which he had witnessed the use of

[29] See Morgan, "The Privilege Against Self-Incrimination," 1–45.
[30] For a list of titles of early articles on the "third degree," see Keedy, "The Third Degree and Legal Interrogation of Suspects," 761, 762.
[31] See Report of Committee on Lawless Enforcement of Law, Section of Criminal Law and Criminology of the American Bar Association, *American Journal of Police Science* 1 (1930), 575, 593.

"third degree" techniques.[32] This book received considerable public notice and served to dramatize an increasingly controversial subject. It was followed in 1931 by two additional studies of police malpractice, both furnishing strong support for the conclusion that force, either physical or psychological, was frequently, if not regularly, used to obtain confessions and other incriminating statements. One of these, a volume by Ernest J. Hopkins entitled *Our Lawless Police*, asserted that illegal methods of law enforcement characterized the nation's "struggle against crime."[33] Although Hopkins analyzed a variety of police abuses, ranging from false arrest to perjured testimony, he gave major attention to abuses accompanying the interrogation of suspects. He maintained that "some form" of the "third degree" existed "everywhere," and further insisted that it was the "predominating type of trial for crime" in this country.[34] The other 1931 study was the eleventh report of the famous *National Commission on Law Observance and Enforcement*, better known as the Wickersham Commission.[35] On the basis of evidence which included surveys of police practices in fifteen major cities in the United States, the commission documented an impressive number of instances in which physical brutality or psychological compulsion were employed by police to extort confessions later used as evidence of guilt.

These and other revelations of police brutality naturally raised serious doubts about the adequacy of procedural safeguards generally assumed to be inherent in a constitutional system of government. If the police themselves could not be depended upon to honor such guarantees as the individual's right to remain silent and to be informed of the reason for his arrest, what alternative, if any, existed to assure his protection? This question was a source of increasing concern to many observers of American society during

[32] Emanuel H. Lavine, *The "Third Degree," A Detailed and Appalling Exposé of Police Brutality* (New York: Vanguard Press, 1930).
[33] Ernest J. Hopkins, *Our Lawless Police* (New York: Viking, 1931), 4.
[34] *Ibid.*, at 189, 204.
[35] National Commission on Law Observance and Enforcement, *Report on Lawlessness in Law Enforcement.*

this period.[36] On the other hand, a great many people, by no means all of them law enforcement officials, denied that the principles of individual liberty were seriously threatened by the judicious use of "third degree" methods. They refused to believe that these practices were of such significance as to justify concern. The police, they argued, must use effective techniques in combatting the real public menace: crime itself. And no one denied that the use of force, physical or psychological, was indeed effective in extracting confessions. Then as now, many people equated such tangible results with actual "progress" in the "war against crime." They further argued that the persons against whom such methods were employed had no respect for the laws of the community and thus did not really deserve the constitutional rights and immunities accorded other individuals. The possibility that a statement beaten or frightened out of a person might be false did not appear to be important to many such defenders of "law and order," and they were even less impressed by the argument that all persons, irrespective of guilt or innocence, should be treated in accordance with basic standards of human decency.[37]

But those who refused to recognize the existence of a serious problem in this area were hard pressed to explain away facts disclosed by the Wickersham Commission, by a growing number of judicial opinions, and by other sources previously noted. Many doubts and misconceptions about the widespread incidence of police misconduct were dispelled, and a growing awareness of the dangers inherent in such practices became apparent during the early 1930s. This awareness was further stimulated by the rise of totalitarian regimes, first in Russia and Italy, then in Germany, in which dictatorial rule was largely dependent upon similar "strong-arm" methods. By the mid-1930s the "police state" in Germany had acquired startling power; and many thoughtful people saw in

[36] A number of shortcomings and uncertainties in the operation of the criminal justice system were graphically illustrated in Edwin M. Borchard, *Convicting the Innocent* (New Haven: Yale Univ. Press, 1932). For a more recent compilation of the same type, see Jerome Frank and Barbara Frank, *Not Guilty* (Garden City, N. Y.: Doubleday, 1957).

[37] See *New York Times*, Sept. 27, 1931, Sec. 3, p. 5, col. 4.

the practice of the "third degree" by American police, with its emphasis on incommunicado detention and secret questioning, a close parallel to methods of the *Gestapo*.

It is thus clear that by 1936 a variety of conditions favored a decision by the United States Supreme Court placing a constitutional ban upon tactics so often employed in police interrogation, especially at the local level. In light of widespread concern with the problem for several years prior to the *Brown* decision, plus the Court's willingness to reverse state convictions on other grounds, one may suspect that the justices were disposed to hand down such a ruling at an earlier date. But the Court cannot always choose the moment at which it will act upon even the most pressing questions, despite the willingness of some or all of its members to do so. It must await an appeal or application for certiorari presenting for review a case in which the question is properly raised. If it is venturing into new territory, the Court is apt to insist that the case which is to serve as the basis for its initial pronouncement set forth in the most unequivocal and convincing form the abuse against which constitutional protection is sought. An examination of the denials of certiorari during the decade prior to the *Brown* decision reveals no case in which the admissibility of a confession was at issue.[38] Considering the large number of coerced confessions challenged in state courts during this period, it is somewhat surprising that prior to 1936 no visible attempt was made to bring such a case before the Court.

In any event, when the occasion did present itself, a unanimous Supreme Court did not hesitate to bring within the "fair trial" requirement prohibitions against the use of coerced confessions. The willingness of Justices James C. McReynolds and Willis Van Devanter, who had dissented in the *Dempsey* and *Powell* cases, to vote with their colleagues attests to the Court's serious concern for the way in which police went about the business of interrogating suspects.

---

[38] This survey was confined to cases in which a state or a law enforcement officer appeared as a party. There is only a bare possibility that this classification excludes a case or cases involving the confession issue.

A better opportunity to extend the scope of a constitutional doctrine could hardly have been found than that presented by *Brown v. Mississippi.* The undisputed acts of brutality revealed by the record were antithetical to the basic ideals of the American legal tradition and to the very idea of civilization itself. Without the "forced confessions" of the three defendants there was little if any evidence upon which to convict them of murder. Furthermore, it is beyond doubt that the trial judge and jury knew of the circumstances of coercion well in advance of the time for rendering a verdict. The convictions, carrying with them sentences of death, were twice affirmed by the Mississippi Supreme Court. On both occasions, however, powerful and persuasive dissenting opinions were filed. These assuredly influenced the federal Supreme Court in its grant of certiorari and its ultimate reversal of the convictions.[39] A closer look at the uncontroverted facts in this case should account for the angry and indignant tone characterizing these dissents, as well as Chief Justice Hughes' opinion for the Supreme Court.

Early on Friday afternoon, March 30, 1934, Raymond Stewart, a white farmer in Kemper County, Mississippi, was found in his home brutally murdered.[40] The crime evoked a wave of public outrage, and within a few hours the wheels of mob-dominated justice were in full motion. Guided by scanty and dubious circumstantial evidence,[41] a deputy sheriff named Dial, accompanied by several other white men, seized Yank Ellington, one of the subsequent Negro defendants, and took him to the home of the murdered man where a number of other vigilantes awaited him. The assembled mob began to accuse Ellington of the crime; and when he protested his innocence, they hanged him from the limb of a

---

[39] See Charles T. McCormick, "Some Problems and Developments in the Admissibility of Confessions," *Texas Law Review* 24 (Apr. 1946), 239–78.

[40] This description of the facts is drawn from the dissenting opinions of Justices Anderson and Griffith in the Mississippi Supreme Court's two reviews of the convictions: *Brown v. State,* 158 So. 339 (1935); *Brown v. State,* 161 So. 465 (1935).

[41] A blood-stained axe and an article of clothing with gray hairs and blood on it were found near the house of the defendant Henry Shields. For a description of the "evidence" used by the prosecution, see Justice Cook's majority opinion in the first affirmance of conviction: *Brown v. State,* 158 So. 339, 342.

tree. Taken down and again accused, he persisted in disclaiming any part in the murder and was accordingly hanged a second time. Still he refused to confess, and the severe whipping that followed did not bring a change in his story. At length the mob released him, but the same deputy sheriff placed him under arrest a day or two later. Driving with him into Alabama, Dial administered another severe beating, assisted by a fellow officer. At last, Ellington agreed to sign whatever statement Dial wished to dictate, and this detail completed, he was placed in jail to await trial.

The two other defendants, Ed Brown and Henry Shields, were first put in jail and later visited by the unstinting deputy, whose companions this time included the jailer and another police officer, as well as several private citizens. Brown and Shields were forced to strip and were then severely whipped with a leather strap to which metal buckles were attached. Assured that this torture would continue until they confessed, the prisoners not only admitted having murdered Stewart, but "confessed in every matter of detail as demanded by those present . . . ." As the whippings continued, "they changed or adjusted their confessions in all particulars of detail so as to conform to the demands of their torturers."[42] When the desired statements had been obtained, the defendants were warned that if they were so imprudent as to alter or deny their stories, the whippings would be resumed.

On the following day the three prisoners were forced to go through the empty form of reciting their "free and voluntary" confessions before two sheriffs and one other person. The testimony of these witnesses at the trial served as the formal authority upon which the confessions were admitted into evidence. On the evening before the trial opened the court appointed four members of the local bar to serve as counsel for the accused. Failure to single out one attorney to perform this function had the apparent effect of absolving all of them of explicit responsibility and diminished what little effectiveness the appointment might otherwise have had. This very kind of laxness in providing indigent defendants with counsel had been condemned two years earlier by the Su-

[42] 161 So. 465, 470.

44

preme Court in the first of the famous Scottsboro cases.[43] It is hard to believe that the trial judge was unaware of this highly publicized decision. His arbitrary disregard of its central requirement illustrates and underscores one of the limitations inherent in the impact of even the most basic constitutional ruling by the Supreme Court. It appears from the record that only two of the appointed lawyers made any effort to discharge the unpopular duty assigned them, and this effort could hardly have been effectual given the short time allowed for preparation. The trial and predictable verdict of guilty required less than two days of argument and deliberation. Within one week after commission of the crime the defendants were convicted and sentenced to death.

At the trial the Kemper County sheriff testified that he had heard about the treatment of the defendants, but that he had no personal knowledge of it. He had noticed one of the prisoners limping, and this man had told him of the severe whippings. On his neck the defendant Ellington bore the marks of the rope used to hang him, and these were "plainly visible to all" during the trial.[44] Deputy Sheriff Dial, who openly acknowledged that the whippings had taken place, was asked how severely he had beaten Ellington. He replied bluntly: "Not too much for a Negro; not as much as I would have done if it were left to me."[45] Two other witnesses testified that they had taken part in the whippings, and no one denied that the brutality described above did in fact occur. The defendants took the witness stand and described to judge and jury the sordid details of their treatment.

The convictions were appealed to the Mississippi Supreme Court on the ground that the trial court had erred in admitting the confessions into evidence. This seemingly irrefutable argument was rejected on the basis of a procedural technicality. A majority of the justices agreed that because defense counsel had failed to move formally at the trial for the exclusion of confessions, the question of whether they had been obtained by force could not be

[43] *Powell* v. *Alabama*, 287 U. S. 45 (1932).
[44] 161 So., at 471.
[45] *Ibid.*

reviewed by an appellate court. From the record it appears that during the trial the defense had in fact raised objections to the methods used in extracting the confessions, but had failed to move formally for the exclusion of this evidence. By placing exclusive emphasis upon this omission the state Supreme Court managed to evade consideration of the fundamental question at issue. It was pointed out that the confessions had been duly admitted by the trial judge after a preliminary examination to determine their voluntariness. In accordance with the procedure then followed in Mississippi and a number of other states,[46] this evidence had been presented to the jury with the instruction that it be disregarded if, in the opinion of that body, it had not been freely and voluntarily given. The jury's finding of "voluntariness" was regarded as conclusive, and no question was raised concerning the basic fairness of the proceeding. One of the ironies of this mechanistic ruling was the Court's failure to question the casual manner in which defense counsel was appointed and yet to base its ruling squarely on counsel's inefficiency at the trial.

In a strongly worded dissent, Justice W. D. Anderson criticized the rigid application of evidentiary rules. "It is a common saying," he observed, "that there are exceptions to all rules. If that be true, this is one case that ought to come within the exception. Wipe out these confessions, and the court would have been forced to direct a verdict of not guilty."[47] He pointed out that the inadequate time afforded defense counsel to prepare for trial should be taken into account in weighing the importance of the failure to move for exclusion. Relying on the Scottsboro decision, he concluded that the defendants had been denied a "fair and impartial trial."[48]

The convictions were once more appealed to the state Supreme

---

[46] For description and evaluation of the methods of procedure followed in various states with respect to the admission of confessions into evidence, see Warren L. Swanson and Roger W. Eichmeier, "The Role of Judge and Jury in Determining a Confession's Voluntariness," *Journal of Criminal Law, Criminology and Police Science* 48 (May–June 1957), 59–65. For the Supreme Court's more recent establishment of constitutional requirements governing the method by which state trial courts determine the voluntariness of confessions, see *Jackson* v. *Denno*, 378 U. S. 368 (1964).

[47] 158 So., at 343.

[48] *Ibid.*

Court on the grounds that both the use of the confessions and the denial of effective assistance of counsel violated their constitutional rights. For the second time that Court affirmed the convictions, employing the same reasoning as that followed in its first decision. While acknowledging the facts disclosed by the record, the Court continued to treat as immutable the procedural rule on which its judgment rested.

Justice V. A. Griffith, joined in dissent by Justice Anderson, rejected this narrow approach and examined the combination of circumstances leading to the convictions. He refused to regard the formal courtroom proceedings as a trial, maintaining that it was nothing more than a "fictitious continuation of the mob which originally instituted and engaged in the admitted tortures." Anticipating the potential constitutional significance of the case, he observed that:

> If this judgment be affirmed by the federal Supreme Court, it will be the first in the history of that court wherein there was allowed to stand a conviction based solely upon testimony coerced by barbarities of executive officers of the state, known to the prosecuting officers of the state as having been coerced, when the testimony was introduced, and fully known in all its nakedness to the trial judge before he closed the case and submitted it to the jury, and when all this is not only undisputed, but is expressly and openly admitted.[49]

Whether the justice suspected that this case would be reviewed by the Supreme Court is, of course, an open question. But the inescapable impression is that he was addressing himself to that tribunal. He went on to compare the circumstances in this case with those in *Moore* v. *Dempsey* and described the Scottsboro cases as "models of correct constitutional procedure" by comparison with the proceeding under review. This dissent, like that of Justice Anderson, clearly endorsed the "fair trial" standard.

On February 17, 1936, the United States Supreme Court handed down its unanimous decision reversing the convictions. Writing for the Court, Mr. Chief Justice Hughes adopted the

[49] *Brown* v. *State*, 161 So. 465, 472 (1935).

47

position of Justices Griffith and Anderson, making, however, some additional constitutional objections to those raised at the state level. The main point of his opinion set forth broad principles that served as much of the basis for Supreme Court review of state confession cases until the mid-1960s. Hughes relied heavily on the statement of facts presented in Justice Griffith's dissenting opinion. It is significant that in the majority opinions of both state Supreme Court decisions, by contrast, no description of the facts is to be found. Griffith's dissent, and to a lesser extent that of Anderson, served to bring to the Supreme Court's attention critically important facts that might otherwise have received little official notice.

The state, in its argument before the Court, relied on two major contentions—both of which Hughes flatly rejected. The first of these rested on the assumption that coerced confessions conflicted with only one provision of the federal Constitution; namely, the Self-incrimination Clause of the Fifth Amendment. The state argued that since this provision had been held not to apply to the states through the Fourteenth Amendment, the *Brown* case lay outside the Court's proper sphere of review. Hughes responded by asserting that the immunity against self-incrimination had no bearing on questions at issue in this proceeding. The Self-incrimination Clause, admittedly inapplicable to the states in 1936, referred to the "processes of justice by which the accused may be called as a witness and required to testify."[50] The extraction of a confession by torture was quite a different matter. The clear inference from Hughes' statements is that even if the Fifth Amendment guarantee had been applicable to the states, the confession issue raised by this record would not have been decided under this rationale. His language indicates how far the Court had withdrawn from its position in the *Bram* case, where exclusive reliance was placed upon the Self-incrimination Clause as the proper standard for determining the admissibility of an out-of-court confession. For Hughes the state had some freedom in establishing its criminal procedure, but this latitude was only the "freedom of constitutional government . . . limited by the requirement of due

[50] 297 U. S. 278, 285 (1936).

process of law." Thus, just because a state might abolish the procedure of grand jury indictment or even jury trial itself, it did not follow that the state could "substitute trial by ordeal."[51]

The state's second contention turned on the previously mentioned failure of defense counsel to move formally for exclusion of the confessions at trial. Hughes concluded that this argument was based on a "misconception of the nature of petitioner's complaint." Applying the "fair trial" rationale, he pointed out that the complaint was "not of the commission of mere error, but of a wrong so fundamental that it made the whole proceeding a mere pretense of a trial and rendered the conviction and sentence wholly void."[52] Under such circumstances and in view of the due process requirement of the Fourteenth Amendment, the proceedings "could be challenged in any appropriate manner."[53]

Thus the door was opened, if only slightly, to a broad area of adjudication involving the powers of police and the immunities of prisoners. In this initial Fourteenth Amendment decision the Court did not define the term "coercion" in detail. It did not specify the precise limits beyond which police interrogation could not constitutionally extend. It simply ruled that the Due Process Clause prohibited the use in state courts of confessions extorted by such extreme forms of physical violence as hanging and whipping. This case was made unique, not so much by the excessive brutality of law enforcement officers, but by their willingness to acknowledge their treatment of the defendants. It was hardly representative of the kinds of controversies involving confessions that began to come up for review within a few years. But without this initial step, the Court might have found it more difficult to deal with the complex situations that typically characterized disputed allegations of coercion.

Despite the landmark proportions of this decision, its immediate practical results were by no means spectacular. The Court could do no more than condemn the confessions and reverse the convictions. Nothing prevented the state from initiating a new

[51] *Ibid.*, at 286.
[52] *Ibid.*
[53] *Ibid.*, at 287.

49

proceeding so long as the confessions were not used as evidence. Given the prevailing climate of opinion in Mississippi, the prosecution might still hope to obtain murder convictions, despite the insufficiency of additional evidence. But it chose to compromise, giving the defendants the option of pleading *nolo contendere* to charges of manslaughter. Considering the hostile atmosphere in which the original trial was held and the two affirmances of conviction by the Mississippi Supreme Court, this arrangement amounted to a meaningful concession.[54]

Although *Brown* v. *Mississippi* constituted a significant extension of the scope of the Due Process Clause, it did not precipitate an immediate torrent of Supreme Court activity in the confession field. No related cases came before the Court until 1940, but in that year three were decided. The first and by far the most important of these, *Chambers* v. *Florida*,[55] extended the application of the "fair trial" doctrine to a less violent though equally sinister form of police intimidation. Here the elements of coercion reviewed by the Court were: the instilling of fear; long and exhaustive questioning accompanied by frequent threats; and the isolation of the defendants from relatives, friends, and counsel throughout a lengthy period of interrogation.

As in the *Brown* case, the Court chose not to identify due process restrictions against coerced confessions with such guarantees of the Bill of Rights as immunity against self-incrimination and the right to counsel. Justice Benjamin N. Cardozo, in the famous decision of *Palko* v. *Connecticut*,[56] had restated the Court's rationale for inclusion of provisions of the first eight amendments within the Due Process Clause of the Fourteenth Amendment in terms of a "scheme of ordered liberty." Under this rationale of "selective incorporation," as of 1940 the right to assistance of counsel—for capital offenses, and perhaps in noncapital cases—was recognized as applicable to the states via the Due Process

---

[54] See Alan Barth, *The Price of Liberty*, 54. "Brown was sentenced to seven and a half years, Ellington to three, Shields to two and a half."
[55] 309 U. S. 227 (1940).
[56] 302 U. S. 319 (1937).

Clause of the Fourteenth Amendment.[57] The Court, however, gave no indication of the recognition of any clear connection between this right and the protection of suspects against coercive tactics of police interrogation. By the time that a minority of Court members, led by Justice William O. Douglas, began to urge the linking of the right to counsel with the ban on coerced confessions, the Court had adopted the rule of *Betts* v. *Brady*[58] by which the right of indigent persons to counsel in noncapital state cases was made to depend upon the "totality of facts" presented in each case reviewed by the Court. In the early state confession cases—all involving capital offenses—the Court found the circumstances of coercion so overwhelming that anything beyond the rudimentary guarantees of due process probably appeared superfluous as a basis of constitutional protection. The Court began to look at somewhat more complex combinations of circumstances in the confession field at about the time that it narrowed the right-to-counsel protection in state cases. This factor may account in large part for the independent development of constitutional guarantees in the two areas until their fusion in the mid-1960s.[59]

The *Chambers* case revealed a familiar pattern of racial prejudice and police brutality. Isaiah Chambers was one of four Negro suspects arrested along with some thirty other persons for questioning in connection with the robbery and murder of Robert Darsey, an elderly white man in the small town of Pompano, Florida. The crime occurred on Saturday night, May 13, 1933; and as in the *Brown* case, great public wrath was aroused. The direct parallel between the Mississippi and Florida cases, however, seems to extend no further. The prisoners were not seized by a mob of private citizens and police officers; and, despite their allegations, the undisputed record does not indicate the use of physical torture to extract confessions. They were nevertheless clearly threatened

[57] For discussion of the imprecise scope of the Fourteenth Amendment right-to-counsel guarantee at this time, see Beaney, *The Right to Counsel in American Courts*, Ch. 5.

[58] 316 U. S. 455 (1942).

[59] See *Escobedo* v. *Illinois*, 378 U. S. 478 (1964); *Miranda* v. *Arizona*, 384 U. S. 436 (1966).

with mob vengeance and were taken by the police to the Dade County jail in Miami, ostensibly for their own protection. There the suspects were held overnight; and at least one of them was deliberately lodged in the "death house." Brought back the following day to the county in which the crime was committed, they were questioned in intermittent sessions for a period of one week. Although the long sessions of interrogation—sometimes extending through the night—were physically exhausting, the coercion appears to have been primarily psychological. Fear was created in the minds of the prisoners, not only by the threat of mob violence, but also by the surroundings in which the questioning took place and by prolonged isolation from those presumably able to assist them.

Each of the suspects was questioned singly by a battery of four officers in a fourth floor room of the county jail in Fort Lauderdale. Early on Sunday morning, May 21, after an all-night "grilling," one of the prisoners "broke." The district attorney was called at his home and summoned to the jail to hear the confession. Finding the statement unsatisfactory, he ordered the police to continue the interrogation and to call him again when they had obtained the desired modifications. This official encouragement of "third degree" practices indicates the extent to which constitutional processes were subverted in this case. Confessions were ultimately obtained from all four defendants, and only after these statements were adjusted to the demands of the inquisitors did the questioning cease. The confessions were admitted into evidence and were the basis of subsequent convictions of murder in the first degree.

The Florida Supreme Court affirmed the convictions and their accompanying sentences of death.[60] Before the cases finally reached the United States Supreme Court, however, the issue of the voluntariness of the confessions, not considered at the original trial, was twice submitted to a jury. On both occasions the confessions were found to have been freely made and verdicts of guilty were again returned. The state Supreme Court twice re-

---

[60] *Chambers v. State*, 151 So. 499 (1933).

affirmed the convictions.[61] One justice dissented from the Florida Supreme Court's final affirmance, but his position was based on a point of procedure unrelated to the issue of coercion.[62]

The press made much of the fact that the federal Supreme Court's decision was handed down on the anniversary of Lincoln's birthday; and that the unanimous opinion was written by Justice Hugo L. Black, who, on the occasion of his appointment to the High Bench less than three years earlier, had been sharply assailed for his previous membership in the Ku Klux Klan.[63] Any lingering doubt about his complete repudiation of the racist credo expounded by that group should have been thoroughly dispelled by the tone of his opinion. The eight justices who participated in reversal of the convictions[64] significantly extended the scope of the "fair trial" doctrine, enlarging in two respects the Court's exercise of authority in reviewing coerced confession cases.

First of all the Court asserted its authority to determine for itself "by review of the facts upon which that issue necessarily turns,"[65] the presence or absence of coercion. In *Brown* v. *Mississippi* the question of coercion had never been in doubt, even in the state courts. No one at any point in the proceedings had denied the facts of physical torture, and it was thus unnecessary for Chief Justice Hughes to consider whether the Supreme Court could make an independent judgment on the basis of the undisputed record. But because the Florida court ruled in the *Chambers* case that the confessions were not coerced, it was necessary for Black and his colleagues to answer this question. Since the Court had already exercised this authority in reviewing certain

[61] *Chambers* v. *State*, 152 So. 437 (1933); *Chambers* v. *State*, 187 So. 156 (1939). Chambers was committed to a mental institution before his conviction was reviewed by the Federal Supreme Court. See Bennett Boskey and John H. Pickering, "Federal Restrictions on State Criminal Procedure," *University of Chicago Law Review* 13 (Apr. 1946), 266–99.

[62] The dissenting judge did not question the admissibility of the confession. He contended that error resulted from failure to grant a new trial. 187 So. 156.

[63] See, for example, *New York Times*, Feb. 13, 1940, p. 1., col. 6; p. 22, col. 2; Feb. 15, 1940, p. 18, col. 3.

[64] Justice Frank Murphy took no part in the consideration or decision of this case.

[65] 309 U. S. 227, 229.

other aspects of criminal procedure,[66] its extension of the prerogative of independent judgment to confession cases was supported by precedent. Secondly, the justices branded as coercive a form of treatment less extreme than overt physical torture. By focusing on the fear-inducing elements of incommunicado detention and relentless questioning, they began to come to grips with the elusive phenomenon of psychological coercion. Although the record here left no doubt that the confessions were involuntary, the justices were soon to encounter situations in which the answers were not so easy.

In many of these subsequent cases the form of police malpractice closely resembled that in the *Chambers* case; but great differences appeared with respect to the defendants' experience, education, financial resources, and social status. Thus, in trying to determine whether psychological coercion had occurred, the Court found itself placing greater and greater emphasis upon a variety of factors much less tangible than direct physical brutality or threats. Of course, some importance was accorded in the *Brown* case to the defendants' youth, poverty, lack of education, and membership in a vulnerable racial minority. But these elements were less decisive than the bare facts of physical torture. The status of the defendants in the *Chambers* case, on the other hand, was of somewhat greater relative importance than the actions of the police per se. Black's opinion is replete with references to the "helpless" condition of the defendants, their lack of education, their poverty, their youth, and their membership in an exploited minority group.[67] Although he stated flatly that the Constitution proscribed the police methods used to extract these confessions, it is unlikely in view of later decisions that all the justices shared the view implicit in this assertion. Black seems to have regarded the conduct of the police alone as sufficient basis for reversal of the convictions. But his position was somewhat obscured by the emphasis that he placed on the status of the defendants. Within a few years, as we shall see, Black began to urge that certain meth-

---

[66] *Pierre v. Louisiana*, 306 U. S. 354 (1939); *Norris v. Alabama*, 294 U. S. 587 (1935).
[67] 309 U. S., at 238.

ods of law enforcement were "inherently coercive" irrespective of their supposed effect upon a particular individual.[68] While a Court majority briefly accepted this rationale, most of the justices soon returned to a form of balancing test, by which methods of psychological police pressure were weighed against the presumed capacity of the suspect to withstand pressure to confess. Much of the confusion characterizing Supreme Court performance in the state confession field resulted from a failure to distinguish clearly between these two fundamentally different considerations.[69]

Justice Black's eloquent concluding remarks in the *Chambers* case reflect his commitment to the responsibility of courts in general and the Supreme Court in particular to protect the rights and immunities of the weak and oppressed:

> Under our constitutional system, courts stand against any winds that blow as havens of refuge for those who might otherwise suffer because they are helpless and weak, outnumbered, or because they are non-conforming victims of prejudice and public excitement. Due process of law, preserved for all by our Constitution, commands that no such practice as that disclosed by this record shall send any accused to his death. No higher duty, no more solemn responsibility rests upon this Court, than that of translating into living law and maintaining this constitutional shield deliberately planned and inscribed for the benefit of every human being subject to our Constitution—of whatever race, creed or persuasion.[70]

As an expression of the high ideal of judicial protection of the oppressed, this statement merits commendation. But as an assessment of what courts actually have offered to that vast majority of exploited defendants whose convictions are not reviewed by appellate courts, Black's words have a decidedly hollow ring.

Chambers v. *Florida* substantially enlarged the scope of the "fair trial" doctrine in state confession cases. Although Black's sweeping indictment of illegal police interrogation was not long allowed to go unopposed, it served as the controlling precedent

[68] See his opinion in *Ashcraft* v. *Tennessee*, 322 U. S. 143, 154 (1944).
[69] See *Malinski* v. *New York*, 324 U. S. 410 (1945); *Haley* v. *Ohio*, 332 U. S. 596 (1948); *Fikes* v. *Alabama*, 352 U. S. 191 (1957); *Culombe* v. *Connecticut*, 367 U. S. 568 (1961).
[70] 309 U. S., at 241.

for two additional decisions handed down during the same Supreme Court term and for three cases decided during the next two years. In the first four of these cases the judgments of the Court were announced without comment in *per curiam* decisions.[71] Each of these rulings reversed a state conviction carrying with it a sentence of death. Incommunicado detention, secret sessions of interrogation often lasting for many hours, threats of mob violence, removal of suspects at night to unfamiliar places as a further means of instilling fear—such were the elements of coercion common to all these cases. Without exception the defendants were uneducated, indigent Negroes, tried in southern states. Each conviction rested primarily, if not entirely, upon a challenged confession. Allegations of the use of physical force to obtain the confessions were denied by the police and were not clearly substantiated by other evidence. *Ward* v. *Texas,* the fifth case directly controlled by the *Chambers* ruling differed only in that it involved a conviction for "murder without malice," carrying a three-year prison sentence, not a sentence of death.[72] Writing for a unanimous Court, Justice James Byrnes concluded that the confession "was not free and voluntary but was the product of coercion and duress, that petitioner was no longer able freely to admit or to deny or to refuse to answer and that he was willing to make any statement that the officers wanted him to make."[73] It should be noted that the emphasis of this opinion, by contrast with that in *Chambers* v. *Florida,* was placed exclusively and unequivocally upon the defendant's response to police pressure, not upon the methods of coercion as such. The unanimity of both decisions suggests that the Court did not yet recognize any significant distinction between these two facets of coercion.

The Supreme Court's first affirmance of a state conviction based in part on a challenged confession occurred on December 8, 1941, some six months prior to the *Ward* decision. In *Lisenba* v.

[71] *Canty* v. *Alabama,* 309 U. S. 629 (1940); *White* v. *Texas,* 309 U. S. 631 (1940), 310 U. S. 530 (1940); *Lomax* v. *Texas,* 313 U. S. 544 (1941); *Vernon* v. *Alabama,* 313 U. S. 547 (1941).
[72] 316 U. S. 547 (1942).
[73] *Ibid.,* at 555.

California[74] the limits of the "fair trial" doctrine as a basis for determining confession admissibility were plainly revealed. Here the Court was dealing with the confession of a defendant who was portrayed as a hardened and depraved killer, by no means helpless or easily intimidated by the police. In the previous cases the circumstances of coercion were so overwhelming that even the most cautious of the justices endorsed the application of the "fair trial" standard. Because of the Court's unanimity it was not so obvious that this rationale was highly subjective—and that it provided at best a tenuous and indirect basis for ascertaining confession admissibility.

Seldom has the Court encountered a more grisly set of facts and allegations than those presented in the *Lisenba* case. Raymond Lisenba (who at the time that this case arose went under the name of Robert James) was accused of murdering his wife; and although he confessed to the crime after lengthy and persistent questioning, he later denied guilt, contending among other things, that his confession had been coerced in violation of the Due Process Clause of the Fourteenth Amendment.[75] At his trial he pleaded not guilty, was convicted, and sentenced to death. The California Supreme Court twice affirmed his conviction, but on both occasions two justices dissented.[76] The case was first argued before the federal Supreme Court on February 6, 1941, and the judgment was affirmed *per curiam* by an equally divided Bench.[77] Reargument was held and opinions written the following fall, and, with Justices Black and Douglas dissenting, the conviction was again sustained. It is noteworthy that the brief filed by the prosecution was joined by Earl Warren, at that time California's attorney general. Later, as chief justice, he explicitly rejected the confession rationale endorsed in that brief and by the Court majority in *Lisenba*.[78]

---

[74] 314 U. S. 219 (1941).
[75] See the dissenting opinion of Justice Emmet Seawell, in *People* v. *Lisenba*, 89 P. 2d 39, 54 (1939).
[76] *People* v. *Lisenba*, 89 P. 2d 39 (1939); *People* v. *Lisenba*, 94 P. 2d 569 (1939).
[77] *Lisenba* v. *California*, 313 U. S. 537 (1941).
[78] See his majority opinion in *Miranda* v. *Arizona*, 384 U. S. 436 (1966).

The death of Mrs. James occurred on or about August 5, 1935, and was at first attributed to accidental drowning. It was not until the following April, when the widower was placed under observation for suspected incest involving his niece, that authorities uncovered and developed the criminal character of his wife's death. An alleged accomplice named Hope made a statement placing primary responsibility on James and describing the crime in full detail. Some of the "facts" set forth in his statement were corroborated by expert testimony at the trial, but much of his story was substantiated only by James's later confession. The account presumably accepted by the jury revealed that James, a Los Angeles barber, married his manicurist, Mary Busch, and insured her life for five thousand dollars with a double indemnity clause for accidental death. To facilitate this "accident" he and his accomplice procured several rattlesnakes and caused one of them to bite the unsuspecting victim. When the poison failed to have an immediately fatal effect, James drowned his spouse in the bathtub, then placed her body in a nearby pond where he and two friends of the family "discovered" it the following day.

The undisputed record shows that the police illegally held James in a "furnished house" next door to his own residence where, for two days, he was intermittently questioned by a state's attorney and other officials. During this time he was not officially placed under arrest or formally charged with any offense. He was kept awake during the first forty-two hours of interrogation and on one occasion was "slapped" by an officer. After his refusal to confess during this period he was booked on a charge of incest and placed in jail. Eleven days later, on May 2, 1936, he was confronted by his alleged accomplice and told that the latter had made a statement implicating him in the murder. From 4:00 P.M. until midnight, James was locked in the district attorney's office and subjected to intensive questioning which ended only with his agreement to confess.

James subsequently alleged that the police had beaten him severely during the course of his detention and interrogation, but this claim was firmly denied by the officers.[79] It was conceded,

[79] In support of James' contention that he was beaten, two witnesses testified

however, that no formal charge of murder was placed against the suspect until after his confession was obtained. The highly publicized trial that followed was characterized by lurid testimony, some of which sought to connect James with the unexplained death of another wife several years prior to the 1935 murder. At one point the prosecution brought two live rattlesnakes into the courtroom, supposedly for purposes of identification. James submitted several depositions tending to show that he was congenitally "weak-minded" and more susceptible to coercive pressure than the average person.[80] He also presented but later withdrew a plea of insanity. It is significant that these latter factors carried no apparent weight with the Supreme Court, although at a subsequent date such characteristics as the mental and emotional condition of the defendant were to receive careful scrutiny. A majority of the justices were concerned only with the question of whether the defendant's freedom of choice "to admit, to deny, or to refuse to answer" was abridged. Because he displayed "self-possession," "coolness," and "acumen throughout his questioning, and at his trial," they concluded, without reference to his mental equilibrium, that freedom of choice had been preserved.[81]

Speaking for the Court, Justice Owen J. Roberts frankly acknowledged that the police had violated state law and voiced disapproval of their conduct. He asserted, however, that the constitutional question before the Court did not turn upon the commission of illegal acts per se. Nor was the question controlled by California's evidentiary rule governing the admissibility of confessions. As in most other states, that rule was based on the common-law standard of trustworthiness, chiefly designed to guard against the introduction of false evidence. It fell far short of the broader concept of fairness to the individual implicit in "due process of law." Accordingly, the Court could not determine confession admissibility simply by applying the common-law test. Here for the first time in a state case the Court explicitly differen-

---

that his ears were noticeably bruised and swollen shortly after the period of incommunicado detention. 314 U. S. 219, 230.

[80] 89 P. 2d 39, 45.

[81] 314 U. S. 219, 241.

tiated between the trustworthiness rationale and the due process requirement: "The aim of the requirement of due process is not to exclude presumptively false evidence, but to prevent fundamental unfairness in the use of evidence, whether true or false." [82]

Roberts attempted further explanation of the meaning of the due process requirement in a criminal trial, identifying it in familiar terms with "that fundamental fairness essential to the very concept of justice." Without attempting to distinguish between police practices that constituted "fundamental" unfairness and those which were merely illegal, he reiterated the view that the "fair trial" requirement was abridged by the use of a coerced confession "as a means of obtaining a verdict." [83] The great difficulty of giving concrete meaning to the "fair trial" standard is made abundantly clear by Roberts' repeated use of such nebulous phrases as "fundamental fairness," "concept of justice," and "due process of law," as if one somehow explained or clarified the other. Obviously, the notion of fairness, in the realm of criminal procedure no less than in other areas of human interaction, is highly elusive. Equally obvious, however, is the inevitability of making subjective judgments in the necessary course of interpreting vague constitutional provisions.

According great importance to considerations of federalism in the field of criminal procedure, Roberts deferred to the state court findings on all disputed questions of fact. While reserving the Supreme Court's authority to make an independent examination of the undisputed record, he likewise adhered to judgments of the California court's rejecting James' contention that his confession was coerced. The majority's conclusion that irregularities in this case were less extreme than those in previous state confession cases could hardly have been based on the actions of the police. In many pertinent respects they were identical to tactics used in *Chambers* v. *Florida* and the four pre-*Lisenba* confession cases that it directly controlled. Incommunicado detention, relentless questioning by batteries of officers at all hours of the day and night with the accompanying deprivation of sleep for a long

82 *Ibid.*, at 236.
83 *Ibid.*, at 237.

period of time—these factors were as prominent in *Lisenba* as in previous cases. The record further revealed a limited amount of admitted physical brutality, an ingredient never clearly established in the *Chambers* ruling.

The *Lisenba* decision was based on the Court's impression of the defendant's reaction to his treatment. He did not appear to be as frightened of the power of the police as were defendants in earlier cases, and he was not under the additional threat of mob violence. He did not belong to a racial minority and did not occupy a particularly low social status. Although lacking formal education, he was described as "clever" and apparently displayed self-confidence. Moreover, he did not confess until after his accomplice implicated him, although he had already been subjected to the most exhausting part of his interrogation.

Important as these factors were in bringing about a break in the pattern of reversal, one cannot read the Court's extensive account of facts and allegations bearing on the crime without reaching the conclusion that the majority viewed the defendant as a ruthless and designing murderer. He was portrayed as an experienced criminal, by contrast with defendants in the *Brown* and *Chambers* cases who were repeatedly described as the helpless victims of police brutality.

Although Justice Roberts concluded that the illegal acts of the police "here took them close to the line,"[84] he did not specify what additional circumstances would have rendered the proceeding unconstitutional. On the other hand, Justice Black, joined in dissent by Justice Douglas, was equally indefinite in his assertion that the case was controlled by *Chambers* v. *Florida*. In a brief opinion he stressed the similarities between this and preceding cases but failed to acknowledge the obvious differences.[85] This omission adds weight to the belief that even at this early date, Justice Black was willing to reverse any conviction based in whole or in substantial part on a confession obtained by law enforcement officers in violation of state law.

Soon after this decision other sources of disagreement began to

[84] *Ibid.*, at 239.
[85] *Ibid.*, at 241–43.

divide the Court more sharply in its determination of the admissibility of state confessions. During the same period the Court also introduced a new standard of confession admissibility for federal prosecutions.[86] By the mid-1940s the "fair trial" doctrine had largely run its course as the principal basis for deciding Fourteenth Amendment confession cases. Although reliance was occasionally accorded it for more than a decade after *Lisenba*, that decision clearly exposed its deficiencies. Justice Black, usually joined by Justices William O. Douglas, Frank Murphy, and Wiley B. Rutledge, found the "fair trial" standard too limited as a basis of procedural guarantees.[87] On the other hand, several members of the Court, led by Justice Robert H. Jackson, came to rely in part on the common-law rule of trustworthiness and to accord more importance to the probable guilt or innocence of given defendants.[88] Justice Felix Frankfurter, the leading exponent of the "due process" approach in this, as in many other areas of adjudication, seldom expressed his views exclusively in terms of the "fair trial" doctrine. By contrast with the Court's growing multiple alignment in state confession cases, it achieved nearly complete unanimity in articulating a more rigorous and far more controversial confession standard for federal trials. Analysis of this simultaneous development of dual standards—state and federal—provides the central theme for the two following chapters.

[86] *McNabb* v. *United States*, 318 U. S. 332 (1943); *Anderson* v. *United States*, 318 U. S. 350 (1943).

[87] It should be noted, however, that Justice Murphy voted with the majority in affirming the *Lisenba* conviction on the basis of the fair trial rationale and that Justices Douglas and Rutledge voted for affirmance on similar grounds in *Lyons* v. *Oklahoma*, 322 U. S. 596 (1944).

[88] At one time or another during the 1940s this position received the additional support of Chief Justices Stone and Vinson and Justices Roberts, Reed, and Burton. It achieved brief majority status in the early 1950s with the endorsement of Justices Minton and Clark.

4

The McNabb-Mallory Rule

IN 1943 the newly constituted Roosevelt Court[1] introduced a separate standard of confession for federal cases. Articulated by Justice Felix Frankfurter in *McNabb* v. *United States,* this test focused directly on police procedures and greatly widened the scope of judicial surveillance over the interrogation process. During the same period the Court also began to broaden the due process requirements of state confession admissibility well beyond the narrow confines of the "fair trial" doctrine. Although these new federal and state standards developed along separate lines of formal interpretation, they were alike in reflecting the Court's growing concern during World War II with the glaring gap between ideal and reality in the administration of American criminal justice.

By contrast with state confession requirements the federal standard rested on no provision of the Constitution but solely on the Supreme Court's supervisory authority over the administration of justice in federal courts. The *McNabb* decision drew sharp criticism from numerous federal law enforcement spokesmen and from many members of Congress. This response in fact set the tone for later campaigns against several interrogation rulings, most notably *Miranda* v. *Arizona.* Out of initial intra-Court division and persistent public controversy, the federal standard ultimately gained unanimous endorsement of the justices in the 1957 decision of *Mallory* v. *United States.* This chapter traces the development of the *McNabb-Mallory* Rule and examines congressional reaction to this effort at interrogation reform via judicial decision.

As we have seen, the Supreme Court's earliest rulings in the

[1] For general background, see C. Herman Pritchett, *The Roosevelt Court* (New York: Macmillan, 1948), especially Ch. 6.

confession field were confined to federal prosecutions. With the important exception of the *Bram* case[2] these federal decisions were not explicitly based on constitutional provisions, although in the 1920s the Court occasionally spoke in vague terms of a connection between the concept of due process of law and the proper standard of admissibility of federal confessions.[3] This suggested line of development did not materialize, however, the Court in fact deciding no more federal confession cases per se until the *McNabb* ruling of 1943. In the meantime, of course, the due process standard intimated in earlier federal cases was applied to the states through the Fourteenth Amendment and developed in the sequence of decisions analyzed in the preceding chapter. By the time that the Court once again turned its attention to the federal level, the "fair trial" requirements of due process had been fully articulated in the confession field. A strong indication that the limits of this approach were recognized by a Court majority is apparent in its failure to invoke the Due Process Clause of the Fifth Amendment in *McNabb* v. *United States*. The facts of the case were apparently amenable to the due process standard. Circumstances suggesting psychological coercion and the inability of the defendants to withstand police pressure were abundant. But the Court chose not to invoke the due process standard, or, for that matter, any constitutional test at all. It based its decision on its long recognized extraconstitutional supervisory authority over the administration of criminal justice in federal courts.[4] In adopting this approach, moreover, Justice Frankfurter, consistent with his own constitutional and judicial philosophy, made a sharp distinction between the Court's role in reviewing federal as opposed to state criminal convictions. In the former area its supervision might be highly detailed and might well reflect a conscious choice

---

2 *Bram* v. *United States*, 168 U. S. 532 (1897).

3 See *Ziang Sung Wan* v. *United States*, 266 U. S. 1 (1924).

4 Speaking for the majority, Justice Frankfurter stated that in exercising this power, the Supreme Court had, "from the very beginning of its history, formulated rules of evidence to be applied in federal criminal prosecutions." 318 U. S., at 341. In support of this contention he cited a number of prior rulings, the earliest and perhaps most famous of which arose out of the notorious Burr conspiracy, *Ex Parte Bollman and Swartwout*, 4 Cranch 75 (1807). Cf. *Nardone* v. *United States*, 308 U. S. 338, 341–42 (1939).

among policy alternatives. As he saw it, the Court's duty in federal cases was that of "establishing and maintaining civilized standards of procedure and evidence." Such standards could not be satisfied "merely by observance of those historic safeguards for securing trial by reason which are summarized as 'due process of law' . . . ."[5] This narrower, more restricted due process approach he found compatible with principles of federalism under which state trial and appellate courts were to be given a high degree of autonomy.

Like the early state confession cases, the *McNabb* case originated in the South and involved defendants of limited education who confessed only after "protracted and repeated questioning . . . ." But the parallels with earlier cases go no further. The McNabbs were members of a Tennessee mountain clan engaged in the illegal whisky business. Late in July, 1940, a federal revenue officer was shot and killed during a nighttime raid of the family enterprise. Over the next two or three days Freeman, Raymond, Benjamin, Emuil, and Barney McNabb were questioned in connection with the crime. On the basis of subsequent confessions, the first three named were convicted of second-degree murder.

Although the exact circumstances surrounding the interrogations are not clear from Frankfurter's opinion, it is apparent that the periods of questioning were lengthy and that the suspects were not afforded an opportunity to consult a lawyer or to contact relatives and friends. Frankfurter found it unnecessary to determine whether the Due Process or Self-incrimination Clauses of the Fifth Amendment prohibited this method of investigation. Rather, he concluded that it was condemned by acts of Congress which, either directly or by implication, required that persons arrested by federal officers be taken promptly before a commissioner or other judicial officer, advised of the accusation, and informed of their procedural rights.[6] Such safeguards as prompt arraignment, he insisted, "must be provided against the dangers of the over-zealous as well as the despotic." Legislation demand-

[5] 318 U. S., at 340.
[6] See Act of Mar. 1, 1879, Ch. 125, Sec. 9, 20 Stat. 327, 341–42; Act of Aug. 18, 1894, Ch. 301, 28 Stat. 416; Act of June 18, 1934, Ch. 595, 48 Stat. 1008.

ing that police show "with reasonable promptness" some legal cause for holding persons "constitutes an important safeguard—not only in assuring protection for the innocent but also in securing conviction of the guilty by methods that commend themselves to a progressive and self-confident society."[7] Thus the Court's decision did not rest on a finding that the McNabbs' confessions were made involuntarily or that they had actually been subjected to third-degree tactics. The suggestion of the third degree existed only in the presence of conditions of incommunicado detention often associated with it. This at least appeared to be Frankfurter's rationale, but other language in the opinion emphasized the low level of the McNabbs' education (none of them had gone past the fourth grade), their youth, and unfamiliarity with the law enforcement process.[8] Just what relationship existed between these individualized human factors and the investigating officers' alleged violations of law, remained very much in doubt.

The federal statutes on which this ruling was based required in very general terms that an arrested person be taken before a judicial officer for a preliminary hearing. Although two of the measures required promptness, none of them prohibited the use of evidence obtained in violation of this requirement. Frankfurter concluded, however, that no person could be convicted "upon evidence secured under the circumstances revealed here." He thus laid down an exclusionary rule implementing the "prompt arraignment" requirement in the same way that the *Weeks* Exclusionary Rule, announced thirty years earlier, put teeth into the Fourth Amendment restriction against unreasonable searches and seizures.[9] Frankfurter summarized the rationale underlying the *McNabb* Rule by stating that:

> The history of liberty has largely been the history of observance of procedural safeguards. And the effective administration of criminal justice hardly requires disregard of fair procedures imposed by law.[10]

[7] 318 U. S., at 343–44.
[8] *Ibid.*, at 334–35, 337.
[9] *Weeks v. United States*, 232 U. S. 383 (1914).
[10] 318 U. S., at 347.

The *McNabb* Rule was reiterated in the companion case of *Anderson* v. *United States*,[11] and again Mr. Justice Frankfurter was the majority spokesman. This case, also originating in Tennessee, grew out of the dynamiting of TVA property by striking coal miners. Under a "working arrangement" with the FBI, local authorities in Polk County arrested a number of strikers without warrant and subjected them to long, incommunicado sessions of questioning, in clear violation of state law. The confessions thus obtained were turned over to federal authorities who then arrested and formally charged eight of the suspects. In Frankfurter's words "the fact that the federal officers themselves were not formally guilty of illegal conduct [did] not affect the admissibility of the evidence which they secured improperly through collaboration with state officers."[12]

In both the *McNabb* and *Anderson* cases Justice Stanley F. Reed was the lone dissenter. He strongly objected to the Court's use of its supervisory authority as a basis for "broadening the possibilities of defendants escaping punishment by these more rigorous technical requirements in the administration of justice."[13] His critical view of "technical requirements" in the realm of criminal law was, of course, enthusiastically supported by many law enforcement spokesmen and rapidly gained support in Congress and among a growing minority of Supreme Court justices.[14] According to this argument, any extension of procedural safeguards beyond the time-honored test of voluntariness seriously threatened the effectiveness of law enforcement. And as Reed developed and refined his views in a number of subsequent opinions, it became clear that his idea of voluntariness was closely connected to reliability or trustworthiness of a given confession—a far more restricted view of voluntariness than the Court was then taking.

[11] 318 U. S. 350 (1943).
[12] *Ibid.*, at 356.
[13] *McNabb* v. *United States*, 318 U. S. 332, 349.
[14] For a penetrating analysis of the *McNabb* decision and its aftermath, see James E. Hogan and Joseph M. Snee, "The *McNabb-Mallory* Rule: Its Rise, Rationale and Rescue," *Georgetown Law Journal* 47 (Fall 1958), 1, 3–10. See also "Note," *Wisconsin Law Review* (Jan. 1945), 105–11.

The *McNabb* Rule, unlike earlier state confession decisions, produced substantial negative reaction in Congress. Congressman Samuel F. Hobbs, (D., Ala.) introduced legislation designed to overrule the new judicial requirement; and late in 1943, some eight and one-half months after the *McNabb* decision, a subcommittee of the House Committee on the Judiciary held hearings on this measure.[15] The Hobbs bill, H.R. 3690, stated in part

> that no failure to observe the requirement of law as to the time within which a person under arrest must be brought before a magistrate, commissioner, or court shall render inadmissible any evidence that is otherwise admissible.[16]

This was the first in a long line of congressional measures aimed at overturning Supreme Court standards in the confession field— first at the federal level only, but, following the *Miranda* ruling, at the state level as well. The hearings on H.R. 3690 contained most of the elements that have come to be so familiar in the public criticism of Court performance in this field. Major Edward J. Kelly, superintendent of police in the District of Columbia, where application of the new rule aroused greatest controversy, appeared as the first witness before the subcommittee. His testimony was replete with allegations of the devastating effect of the *McNabb* Rule on the efficiency of police work. After characterizing the decision as "one of the greatest handicaps that has ever confronted law enforcement officers," he made the free-swinging assertion— based on nothing in the decision itself—that the new procedure was a "very grave and dangerous handicap to all law enforcement officers throughout the entire country . . . ."[17] This claim was ludicrous in view of Justice Frankfurter's careful distinction between the new federal requirement outlined in *McNabb* and the far more limited due process guarantee afforded by the Fourteenth Amendment in state confession cases. Referring in particular to what he saw as the adverse effect of the *McNabb* Rule on

[15] See U. S., Congress, House, *Admission of Evidence in Certain Cases*, Hearings before Subcommittee Number 2 of the Committee on the Judiciary, 78 Cong., 1 sess., Nov. 24–Dec. 10, 1943.

[16] *Ibid.*, at 1.

[17] *Ibid.*, at 1, 3.

law enforcement in Washington, D. C., Major Kelly insisted on the necessity of a period during which the police should have exclusive control over the suspect.[18]

Subcommittee Chairman Zebulon Weaver (D., N. C.) shared Kelly's view and sized up the situation as one in which "judges" (presumably the *McNabb* majority) were "undertaking to run the police department," and were apparently more concerned "about some fellow . . . charged with the crime than . . . with protecting the decent, law-abiding citizens of this community."[19] This fallacy of presuming the almost certain guilt of anyone suspected by the police has been repeated endlessly by many of the court's law enforcement critics over the years.[20] Agreeing with Weaver, Major Kelly employed another anti-Court device, this one reflecting the highly defensive posture so often assumed by the police. If a series of murders occurred in the District of Columbia, the police department, he insisted, could not be held responsible for failure "to solve these cases," since the officers were "absolutely prevented and handicapped to proceed with a proper, efficient, and necessary investigation . . . ."[21]

In a detailed statement the bill's sponsor, Congressman Hobbs, himself a former trial judge, stated a strong preference for the

[18] "I do not feel, as Superintendent of Police of this city, that we should be interfered with until we have had a reasonable time to investigate properly and sufficiently all serious crimes that are committed in the nation's capital." *Ibid.*, at 6.
[19] *Ibid.*, at 7.
[20] We are told, for example, that "criminal interrogators must deal with criminal offenders on a somewhat lower moral plane than that upon which ethical, law-abiding citizens are expected to conduct their everyday affairs." Apparently the interrogator, according to this line of argument, is capable of determining in advance whether he is dealing with a criminal offender or an innocent person, although precisely how he manages this bit of magic remains shrouded in mystery. Fred E. Inbau, "Police Interrogation: A Practical Necessity," in *Police Power and Individual Freedom: The Quest for Balance*, ed. by Claude R. Sowle (Chicago: Aldine Publishing Company, 1962), 151. In a similar vein another critic pointed out that the greatest chance of getting a confession is at the time of arrest, "when the shock of being caught is greatest and before he has a chance to think things over; particularly before he gets in jail and has a chance to talk the matter over with other experienced criminals." Somehow the arrested person is presumed not only to be guilty but also to be an experienced criminal. Cornelius W. Wickersham, Jr., "The Supreme Court and Federal Criminal Procedure," *Cornell Law Quarterly* 44 (Fall 1958), 14–31, at 29–31.
[21] U. S., Congress, House, Hearings before Subcommittee Number 2 of the Committee on the Judiciary on H. R. 3690, 8.

voluntariness test of confession admissibility. Irrespective of the treatment of the prisoner and of the amount of incriminating evidence against him, Hobbs argued, any confession made prior to arraignment must be excluded from evidence, with the result that some obviously guilty defendants "must go scot free."[22] He could not believe that this implementation of federal laws calling for prompt commitment and arraignment truly reflected the intent of Congress. Besides his criticism of the *McNabb* Rule itself, Hobbs tried to undermine its authority by attacking the professional qualifications of its author in the field of criminal procedure. Some of the worst elements of the argument *ad hominem* are apparent in the following excerpt:

> With all due respect to Mr. Justice Frankfurter, if my information be correct, he has never tried a criminal case in his life. He has had no experience to make him familiar with the procedure in criminal cases. He does not know from experience what problems our law enforcement officers are up against, nor [sic] know the necessity for thorough investigation before charges are preferred. I doubt if he knows what it means for a man to be suspected and immediately arraigned and charged of record with a heinous crime, when thorough investigation would show him innocent.[23]

Frankfurter's recognized brilliance as a legal scholar whose published work included critical analysis of several aspects of criminal procedure[24] easily refuted this charge of inexperience. The congressman's remarks appear even more unwarranted when it is remembered that several other members of the *McNabb* majority —Justices Black and Murphy to name just two—had considerable first-hand experience with the routine activities of law enforcement, from such vantage points as "city judge," "recorders court judge," public prosecutor, and attorney general.[25]

[22] *Ibid.*, at 19.
[23] *Ibid.*, at 25.
[24] See, for example, Felix Frankfurter, *The Case of Sacco and Vanzetti: A Critical Analysis for Lawyers and Laymen*, (Boston: Little, 1927; Universal Library Ed., 1962).
[25] See generally, John P. Frank, *Mr. Justice Black—The Man and His Opinions* (New York: Knopf, 1949), 17, 22–31; J. Woodford Howard, Jr., *Mr. Justice Mur-*

H. R. 3690 was also supported by the testimony of Judge Harold M. Stephens of the District of Columbia Court of Appeals, who confined his observations to an endorsement of the soundness of the voluntariness test and what he saw as the misplaced emphasis of the *McNabb* Rule. He contended that the "third degree," against which the rule was directed, occurred as frequently *after* formal commitment as before. Such abuses could be stopped, not by rules excluding voluntary confessions from evidence, but by "improved personnel and facilities for police forces so that character and efficiency and scientific methods rather than brutality will be used to obtain evidence."[26]

Attorney General Francis Biddle, while sharing some misgivings about the new requirement, failed to give the Hobbs bill his endorsement. Referring to the pending Washington, D. C., case of *United States* v. *Mitchell,* mentioned in previous testimony as one of many prosecutions adversely affected by the *McNabb* Rule, he indicated that the Court might have occasion to "clarify its new doctrine." He pointed out that the Hobbs bill, even if enacted, "would leave unaltered the underlying law with respect to the duty to arraign and the illegality of detention when that duty has not been fulfilled."[27] As an alternative he suggested that Congress soften the prompt arraignment requirement itself by specifying merely that arraignment occur within a "reasonable time" after arrest. He proposed a substitute measure embodying this approach that would, in effect, recognize the authority of the police to question a suspect in private during a reasonable period prior to a preliminary judicial proceeding at which the suspect would be advised of his rights and formally charged.[28] Beyond conceding that seven or eight days of prearraignment detention would probably be excessive, Biddle made no effort to specify what he meant by the term "reasonable time."

The principal sources of organizational support for the Hobbs bill were largely restricted to the field of law enforcement, led by

---

phy: A Political Biography (Princeton: Princeton Univ. Press, 1968), 22–30, 180–228.

[26] *Hearings* on H. R. 3690, 13.

[27] *Ibid.*, at 34.

[28] For the full text of Biddle's substitute bill, see *ibid.*, at 36–37.

the National Sheriffs Association and the International Association of Chiefs of Police. Opposition to the measure was voiced by
The Railway Labor Executives' Association, the Brotherhood of
Locomotive Engineers, the Brotherhood of Railroad Trainmen,
the American Civil Liberties Union, and a number of private
attorneys. Although efforts to enact the Hobbs bill were ultimately
unsuccessful, the debate surrounding it provided some indication
of the dimensions of public controversy aroused by the *McNabb*
Rule.

Criticism of the decision was also reflected in the deliberations
over the Federal Rules of Criminal Procedure, authorized by congressional enactments and Supreme Court orders in the years immediately preceding the *McNabb* ruling but not put into effect
until 1946.[29] Rule 5(a) codified existing federal statutes respecting
arraignment—the same statutes upon which the *McNabb* Rule
rested. It reads as follows:

> An officer making an arrest under a warrant shall take the arrested
> person without unnecessary delay before the nearest available
> commissioner or before any other nearby officer empowered to
> commit persons charged with offenses against the laws of the
> United States. When a person arrested without a warrant is
> brought before a commissioner or other officer, a complaint shall
> be filed forthwith.[30]

An early draft section 5(b), embodying the *McNabb* Rule by requiring the exclusion of evidence obtained in violation of 5(a),
was strongly opposed by the American Bar Association and was
omitted from the draft ultimately approved by the Supreme
Court.[31]

Some sharp anti-*McNabb* reaction came from academic circles.
Writing in the February, 1944, issue of the *Michigan Law Re-*

---

[29] For a comprehensive discussion of their evolution and content, see Lester B. Orfield, "The Federal Rules of Criminal Procedure," *Nebraska Law Review* 26 (May 1947), 570–627. For additional background see Albert J. Harno, "Proposed Rules of Criminal Procedure: Final Draft," *Michigan Law Review* 42 (Feb. 1944), 623–30.

[30] 327 U. S. 821 (1946).

[31] See "Note," *American Journal of Police Science* 36 (Sept.–Oct. 1945), 222–26, at 225.

view, Professor John Barker Waite charged that the decision pro-
pounded "the wisdom of a judicial policy which turns known
criminals loose upon society as a means of punishing the police."
The *McNabb* Rule, he argued, was just as impractical, just as
visionary, as the *Weeks* Exclusionary Rule. Far from improving
police methods, the latter had, he insisted, "conduced to serious
police misbehavior."[32] While conceding that it might be too late
to repudiate the *Weeks* Rule, he nevertheless urged the rejection
of the *McNabb* approach, which he regarded as both ineffective
and dangerous.

Without directly acknowledging the widespread criticism of its
new evidentiary rule, the Court in *United States* v. *Mitchell*[33]
gracefully gave ground, as anticipated in hearings on the Hobbs
bill. Once more Justice Frankfurter acted as spokesman for the
majority, this time holding challenged evidence admissible and
overturning the D. C. Court of Appeals reversal of James Mitchell's housebreaking and larceny convictions. The evidence in
question consisted of an admission of guilt and recovered items of
stolen property. According to the police, Mitchell's admission and
consent to the search of his house were made shortly after his
arrest, immediately upon his arrival at the station house. They
acknowledged that Mitchell was subsequently held illegally, without arraignment, for eight days. The Court ruled, however, that
Mitchell's illegal detention did not "retroactively change the circumstances under which he made the disclosures."[34] Frankfurter
insisted that this conclusion was consistent with the principle laid
down in *McNabb* v. *United States.*

> Inexcusable detention for the purpose of illegally extracting evi-
> dence from an accused, and the successful extraction of such ex-
> culpatory statements by continuous questioning for many hours
> under psychological pressure, were the decisive features in the
> *McNabb* case which led us to rule that a conviction on such evi-
> dence could not stand.[35]

[32] John Barker Waite, "Police Regulation by Rules of Evidence," *Michigan Law Review* 42 (Feb. 1944), 679–93, at 681, 685.
[33] 322 U. S. 65 (1944).
[34] *Ibid.,* at 70.
[35] *Ibid.,* at 67.

In the closing sentence of his opinion, Frankfurter replied obliquely to some of the criticism leveled at the *McNabb* rationale. The Court's power to formulate rules of evidence, he said, was "not to be used as an indirect mode of disciplining misconduct."[36]

Despite the attempt to square this holding with *McNabb*, it clearly offered trial judges an added opportunity to avoid the far-reaching implications that many initially read into that decision. The Mitchell case made it clear that at least some admissions and confessions made prior to arraignment were admissible and that even reasonably prompt arraignment was not required under all circumstances. The Court seemed to be restricting the *McNabb* Rule to circumstances in which psychological coercion accompanied illegal detention and thus to be moving back toward the traditional voluntariness criterion.

Nevertheless, Justice Reed, who filed a separate concurring opinion, objected even to this narrowed version of the rule. "The juristic theory under which a confession should be admitted or barred," he stated, "is bottomed on the testimonial trustworthiness of the confession."[37] Thus Reed expressed for the first time a view which he and a growing number of justices adopted in later confession cases, both federal and state—a view which, as we shall see, received the brief support of a Court majority in the early 1950s. Reed, falling back on the original common-law rationale, believed that the voluntariness requirement was justified mainly because it guarded the defendant against use of a false confession.

After the *Mitchell* case those federal judges who had been critical of the *McNabb* Rule apparently felt free to ignore it.[38] The Hobbs bill, slightly amended but retaining its flat negation of the *McNabb* requirement, was favorably reported one month later by the House Committee on the Judiciary, and was subsequently approved by the House. Although the measure died in the Senate, it was reintroduced during the Seventy-ninth and Eightieth Con-

---

[36] *Ibid.*, at 70–71.
[37] *Ibid.*, at 71.
[38] See Hogan and Snee, "The *McNabb-Mallory* Rule," at 8–10.

gresses, and on both occasions the House again approved the measure. It was under serious consideration in Congress until the summer of 1947 when, for a third time, the bill was rejected by the Senate.[39] During this period, moreover, the scholarly debate regarding Supreme Court performance in the confession field generally, and at the federal level in particular, continued unabated.[40]

As it turned out, the Supreme Court was not content to allow, either through its own silence or remaining uncertainty, the gradual erosion of the new federal confession standard. In the 1948 case of *Upshaw* v. *United States*,[41] it reaffirmed by the narrow margin of five to four the *McNabb* Rule in even more positive terms than those of Justice Frankfurter's initial pronouncement. At issue was the confession of Andrew Upshaw, a Negro defendant in the District of Columbia, to the crime of grand larceny after a thirty-hour period of detention, during which he was not taken before a committing magistrate. Although the Court accepted no allegations of coercion and Upshaw was apparently not put through the intensive "grilling" process to which the McNabbs were subjected, this lengthy period of detention was in clear violation of Rule 5(a) of the Federal Rules of Criminal Procedure. Brushing aside the lower court's attempt to confine the McNabb precedent to circumstances of psychological coercion, Justice Black for the majority held that the *Upshaw* case fell "squarely" within that ruling irrespective of "what was decided in the Mitchell case."[42] The crucial element of the *McNabb* decision, as he interpreted it, was the making of a confession "during illegal detention due to failure promptly to carry a prisoner before a committing magistrate," regardless of whether the confession was extracted by physical or psychological force.[43] The police gave

---

[39] For further discussion of the Hobbs bill and the unsuccessful effort to bring about its enactment, see "Note," *Cornell Law Quarterly* 32 (June 1947), 594–600; and "Comment," *Journal of Criminal Law and Criminology* 38 (July–Aug. 1947), 136–38.

[40] See, for example, Fred E. Inbau, "The Confession Dilemma in the United States Supreme Court," *Illinois Law Review* 43 (Sept.–Oct. 1948), 442–63; Charles T. McCormick, "Some Problems and Developments in the Admissibility of Confessions," 239–78.

[41] 335 U. S. 410.

[42] *Ibid.*, at 412.

[43] *Ibid.*, 413.

as their only justification for holding Upshaw on suspicion their lack of evidence against him. They simply wished to question him in the hope that something more tangible might be produced and contended that this method was fully consistent with the "usual police procedure of questioning a suspect." Usual or not, as Black put it bluntly, this practice "is in violation of law and confessions thus obtained are inadmissible under the *McNabb* Rule."[44]

In a long dissenting opinion, Justice Reed, supported by Chief Justice Fred M. Vinson and Justices Robert H. Jackson and Harold H. Burton, took sharp exception to what he saw as an extension of the *McNabb* doctrine. Once again he insisted that exclusion of a confession was justified only if it could be shown that some form of compulsion accompanied detention, whether or not the detention itself conformed to prompt arraignment requirements. "In criminal trials," he argued, "the method of obtaining evidence has never been a reason for barring its use except where constitutional rights were violated."[45] By the Court's own definition constitutional rights were not at issue unless some form of coercion existed, in which case the Due Process and Self-incrimination clauses protected the defendant. By this line of reasoning, Reed sought to undermine the rationale of the *Mc-Nabb* Rule as applied in *Upshaw*. He did not deny the Court's supervisory power over the administration of criminal justice. But he tried to show that such authority did not provide a legitimate basis for excluding confessions based on nothing more than the justices' own notions of propriety in the conduct of criminal investigations. Far from strengthening the administration of criminal justice, this decision, according to Reed, actually placed "another weapon in the hand of the criminal world." He viewed the *Upshaw* requirement of commitment "without unnecessary delay" as an "iron rule," lacking the flexibility he assumed to be essential to effective law enforcement. The Court failed, in his estimation, to recognize a vital distinction between "necessary and unnecessary delay in commitment."[46] In Reed's scale of

44 *Ibid.*, at 414.
45 *Ibid.*, at 427.
46 *Ibid.*, at 436.

values, society was far more gravely threatened by the judge-made policy of "prompt arraignment" than by abuse of discretion on the part of the police in holding suspects for private questioning.

No doubt Justice Reed correctly assessed the *Upshaw* decision as an extension of the original *McNabb* Rule. But he probably overstated the inflexibility of the requirement of commitment "without unnecessary delay." All that the Court actually held in *Upshaw* was that a thirty-hour period of detention, on mere suspicion without bringing the suspect before a judicial officer, rendered any resulting confession inadmissible. It went no further in spelling out the meaning of the phrase "unnecessary delay." The great importance of the *Upshaw* decision as a milestone in the development of a federal confession standard was that it made a sharp distinction between the new requirement of prompt preliminary hearing and traditional considerations of coercion and voluntariness.[47]

It remained for the Warren Court nearly a decade later to attempt clarification of "unnecessary delay" as required by the Federal Rules of Criminal Procedure. Moving logically from the *McNabb* and *Upshaw* precedents, a unanimous Court in *Mallory v. United States*[48] set forth more explicitly the meaning of the "prompt arraignment" requirement. For the first time it attempted a precise definition of "unnecessary delay," and in doing so, aroused even more controversy than the *McNabb* decision itself had produced. Nevertheless, "the Mallory decision left much uncertainty as to its import in fact situations not on all fours with it."[49] While it outlawed delay in arraignment, solely for purposes of interrogation, it did not indicate how much leeway the police would have when the arrest took place at a time when no committing magistrate was on duty.

From the standpoint of timing and factual circumstances, the

---

[47] For further discussion of the *Upshaw* ruling and its implications, see Hogan and Snee, "The *McNabb-Mallory* Rule," 10–15. See also "Note," *North Carolina Law Review* 27 (June 1949), 552–58; "Note," *Utah Law Review* 1 (1949), 82–89; "Note," *Dickinson Law Review* 53 (Mar. 1949), 206–209; "Note," *Boston University Law Review* 29 (Apr. 1949), 250–53.

[48] 354 U. S. 449 (1957).

[49] Hogan and Snee, "The *McNabb-Mallory* Rule," 26.

case of *Mallory* v. *United States* was tailor-made for critics of the Court. Announced on June 24, 1957, it provided one more convenient target for those who were already branding the Warren Court as an agent of "race-mixing" or a "tool of Moscow."[50] It is hardly a coincidence that many of those who lashed out at the *Mallory* decision were foremost critics of the Court's rulings in areas of race relations and internal security. This parallel was especially evident in congressional efforts to overturn or modify leading decisions in each of these areas.

The *Mallory* case grew out of the rape of a thirty-eight-year-old white housewife in the basement of a Washington, D. C., apartment building. Suspicion immediately centered on Andrew R. Mallory, the nineteen-year-old son of a Negro janitor who lived in the basement, near the resident laundry facilities where the crime occurred. Mallory was arrested along with two other suspects shortly after 2:00 P.M. and was immediately questioned for a period of from thirty to forty-five minutes. At about 4:00 P.M., according to the undisputed record, he agreed to take a "lie detector test," but this phase of his questioning did not begin until about eight o'clock that evening. The polygraph operator later testified that after about an hour and a half of questioning, Mallory began to "break" and soon made a full confession, which he repeated to other officers at 10:00 P.M. At this point, some seven and one-half hours after his arrest and subsequent to his confession, the police made their first attempt to contact a United States commissioner for the purpose of arraigning the suspect. Finding no commissioner on duty at that hour, they secured Mallory's "consent to examination by the deputy-coroner who noted no indicia of physical or psychological coercion." After confrontation by the complaining witness and "practically every man in the sex squad," Mallory, in response to further questioning by three

---

[50] For analysis of congressional reaction to Court decisions in these and related areas, see Clifford M. Lytle, *The Warren Court and Its Critics* (Tucson: Univ. of Arizona Press, 1968), Chs. 2 and 3. The vehemence of such criticism can be attributed in part to the normal political motive of appealing to "the constituents back home . . . ." Lytle provides ample support for the belief that this tendency has been particularly strong "when the protests have concerned the trend of civil rights decisions." *Ibid.*, at 11. See also C. Herman Pritchett, *Congress versus the Supreme Court, 1957–1960* (Minneapolis: Univ. of Minnesota Press, 1961), 34–40, 117.

officers again repeated the confession and dictated it to a stenographer between 11:30 and 1:30 that night. On the following morning he was brought before a commissioner and arraigned. Mallory's trial was delayed for one year because of doubt about his "capacity to understand the proceedings against him," a factor connected to Frankfurter's description of the defendant as a person of "limited intelligence."[51] The prosecution, relying heavily on the confession, was ultimately completed, however, and Mallory's conviction, carrying with it a recommended sentence of death, was affirmed by the District of Columbia Court of Appeals.[52]

In reversing this judgment, the Supreme Court acknowledged that the prompt arraignment requirement of Rule 5(a) did "not call for mechanical or automatic obedience." A "brief delay" might be permitted if, for example, the suspect's "volunteered" story could be quickly verified by third parties. But delay could not be condoned if it gave police an "opportunity for the extraction of a confession."[53] Once again attention was directed to the conditions under which coercive pressure might be secretly applied, rather than to the question of whether impermissible force had been used in a discrete situation. Frankfurter summarized the Court's objective in the following language:

> It is not the function of the police to arrest, as it were, at large and to use an interrogating process at police headquarters in order to determine whom they should charge before a committing magistrate on "probable cause."[54]

The Court's recognition of a margin of flexibility in the prompt arraignment requirement, far from justifying the action of the police in detaining and questioning Mallory, served to underscore its illegality. The Court did not attempt a sweeping condemnation of all police questioning of suspects—not even all private questioning. It raised no objection to any form of *post-arraignment* interrogation. What it did insist upon, and what

[51] 354 U. S., at 451.
[52] 236 F. 2d 701 (1956).
[53] 354 U. S., at 455.
[54] *Ibid.*, at 456.

critics of the decision found so objectionable, was a procedure that permitted at least minimal judicial surveillance of detention—a procedure that gave the suspect an opportunity to be informed of his right to remain silent and to be assisted by a lawyer. Typical of the negative responses on this point was Assistant Attorney General Warren Olney's quoted remark in the *Washington Evening Star* two days after the decision: "This opinion says in so many words that police can't question a suspect after his arrest."[55] At stake here was not the authority to question, in the abstract, but the power to question in private (or in secret) under conditions highly favorable to the police, indeed conditions within their exclusive control.

The reversal of Mallory's conviction did not, of course, result automatically in his release, although some critics of the decision either jumped to this erroneous conclusion or sought to convey such an impression. The ruling declared Mallory's confession inadmissible because it was obtained in violation of Rule 5(a) of the Federal Rules of Criminal Procedure. The prosecution was not prohibited from pressing for a new trial, provided this portion of the evidence was disregarded. As it turned out, Department of Justice officials ordered Mallory's release, concluding that without the confession a second successful prosecution would be impossible. It was easy enough to blame the Supreme Court for this result, thereby sidestepping the embarrassing question of whether,

[55] Olney went on to assert that the decision would have its greatest impact in the area of "gangster crimes." The "hardened professional criminals" would be the chief beneficiaries of the decision. *Washington Evening Star*, June 26, 1957, quoted in 103 *Congressional Record* 10472, 85 Cong., 1 sess. (June 27, 1957.) This line of argument has strong emotional appeal but is of highly doubtful validity. Studies clearly indicate that those most likely to be affected by judicial restrictions on police interrogation are not the seasoned professional criminals, especially those identified with "organized crime." Such persons are usually fully aware of their procedural rights and are likely to have access to competent legal counsel. Those who stand to benefit from such decisions are typically suspects like Mallory himself—people who lack education, money, social or political influence, or who are vulnerable because of unfamiliarity with criminal procedure, subnormal intelligence, psychological abnormality, and related factors. For documentation of this conclusion with specific reference to the Negro minority, see United States Commission on Civil Rights, Bk. Five, *Justice* (Washington, D. C.: United States Government Printing Office, 1961). See generally Jerome Hall, "Police and Law in a Democratic Society," 133–77; and David L. Sterling, "Police Interrogation and the Psychology of Confession," *Journal of Public Law* 14, no. 1 (1965), 25–65.

in view of the alleged certainty of Mallory's guilt, police and prosecution could have built a stronger case to begin with. For such Court-baiters as Senator Strom Thurmond, the possibility of law enforcement error, even as a partial explanation for Mallory's release, carried no weight at all. In a characteristic denunciation from the Senate floor on June 27, three days after the decision, he expressed "regret" that the Court showed "more concern for the rights of Communists and criminals, including rapists and murderers, than . . . for the protection of innocent American citizens." He also regretted that Congress had "wasted so much time over a so-called civil rights bill when the very lives of innocent women in our capital city [were] being endangered by decisions such as that in the Mallory case."[56]

A more tangible congressional response to the Court's ruling followed in short order. On July 9, 1957, two bills designed to overturn the *Mallory* Rule were introduced respectively by Congressmen William C. Cramer (D., Fla.) and Kenneth B. Keating (R., N. Y.). These virtually identical measures set the pattern for numerous anti-*Mallory* proposals in succeeding congressional sessions. They provided that confessions and related statements not be excluded from evidence "solely because of delay" in bringing an arrested person before "the appropriate committing officer."[57] The legislative response to *Mallory* was thus almost identical to the Hobbs bill. The overall objective of both *McNabb* and *Mallory* critics in Congress was to sever the automatic connection between delay in arraignment and the use at trial of confessions obtained during such periods of delay.[58] Although the original Cramer and Keating bills died in the House judiciary committee, a similar measure was passed by the House during the next session of Congress. This bill, H. R. 11477, was cosponsored by Congress-

---

[56] 103 *Congressional Record* 10471 (June 27, 1957).

[57] See H. R. 8596 and H. R. 8600, 103 *Cong. Rec.* 11163. See also Digest of Public General Bills, 85 Cong., 1 sess., at 488. Cf. the Poff bill, H. R. 8624, introduced the following day, July 10, 1957, 103 *Cong. Rec.* 11284.

[58] For further elaboration of this point of view and some of the opposition it aroused, see U. S., Congress, House, *Supreme Court Decisions*, Hearings before the Special Subcommittee to Study Decisions of the Supreme Court of the United States of the Committee on the Judiciary, 85 Cong., 2 sess., 1958. Although published in 1958, these hearings were conducted during July, August, and October, 1957.

man Edwin E. Willis (D., La.) and by Keating himself. It provided that "Evidence, including statements and confessions, otherwise admissible, shall not be inadmissible solely because of delay in taking an arrested person before a commissioner or other officer empowered to commit persons charged with offenses against the United States."[59] This sweeping provision was counterbalanced in part by a second section which declared inadmissible any statement made to an interrogating officer prior to advising a suspect that he could remain silent and that any statement he made might be used against him. Some observers saw this second provision as a negation of the first, and, admittedly, it added confusion to a measure already lacking in clarity. One essential difference between the *Mallory* Rule and the bill's Section (b) was that the latter presumably permitted police to give the necessary advice to suspects, while the former entrusted this responsibility, consistent with Rule 5(a), to a judicial officer. The Willis-Keating bill came under criticism in the House for its failure to limit or qualify the phrase "delay in taking an arrested person before a commissioner . . . ." It was pointed out that the Federal Rules of Criminal Procedure referred to "unnecessary delay" and that the bill might easily be interpreted as overruling that requirement and not merely its application in the *Mallory* case.[60] Despite this objection and the failure of leading proponents to resolve the apparent conflict in language, H. R. 11477 was passed by a vote of 294 to 79 on July 2, 1958.

During Senate hearings later the same month, the question over the indefinite wording of the House bill and its Senate counterpart arose once more. The latter measure, S. 2970, better known as the Eastland bill, was identical to Section (a) of the Willis-Keating bill but contained no additional provision requiring that the suspect be advised of his rights. The Senate hearings were conducted by a subcommittee of the Committee on the Judiciary and also covered the Butler bill (S. 3355) and the

[59] Reprinted in U. S., Congress, Senate, *Admission of Evidence (Mallory Rule)*, Hearings before a Subcommittee of the Committee on the Judiciary, 85 Cong., 2 sess., 1958, at 2.

[60] See remarks of Congressman Sidney R. Yates (D., Ill.), June 30, 1958, 104 *Cong. Rec.* 12692.

Morse bill (S. 3325). The first of these measures sought to authorize a twelve-hour delay between arrest and arraignment, during which time the police might, presumably question the suspect in private. By contrast the Morse bill called for the preinterrogation warnings of the nature of the offense under investigation; of the suspect's right to remain silent; that anything he says might be used as evidence against him; and that he has the right to have counsel present during police questioning.[61] In testimony before the subcommittee, Oliver Gasch, United States attorney for the District of Columbia, expressing preference for the Willis-Keating bill, contended that the *Mallory* decision had seriously impaired the administration of criminal justice in the nation's capital. Unlike the Court's most extreme critics in Congress, however, Gasch avoided characterization of the *Mallory* Rule as a device for turning rapists and murderers loose on society. Rather, he stressed the imprecision of the Court's opinion, arguing that it led to confusion and inconsistency in application at trial and intermediate appellate court levels. He submitted a table of cases affected by the *Mallory* Rule, seventeen of them resulting in affirmances of convictions and five in reversals—hardly overwhelming support for critics of the decision.[62] Washington, D. C., Chief of Police Robert V. Murray speculated that "a very large number of the most serious crimes that have been committed in the District of Columbia . . . would have gone unpunished and unsolved if we had had to work under the *Mallory* decision."[63] And Professor Fred E. Inbau, a long-time critic of the Court's federal confession standard, strenuously objected to what he viewed as the Court's misguided and impractical effort to discipline the police through rules of evidence. He insisted that the incidence of the "third degree" had diminished greatly since publication of the Wickersham Report and the Court's earliest state confession decisions, contending in effect that the Court had no factual basis for the doubts prompting its *Mallory* decision. He concluded, nevertheless, that "evidence of guilt," even if illegally

[61] *Admission of Evidence (Mallory Rule)*, at 2–3.
[62] *Ibid.*, at 25–27.
[63] *Ibid.*, at 37.

83

obtained, "ought to be usable against that guilty person." Police reform could be better achieved "by other means than turning an obviously guilty person loose . . . ."[64]

Congressman Keating told subcommittee members that the *Mallory* case had "created a crisis in federal law enforcement." He believed that the widespread consternation produced by the decision was fully justified and that it was incumbent upon Congress to "make sure" that residents of the District of Columbia, whom he described as "second-class citizens," received "the same protection from lawlessness as their neighbors in Maryland and Virginia and the rest of the country." Denying any intention of overturning Rule 5(a), he contended that the single objective of H. R. 11477 was "to do away with the mathematical equation devised by the Supreme Court between the promptness of arraignment and the admissibility of evidence." While recognizing the seriousness of the problem of police illegality, Keating charged that the Supreme Court was attempting through the *Mallory* Rule to deal with the problem "in an indirect and thoroughly inappropriate manner." He saw the requirement as, in effect, putting the arresting officer on trial rather than the criminal suspect and regarded "the public" as the ultimate loser:

> The lawless policeman and the lawless citizen are both threats to the community. I do not follow the logic of a judicial process under which their double offenses are deemed to cancel each other out . . . . Whatever the case . . . the suppression of trustworthy evidence is a wholly illogical expedient for dealing with the problem.[65]

Although agreeing that "procedures in the courts" tended "to weigh the scales of justice against the prosecutor," Senator Joseph S. Clark (D., Pa.) expressed misgivings about congressional efforts to redress the balance.[66] Stronger objections to the Willis-Keating bill and related measures were voiced by representatives

[64] *Ibid.*, at 74.
[65] *Ibid.*, at 16–19.
[66] He felt that the problem could be met "far better by the courts on a case-by-case basis than . . . through the intervention of the legislative arm of our government." *Ibid.*, at 12.

of Americans for Democratic Action; the American Civil Liberties Union; and the Washington, D. C., Bar Association. The latter organization was represented before the subcommittee by its president, De Long Harris, who argued that the bulk of anti-*Mallory* sentiment came from the police and that, although they failed "to admit it," what they really wanted was "a right to arrest citizens without probable cause and without penalty of any sort."[67] Thus the *Mallory* decision, although resting on extra-constitutional grounds, offered indirect protection of a Fourth Amendment value. Perhaps Justice Frankfurter had this connection in mind when he said that an arrested person "is not to be taken to police headquarters in order to carry out a process of inquiry that lends itself, even if not so designed, to eliciting damaging statements to support *the arrest* and ultimately his guilt."[68] The "probable cause" requirement of the Fourth Amendment, applicable to arrest warrants as well as to search warrants, was philosophically linked to the prompt arraignment requirement in much the same way as the Fifth Amendment immunity against self-incrimination and the Sixth Amendment right to the assistance of counsel. But because constitutional development in the confession field, both before and after the *Mallory* case, has involved only the latter two provisions in combination with the broad requirement of due process of law, this kinship with Fourth Amendment rights has been obscured. The connection becomes more evident in the context of "field interrogation" and the related "stop and frisk" procedure, both of which began to come under Supreme Court review only in the late 1960s.[69]

Out of the conflicting and largely inconclusive testimony and case tabulations purporting to assess the impact of the *Mallory* decision, enough doubt arose to persuade the subcommittee that the Willis-Keating bill should be amended and that no further action of any kind should be taken on the Eastland, Butler, and Morse bills. The amendment consisted of the single word *reason-*

---

[67] *Ibid.*, at 110.
[68] 354 U. S., at 454. Italics added.
[69] See *Terry v. Ohio*, 392 U. S. 1 (1968); *Sibron v. New York*, 392 U. S. 40 (1968); *Orozco v. Texas*, 394 U. S. 324 (1969).

able, inserted before the word *delay*, thus supposedly placing some limitation on the period of time during which police might obtain admissible evidence through questioning prior to taking the suspect before a committing magistrate. Subcommittee Chairman Senator Joseph C. O'Mahoney of Wyoming insisted that the amended version of H. R. 11477 was aimed not at criticism of the Supreme Court, but simply at clarification of the *Mallory* requirement.[70] Whether the phrase "reasonable delay" was actually an improvement over "unnecessary delay," the language of Rule 5(a) on which the Court had relied, was anybody's guess. And the heated Senate debate that followed did little to dispel the confusion.

Senator Sam J. Ervin, Jr. (D., N. C.) played a leading role in opposing the amended House bill. He regarded the choice as that of accepting the *Mallory* Rule and thus protecting criminals, or returning to the "voluntariness test" of confession admissibility and protecting society. Sounding a theme to which he returned again and again during the succeeding decade, he asserted that "in recent years enough has been done for those who murder, rape, and rob; and . . . it is about time for Congress to do something for those who do not wish to be murdered, or raped, or robbed." Sharply attacking the entire *McNabb-Mallory* sequence of decisions as misguided and unsupported, he said that he was "sometimes . . . inclined to think that the precedent to which some members of the Supreme Court" were "most faithful" was "the precedent set by Josh Billings' mule, which 'didn't kick according to no rule.' " He objected to any device, including the *Mallory* Rule, that substituted "artificiality such as mere time for the free will of the accused as a basis to exclude testimony."[71]

Over these and similar objections, the O'Mahoney amendment was accepted by the narrow margin of forty-one to thirty-nine. On the same day, August 19, 1958, the amended Willis-Keating bill passed the Senate sixty-five to twelve and was duly referred to a Senate-House conference committee.[72] Acting quick-

[70] For background see 104 *Cong. Rec.* 18483, ff. (Aug. 19, 1958).
[71] *Ibid.*, at 18481, 18483.
[72] *Ibid.*, at 18520–21.

ly in the closing days of the congressional session, this group substituted for the one-word O'Mahoney amendment a clause providing that delay in taking a person before a committing magistrate "is to be considered as an element in determining the voluntary or involuntary nature of . . . statements or confessions." On August 23, the day of adjournment, the House agreed to the conference report. But in a dramatic, last-ditch effort, opponents blocked it through a point of order introduced by Senator John A. Carroll (D., Colo.), based on the contention that the conference report added "new matter" to the bill, in violation of Senate Rule 27. In the closing minutes of the session—shortly after four o'clock on Sunday morning, August 24—the point of order was sustained.[73] Thus the first major effort to overturn or, at the very least to modify, the *Mallory* decision barely fell short of success in Congress.

During the following year, the Willis-Keating bill was again introduced and, despite the waning enthusiasm of anti-*Mallory* forces, it was passed by the House 262 to 138.[74] This time, however, the measure died in the Senate judiciary committee. Throughout the extended congressional dispute over the *Mallory* decision, the *Washington Evening Star* waged a formidable campaign against the ruling. Editorials and news items underscoring the alleged restrictions that it placed on Washington, D. C., police and dramatizing the continuing criminal career of Andrew Mallory were inserted into the *Congressional Record* by various sponsors of anti-*Mallory* legislation.[75] The *Washington Post*, on the other hand, lined up in support of the controversial ruling and provided useful ammunition for opponents of the Willis-Keating bill, as the following excerpt from an editorial reprinted in the *Congressional Record* indicates:

> Police and prosecutors have learned to live with the *Mallory* rule. Their effectiveness in convicting the guilty has not been impaired; and the dire predictions that a horde of criminals would

[73] *Ibid.*, at 19555, 19565, 19568, 19574.
[74] 105 *Cong. Rec.* 12880 (July 7, 1959).
[75] See, for example, 103 *Cong. Rec.* 10471–72 (June 27, 1957); 104 *Cong. Rec.* 199 (Jan. 9, 1958); 104 *Cong. Rec.* 946–49 (Jan. 23, 1958); 106 *Cong. Rec.* 8590 (Apr. 25, 1960).

be loosed on the streets of the capital have not been realized. The Willis-Keating Bill passed by the House and pending in the Senate would operate, however, to open the door to serious police trespasses on individual rights; and it would take away from the courts their one effective sanction against such trespasses.

The real vice of the Willis-Keating Bill is that it would deny to the Courts their only effective means of disciplining policemen who usurped the authority to determine what was probable cause in making an arrest . . . .

The police would be enabled, in short, by wresting confessions from suspects during a period of detention prior to arraignment, to establish the probable cause necessary to justify their arrests in the first place. In effect, then, the bill would make the police judges of the validity of their own arrests.[76]

On April 25, 1960, Senator Ervin introduced S. 3411, which provided that "voluntary" admissions and confessions would be admissible against the accused "in any criminal proceeding or prosecution in the courts of the United States or in the District of Columbia" and that the trial judge's determination of voluntariness would be "binding upon any reviewing court" if "supported by substantial evidence."[77] The bill received enthusiastic and highly vocal support from a number of southern senators whose deep resentment toward school desegregation decisions went hand in hand with their repeated denunciations of the Court's "freeing" of a "confessed and convicted rapist" who just happened to be a Negro.[78] Like most of its predecessors this bill died in committee, and Ervin's renewal of the effort in 1961 met a similar fate. In that year, however, the House passed a measure introduced by Congressman James C. Davis (D., Ga.), essentially restating Section (a) of the Willis-Keating bill but confining its application to the District of Columbia.[79] This measure simply narrowed the jurisdiction contemplated in earlier bills, but it like-

[76] 105 *Cong. Rec.* 15993–94 (Aug. 17, 1959).

[77] 106 *Cong. Rec.* 8590.

[78] *Ibid.*, at 8632–34 (remarks of Senator Harry Byrd [D., Va.]). In addition to Senator Byrd, the Ervin bill was cosponsored by Senators John McClellan (D., Ark.), Olin Johnson (D., S. C.), John M. Butler (R., Md.), and Everett Jordan (D., N. C.).

[79] 107 *Cong. Rec.* 10068 (June 12, 1961).

wise failed to receive Senate approval. Additional unsuccessful efforts were made during 1962 and 1963, in both houses of Congress, to bring about legislative reversal of the *Mallory* decision, but they amounted to little more than token gestures.[80] With the *Escobedo* decision of 1964, anti-Court sentiment in the interrogation field was rekindled, and the *Miranda* ruling later provided the catalyst for the strongest congressional reaction thus far in this emotion-charged area. This phase of activity, culminating with passage of the Omnibus Crime Control and Safe Streets Act of 1968, may be better understood after summarizing the erratic course of constitutional development culminating in the *Escobedo-Miranda* sequence.

[80] See, for example, the remarks of Congressman Cramer (108 *Cong. Rec.* 15854 [Aug. 8, 1962]) in support of his bill, H. R. 3248, 87 Cong., 1 sess., introduced on Jan. 25, 1961, but not acted upon by the House. The Cramer and Ervin bills were again introduced as H. R. 3055 and S. 1012, respectively, 88 Cong., 1 sess. (1963).

5

Old Themes, New Variations

DURING THE YEARS in which the Supreme Court was moving toward unanimous endorsement of a confession standard for federal cases, it vacillated between competing Fourteenth Amendment due process approaches in the state confession field. In 1944, Justice Black introduced the test of "inherent coerciveness" as an alternative to the traditional "fair trial" doctrine. Like the *McNabb-Mallory* Rule, Black's test of confession admissibility condemned procedural violations by the police, without primary regard to the supposed effect of these violations on particular suspects. Although briefly supported by a Court majority, the test of "inherent coerciveness" soon became merely one of several divergent rationales through which the justices sought to adjust the conflicting demands of law enforcement efficiency and individual rights. During the middle and late 1940s a sharply divided Court usually struck this balance in favor of the latter, but no single cohesive majority bloc gained a dominant position.[1]

The deaths of libertarian Justices Frank Murphy and Wiley Rutledge in the summer of 1949 marked the close of what might be described as the first period of judicial activism in the state confession field. Their successors, Justices Tom C. Clark and Sherman Minton, joined the old dissenting bloc, which included Chief Justice Fred M. Vinson and Justices Reed and Jackson, to form a new majority that reversed the course of constitutional development in this field. The change of direction took place against the background of growing restrictions on civil liberties

[1] See, for example, *Malinski* v. *New York*, 324 U. S. 401 (1945); *Haley* v. *Ohio*, 332 U. S. 596 (1948); *Watts* v. *Indiana*, 338 U. S. 49 (1949). For general background on the development of Fourteenth Amendment standards in the field of criminal procedure during this period, see John Raeburn Green, "The Bill of Rights, the Fourteenth Amendment and the Supreme Court," *Michigan Law Review* 46 (May 1948), 869–910.

occasioned by the deepening Cold War and the Korean conflict. The easing of Fourteenth Amendment restrictions on police interrogation proved, however, to be of short duration. The appointment of Chief Justice Earl Warren in 1953 ushered in a new era of expansion in the scope of constitutional protections for the individual, in this as in many other fields of judicial involvement. For the next ten years the Court continued to apply a highly flexible due process rationale to questions of state confession admissibility, proceeding on a case-by-case basis and for the most part broadening the definition of police coercion. By considering the "totality of circumstances" surrounding each challenged confession, it recognized a growing number of due process variables, ranging from the age, education, emotional condition, and economic status of a suspect, to the actions of the police and, on occasion, the external influences of local public opinion.

A Court majority first endorsed the test of "inherent coerciveness" in *Ashcraft* v. *Tennessee*.[2] At issue was the admissibility of an alleged confession obtained after a thirty-six-hour period of continuous police interrogation of E. E. Ashcraft in connection with his wife's murder. Writing for a majority of six, Justice Black made no attempt to weigh the probable effect of this long period of questioning on the suspect. He simply held that its length and intensity constituted a "situation . . . so inherently coercive that its very existence is irreconcilable with the possession of mental freedom by a lone suspect against whom its full coercive force is brought to bear."[3] The majority was concerned almost exclusively with the element of arbitrariness implicit in the staging of a long period of unremitting interrogation—the uncertainty of what occurred behind the closed door of the interrogation room, and the absence of legal safeguards under such circumstances. For the first time in a state confession case the justices focused on the

---

[2] 322 U. S. 143 (1944). For general background, see Boskey and Pickering, "Federal Restrictions on State Criminal Procedure," 266–99.

[3] *Ibid.*, at 154. All previous Fourteenth Amendment confession cases originating in southern states had involved uneducated, poverty-stricken, and otherwise disadvantaged Negro defendants. By contrast, and as if to accentuate the sharp break with traditional standards, Ashcraft, a white man, was described as a skilled road-equipment operator, property owner, and "citizen of excellent reputation." *Ibid.*, at 153.

process of private interrogation; and although they did not find the process, as such, unconstitutional, they did insist that it conform to constitutional requirements placing limits on the length and intensity of questioning. The *Ashcraft* doctrine, unlike the *McNabb* Rule, was pegged explicitly to the interrelated questions of coercion and voluntariness. Still the two standards approached a single, overriding question: namely, whether a criminal justice system that assumes the innocence of a defendant and requires the government to prove his guilt is compatible with a practice that permits officials of that government to question the defendant in private and to introduce into evidence statements made under circumstances known only to accuser and accused.

The *Ashcraft* standard was sharply criticized in a dissenting opinion written by Justice Jackson and endorsed by Justices Roberts and Frankfurter. Echoing Frankfurter's language in *McNabb,* Jackson made a sharp distinction between the Court's extensive supervisory power over federal criminal procedure and its limited authority to review state convictions under the Due Process Clause of the Fourteenth Amendment. Such considerations of federalism precluded the Court's attempt to "discipline" local law enforcement officers for conduct that the justices personally deemed objectionable. He invoked the earlier standard of admissibility, contending that the Court could exclude a confession under the Fourteenth Amendment only if its use in evidence had prevented a fair trial. Fairness in this context could exist only if the confessor retained "possession of his own will and self-control at the time of confession." Precisely how a trial or appellate judge would go about determining the emotional state of a suspect at the time of confession, Jackson failed to tell us. He did insist, however, that the term "voluntary confession" need not refer to a statement made in the complete absence of pressure. He believed that such confessions "usually proceed from a belief that further denial is useless and perhaps prejudicial." The question before the Court, then, was not whether pressure was exerted, but whether this pressure destroyed that freedom of choice traditionally regarded as necessary to a voluntary confession. Jackson was convinced that Justice Black's new approach failed to recognize this crucial distinction:

> The Court bases its position on the premise that custody and ex-amination of a prisoner for thirty-six hours is "inherently coer-cive." Of course it is. And so is custody and examination for one hour. Arrest itself is inherently coercive, and so is detention . . . .
> But does the Constitution prohibit the use of all confessions made after arrest because questioning, while one is deprived of freedom, is "inherently coercive?" The Court does not quite say so, but it is moving far and fast in that direction.

Jackson expressed a strong preference for the traditional ap-proach with its emphasis on the individual suspect's presumed ability to withstand pressure. Paradoxically, he refused to acknowl-edge the strong element of uncertainty implicit in this approach while at the same time attacking the new standard on this very point:

> If the constitutional admissibility of a confession is no longer to be measured by the mental state of the individual confessor but by a general doctrine dependent on the clock, it should be capable of statement in definite terms. If thirty-six hours is more than is permissible, what about twenty-four? or twelve? or six? or one? All are "inherently coercive."[4]

Despite its questionable logic, Jackson's critique of the new confession standard was apparently influential. Just over one month after the *Ashcraft* ruling, a majority of five justices, includ-ing the three dissenters in that case, reasserted the "fair trial" doctrine.[5] At issue in *Lyons* v. *Oklahoma* was the admissibility of a confession made to a prison warden some twelve hours after police had extracted an admittedly involuntary confession from the young Negro defendant. This case was reminiscent of *Cham-*

---

[4] *Ibid.*, at 161, 162. For further analysis of the Ashcraft case see "Comment," *Iowa Law Review* 30 (Nov. 1944), 102–107.
[5] *Lyons* v. *Oklahoma*, 322 U. S. 596 (1944). Justice Douglas concurred in the result but did not endorse the opinion of the Court. Justice Murphy wrote a dis-senting opinion endorsed by Justice Black, and Justice Rutledge dissented separately without opinion.

bers v. *Florida* and other early state confession cases in that the obvious intention of the police was to frighten the defendant into confessing.

Lyons and an accomplice were suspected of the murders of a white tenant farmer, his wife, and a four-year-old son. The victims' charred bodies were discovered in a house presumably burned in an effort to conceal the crime. The record indicates that Lyons was arrested, questioned for two hours, and held incommunicado for eleven days. At the end of this period he was again questioned, this time for at least eight hours. He later testified that during both sessions of interrogation he was subjected to physical violence; and although the police denied this allegation, the testimony of "disinterested" witnesses supported it. Moreover, police conceded that the second round of questioning continued until 2:30 A.M. and that "a pan of the victims' bones" was placed in the suspect's lap "to bring about his confession." After returning with Lyons to the scene of the crime for further questioning, the officers drove him to the state penitentiary at McAlester, where he made a second confession that was subsequently introduced into evidence at his trial and was admitted despite his contention that it was involuntary.

In an opinion by Mr. Justice Reed—who, despite his criticism of the *McNabb* Rule, had supported Justice Black's doctrine of "inherent coerciveness"—the Supreme Court affirmed Lyons' conviction. Brushing aside the claim that force was used to obtain the second confession, Reed chose to consider only the question of the continuing effect of the coercive practices just described. He conceded that involuntary confessions might be given either during or after the employment of "unlawful pressures, force or threats."[6] But in either situation, the question of voluntariness would turn, not on illegal acts of the police, but on the individual suspect's "mental freedom" at the time of confession. Thus Reed echoed Jackson's *Ashcraft* dissent by insisting on the individualization of findings of voluntariness. He merely applied this principle to the matter of "continuing coercion," an aspect of the confession problem to which the Court had given no previous attention. Its sud-

[6] 322 U. S., at 600, 602.

den recognition of this factor as one of crucial importance is hardly convincing, since the element of "continuing coercion" was clearly present in earlier cases. To cite one conspicuous example, the confessions introduced against two of the three defendants in *Brown* v. *Mississippi* were made, not at the time of the admitted whippings, but on the following day, after they "had been given time to recuperate somewhat from the tortures to which they had been subjected."[7] The Supreme Court in reviewing these confessions either chose deliberately to ignore the element of "continuing coercion" or failed to recognize the very existence of such a phenomenon. An examination of Reed's opinion in this context supports the conclusion that those justices who endorsed it were looking for some judicially acceptable way in which to abandon the *Ashcraft* standard of "inherent coerciveness." By confining their holding to "inferences as to the continuing effect of . . . coercive practices," they could reassert the more cautious approach of earlier decisions without the embarrassing necessity of overruling a precedent of only one month's standing. Justice Frank Murphy, in a blistering dissent, exposed the artificiality of this novel approach by pointing out that:

> The whole confession technique used here constituted one single, continuing transaction. To conclude that the brutality inflicted at the time of the first confession suddenly lost all of its effect in the short space of twelve hours is to close one's eyes to the realities of human nature.[8]

Because it suggested a position that split the Court in several later decisions, one other feature of Reed's opinion deserves mention. After elaborately deferring to the trial judge and jury in all disputed questions of fact, and according great weight to their respective findings of voluntariness, he reemphasized the probability of Lyons' guilt. The record indicated that several days after his confession to the warden, Lyons "frankly admitted the killings to a sergeant of the prison guards who was a former acquaintance from his own locality . . . ." Reed interpreted this uncoerced admis-

[7] See Justice Griffith's dissenting opinion in *Brown* v. *State*, 161 So. 465 (1935), quoted in 297 U. S. 278, 283 (1936).
[8] 322 U. S., at 606.

sion not only as further acknowledgment of guilt, but also as a strong indication of the voluntariness of the second confession. In other words, Lyons' guilt made his confession more reliable, "trustworthy," and, by implication according to this dubious line of reasoning, free and voluntary. Reed stopped short of an explicit endorsement of the old common-law test, but the language in his opinion leaves little doubt about the direction in which he was moving:

> A coerced confession is offensive to basic standards of justice, not because the victim has a legal grievance against the police, but because declarations procured by torture are not premises from which a civilized forum will infer guilt . . . . We cannot say that an inference of guilt based in part upon Lyons' McAlester confession is so illogical and unreasonable as to deny the petitioner a fair trial.[9]

Thus, in effect, a Court majority disavowed any intention of "disciplining" the police and gave notice that they would consider the probable guilt of a defendant in reviewing the circumstances under which a challenged confession was made. To say the least, this narrow view of Fourteenth Amendment protection was fundamentally inconsistent with the automatic exclusion of a confession produced by thirty-six hours of continuous questioning.

Justice Murphy's dissenting opinion, endorsed by Justice Black, himself, also departed sharply from the *Ashcraft* standard but for very different reasons. The Fifth Amendment prohibition against compulsory self-incrimination, Murphy insisted, should be openly recognized as the proper standard for determining the admissibility of state confessions. He inferred from earlier cases that the Court had, "in effect," held that the Fourteenth Amendment applied this provision to the states.[10] In view of the Court's initial clear-cut distinction between the Self-incrimination Clause and the Fourteenth Amendment due process requirement,[11] Murphy's inference was probably erroneous. Right or wrong from the stand-

---

[9] *Ibid.*, at 604–605.
[10] 322 U. S., at 605. Cf. Justice Black's dissenting opinion, endorsed by Justice Douglas, in *Adamson v. California*, 322 U. S. 46, 68–92 (1947).
[11] *Brown* v. *Mississippi*, 297 U. S. 278, 285 (1936).

point of logic and precedent, however, it marked the beginning of a long-frustrated but ultimately successful effort to fuse restrictions on state confessions and police interrogation with the constitutional immunity against self-incrimination.

Despite the confusion produced by the juxtaposition of the *Ashcraft* decision and the two opinions in the *Lyons* case, a few generalizations are possible. First of all, it seems likely that Justice Reed and Chief Justice Harlan F. Stone, both of whom supported the application of the test of "inherent coerciveness" in the *Ashcraft* case, had begun to fear that the "activist" members of the Court would invoke this standard to frustrate the police in obtaining credible confessions.[12] The position of Justice Douglas in the *Lyons* case is more difficult to explain. He concurred in the judgment of affirmance but did not endorse Reed's majority opinion. Because he wrote no separate opinion, the reasons for his willingness to accept the verdict of the trial Court remain obscure. It is noteworthy that this decision marks the only occasion on which Douglas has rejected a defendant's constitutionally adjudicated claim that a confession used as evidence against him was coerced. Finally, Justice Murphy's assertion of the applicability of the Self-incrimination Clause to state confession cases introduced a new and ultimately decisive element into the process of constitutional development in this area. Most contemporary commentators dismissed his approach as logically and historically unsound, thereby indicating once again the limited value of such criteria in explaining the judicial process or, for that matter, the meaning of the Constitution.

In several important cases decided during the middle and late 1940s the sharp divergence of views revealed in the *Ashcraft* and *Lyons* rulings underwent further elaboration and refinement.[13] A bare majority of five justices managed to agree on reversal of convictions in these cases,[14] but they were united on little else. In

[12] Subsequent opinions by both justices support this tentative conclusion. See Justice Stone's dissent in *Malinski*, 324 U. S. 401, 434–39 (1945); and Justice Reed's opinion in *Gallegos* v. *Nebraska*, 342 U. S. 55 (1951).

[13] See *Malinski* v. *New York*, 324 U. S. 401 (1945); *Haley* v. *Ohio*, 322 U. S. 596 (1948); *Watts* v. *Indiana*, 338 U. S. 49 (1949); *Turner* v. *Pennsylvania*, 338 U. S. 62 (1949); *Harris* v. *South Carolina*, 338 U. S. 68 (1949).

[14] The only break in this pattern occurred in *Watts* v. *Indiana*, 338 U. S. 49

varying degrees they objected to isolated instances of police misconduct, but only Justices Black and Douglas persisted in condemning all confessions obtained as a result of police methods that might be regarded as "inherently coercive."[15] Justice Frankfurter, while voting for reversal, adopted the more flexible point of view that illegal acts of the police violated the Fourteenth Amendment only if they were accompanied by evidence of the defendant's inability to withstand pressure or offended "those canons of decency and fairness which express the notions of justice of English-speaking peoples even toward those charged with the most heinous offenses."[16] Ultimately, Justices Murphy and Rutledge, who

---

(1949) with Justice Jackson deserting the dissenters and concurring in the judgment of reversal. In addition to the five principal cases discussed in the text, the Court during this period handed down two decisions of marginal importance in the state confession field. Both turned on narrow points of procedure and may be summarized briefly. In *Lee v. Mississippi*, 332 U. S. 742 (1948), it was unanimously held that a defendant did not forfeit the right to contend that his confession was coerced because of his testimony that the confession was actually never made. Despite his equivocation on the point of whether he had in fact confessed, Lee insisted that coercive tactics, including threats, were used by his interrogators, and these allegations were not denied. It seemed clear that the conviction of this seventeen-year-old Negro defendant was based on a coerced confession. The Court, through Justice Murphy, found such a conviction "no less void" simply because of the defendant's possible testimony at a pretrial hearing "that he had never in fact confessed, voluntarily or involuntarily. Testimony of that nature," Murphy continued, "can hardly legalize a procedure which conflicts with the accepted principles of due process." 332 U. S., at 745. On the other hand, a divided Court in *Taylor v. Alabama*, 335 U. S. 252 (1948) upheld the state Supreme Court's action in denying the defendant's petition for review by the trial court of its own judgment against him. Taylor contended that although his confession was coerced, the "fear of further reprisals" had prevented him from informing his attorney of this fact. It was not until after the Alabama Supreme Court's affirmance of his conviction that the defendant, acting through different counsel, filed this petition. Justice Burton, for the majority, found nothing to indicate that the defendant had lacked confidence in his first attorney or that he had been justified in withholding information about the alleged coercion. Murphy, in a dissenting opinion endorsed by Douglas and Rutledge, maintained that the petitioner's execution was "no answer to the allegation he raised." 335 U. S., at 279. Frankfurter filed a separate concurring opinion, and Black took no part in the decision.

15 For further analysis of the complexities of intra-Court conflict in the state confession field during this period, see Samuel Bader, "Coerced Confessions and the Due Process Clause," *Brooklyn Law Review* 15 (Dec. 1948), 51–71; William Wicker, "Some Developments in the Law Concerning Confessions," *Vanderbilt Law Review* 5 (Apr. 1952), 507–22.

16 Frankfurter recognized that the "standards of justice" to which he referred were "not authoritatively formulated anywhere as though they were prescriptions in a pharmacopoeia." He insisted on the other hand that, in applying the Due

rounded out the tenuous majority, endorsed Frankfurter's "due process" approach to confession admissibility.[17] Despite two changes in Court membership,[18] a solid minority of four justices dissented from this series of rulings. The new appointees, Justice Burton and Chief Justice Vinson, fully endorsed the views of their predecessors. The dissenters, who also included Justices Reed and Jackson, continued to insist that the Court majority was extending the scope of due process far beyond its legitimate bounds. For the most part they agreed in theory with Frankfurter's due process rationale, but differed with him in its application to particular sets of circumstances. Increasingly, this minority expressed disapproval of what it viewed as undue Supreme Court interference with the normal and necessary processes of local law enforcement and with the proper reviewing functions of state courts.[19] Justice Jackson gave lucid expression to the growing dissatisfaction in a 1949 opinion which sounded the note soon adopted by a Court majority. Commenting on the Court's simultaneous reversal of three murder convictions in widely separated parts of the country, he contended that "no one" suggested "any" means of solving the crimes other than the custodial questioning of the suspects. The only alternative in each case "was to close the books on the crime and forget it, with the suspect still at large." This Jackson viewed as "a grave choice for a society in which two thirds of the murders already are closed out as insoluble." For the first time in a judicial opinion he expressed preference for the test of "trustworthiness" as the proper confession standard:

Process Clause, judges were not "wholly at large." The highly elusive character of this approach is well summarized in his observation that: "The judicial judgement in applying the due process clause must move within the limits of accepted notions of justice and is not to be based upon the idiosyncrasies of a merely personal judgement." 324 U. S., at 416–17. For analysis of Frankfurter's due process approach in this context, see Helen Shirley Thomas, *Felix Frankfurter: Scholar on the Bench* (Baltimore: Johns Hopkins, 1960), 156–58.

[17] They endorsed Frankfurter's opinions in the three companion cases of *Watts v. Indiana,* 338 U. S. 49 (1949); *Turner v. Pennsylvania,* 338 U. S. 62 (1949); and *Harris v. South Carolina,* 338 U. S. 68 (1949).

[18] Justice Roberts retired in 1945 and was replaced by Justice Harold Burton, President Truman's first Supreme Court appointee. Chief Justice Stone died in 1946 and was replaced by Chief Justice Fred M. Vinson.

[19] See, for example, the dissenting opinion of Burton, joined by Vinson, Reed, and Jackson, in *Haley v. Ohio,* 332 U. S. 596, 607–25 (1948).

99

We must not overlook that in these cases, as in some previous cases, once a confession is obtained it supplies ways of verifying its trustworthiness. In these cases before us the verification is sufficient to leave me in no doubt that the admissions of guilt were genuine and truthful.[20]

Although the Court majority failed to speak with a united voice in this series of decisions, it did reach agreement on one additional point. In the 1948 case of *Haley* v. *Ohio* the defendant's youth was explicitly recognized as crucial in determining that his confession was coerced. Justice Douglas, who might have been expected to vote for reversal solely because the record revealed a midnight session of secret interrogation, stressed the fact that Haley was a "lad in his early teens." But he obscured the actual significance of this single factor with the following statement, so typical of the Court's ambivalent confession opinions during this era:

The age of the petitioner, the hours when he was grilled, the duration of his quizzing, the fact that he had no friend or counsel to advise him, the callous attitude of the police towards his rights combine to convince us that this was a confession wrung from a child by means which the law should not sanction. Neither man nor child can be allowed to stand condemned by methods which flout constitutional requirements of due process of law.[21]

The deaths of libertarian Justices Murphy and Rutledge in the summer of 1949 marked the close of this first distinct period of judicial activism in the confession field. Their successors, Justices Clark and Minton, soon aligned with the earlier dissenting bloc to form a new majority strongly committed to a different set of law enforcement priorities. The course of constitutional development in the confession field has roughly mirrored the expansion and contraction of civil liberties protections generally. It is thus not surprising that as the nation moved into the "cold war" era with its initial reaction against what many people saw as excesses of individual freedom, the restrictions surrounding police interrogation should be temporarily relaxed. The period that spawned

[20] *Watts* v. *Indiana*, 338 U. S. 49, 58, 60 (1949).
[21] 332 U. S. 596, 600–601.

Dennis v. *United States*[22] and the McCarthy witch hunt also brought a string of affirmances in the confession field. This change of direction was reflected in other areas of criminal procedure, as well as in the broad area of First Amendment freedoms.[23]

The principal lines of intra-Court division over confession admissibility were pretty well established at this juncture. As it achieved a position of dominance, the Reed-Jackson wing became even more committed to a policy of judicial self-restraint, reflecting concern for what was seen as a growing crime problem. Justices Black and Douglas, on the other hand, continued to vote for reversal of convictions based to any extent on confessions obtained through illegal conduct by the police.[24] Falling somewhere between these two positions was the highly flexible due process standard of Justice Frankfurter. His approach to confession admissibility, as well as to other questions of criminal procedure arising under the Fourteenth Amendment, contained two elements: (1) a separate assessment of constitutional questions in light of all known circumstances in each case; (2) determination of whether, on the basis of this "totality of circumstances," law enforcement officers had violated fundamental standards of fairness, decency, and justice identified with the Anglo-American legal tradition. Frankfurter denounced official conduct "that shocks the conscience," regardless of whether it produced reliable evidence. On this point of reliability, he differed with the Court majority of the early 1950s, and the difference usually resulted in his voting with Black and Douglas in dissent. On the other hand, he shared the views of Reed and Jackson regarding judicial self-restraint and emphasized the principle of federalism as a limitation on Supreme Court review of state convictions. But his notion

---

[22] *Dennis* v. *United States*, 341 U. S. 494 (1951).

[23] See, for example, *United States* v. *Rabinowitz*, 339 U. S. 56 (1950); and *Feiner* v. *New York*, 340 U. S. 315 (1951).

[24] See, for example, the dissenting opinion of Justice Black, joined by Justice Douglas, in *Gallegos* v. *Nebraska*, 342 U. S. 55, 74–75 (1951). Writing in 1949, Douglas urged that the Court "unequivocally condemn" illegal detention "and stand ready to outlaw . . . any confession obtained during [such] period . . . ." He was convinced that the procedure itself produced coerced confessions; that it was "the root of the evil . . . without which the inquisition could not flourish in the country." *Watts* v. *Indiana*, 338 U. S. 49, 57.

of fairness was apparently quite different from theirs. His conservative constitutional philosophy was counterbalanced by a liberal conscience that was more easily shocked than those of several colleagues who shared his judicial outlook. Frankfurter's attempt to square the conflicting demands of conscience and constitutional theory produced uncertainty if not ambivalence in the disposition of individual cases. It was this element of fluidity that most accurately characterized Supreme Court interpretation of due process requirements during the pre-*Escobedo* period.[25]

The trend toward narrower interpretation of the due process requirement was reflected in a series of decisions handed down between late 1951 and mid-1953. The test of "inherent coerciveness," which had been diminishing in influence during the late 1940s, disappeared altogether. The rule of "trustworthiness" finally achieved and briefly held ascendancy. The "fair trial" standard, in a more restricted form than it had previously assumed, was used repeatedly as a rationale for affirmance of convictions. Concern with the question of a defendant's guilt or innocence ultimately manifested itself in the holding that a jury, independent of the trial judge, might convict a person on sufficient "other evidence" and at the same time disregard his confession on grounds of coercion. The only thread of continuity that ran undisturbed during this interlude was the Court's individualization of each case situation in an effort to determine the defendant's ability to withstand police pressure. Even this tendency was weakened, but at no time did the majority formally depart from the established case-by-case approach.

To begin with, the Court in *Gallegos* v. *Nebraska*[26] affirmed the manslaughter conviction of an itinerant Mexican farm worker who could neither speak nor write English and was residing illegally in the United States. The record revealed a familiar pattern

[25] For further discussion of the development of due process requirements governing state confessions during the 1950s, see David Fellman, *The Defendant's Rights*, 179–84. For additional background and analysis, see Albert R. Beisel, Jr., *Control Over Illegal Enforcement of the Criminal Law: Role of the Supreme Court*, Gaspar P. Bacon Lectures on the Constitution of the United States (Boston: Boston Univ. Press, 1955), Ch. 3.

[26] 342 U. S. 55 (1951).

of circumstances: a twenty-five-day period of illegal detention, conflicting allegations of threats, deprivation of food, and other forms of psychological coercion, not all of which were denied by the police. At the request of immigration officials, Agapita Gallegos was arrested by local authorities in El Paso County, Texas, on a charge of vagrancy. Although the record as reviewed by the Supreme Court is incomplete on this point, it appears that he was questioned about a period of time spent in Nebraska. After four days of intermittent interrogation, during which he later insisted that he was threatened and otherwise intimidated, he confessed to the killing of his girl friend in Nebraska. Local authorities in that state were notified and, from information provided by Gallegos, located and identified the body of the victim. After his removal to Nebraska, Gallegos made a second confession and at his subsequent arraignment entered a plea of guilty. During the entire period of illegal detention he was not assisted by counsel. At his trial for manslaughter he contended that the Texas and Nebraska confessions as well as the guilty plea were inadmissible on grounds of coercion. This contention was rejected and his conviction was affirmed by the Supreme Court of Nebraska.[27]

In announcing the judgment of the Court, Justice Reed rejected Gallegos' allegations that his El Paso confession was coerced and further held that under the Due Process Clause of the Fourteenth Amendment neither confession was rendered inadmissible by the prolonged period of illegal detention prior to arraignment and in the absence of counsel. For the same reasons he found no objection to the prosecution's use of the challenged plea of guilty. Reed insisted that the circumstances of alleged coercion were less extreme than those on which the Court had previously reversed convictions. The elusive quality of such a comparison is compounded by the fact that no two sets of circumstances reviewed by the Court were exactly alike. Indeed the *Gallegos* case presented at least two new elements not previously considered: the serious language barrier, and consecutive periods of illegal detention and interrogation by law enforcement authorities of

---

[27] *Gallegos v. State*, 43 N. W. 2d 1 (1950).

two states. Nevertheless, professing that these and other circumstances had been "carefully weighed," Reed concluded that Nebraska did not violate "standards of decency or justice in this conviction."[28]

With only Black and Douglas dissenting, the Court declined to extend the *McNabb* principle, via the Fourteenth Amendment, to the twenty-five-day period of illegal detention revealed by the record. Moreover, in a federal case decided on the same day it pointedly refused to extend the *McNabb* requirement to a confession obtained while the defendant was under lawful arrest in connection with a separate offense. Speaking again through Justice Reed, whose disapproval of *McNabb* was as strong as ever, the Court insisted that such confessions continue to be measured by traditional standards of voluntariness long recognized in federal courts. Justice Douglas, on the other hand, viewed the practice of holding a man on one charge and questioning him in connection with other crimes as a "perversion" of lawful detention:

> This is an easy short-cut for the police. How convenient it is to make detention the vehicle of investigation. Then the police can have access to the prisoner day and night. . . . We should free the federal system of that disreputable practice which has honey-combed the municipal police system in this country.[29]

These two decisions, while not formally overturning precedents, clearly reflected the Court's new priorities. Both revealed paramount concern for the efficacy of law enforcement and an inclination to minimize the seriousness of procedural irregularities. This theme was apparent in Reed's glorification of the voluntariness test, even in federal prosecutions, as "a just and merciful rule" preserving "the rights of accused and society alike." Presumably, in sharp contrast to what he called "the McNabb fixed rule," the voluntariness test did not "sacrifice justice to sentimentality."[30]

Later in the same term the Court's shift in emphasis became

---

[28] 342 U. S., at 68. Jackson, joined by Frankfurter, filed a separate concurring opinion.

[29] *United States* v. *Carignan*, 342 U. S. 36, 46 (1951).

[30] *Ibid.*, at 45.

even more apparent. In *Stroble* v. *California*[31] a majority of six not only affirmed a conviction based in part on a confession obtained under highly questionable circumstances, but in doing so rejected the State Supreme Court's assumption that this confession was, in fact, coerced. Under review was the first-degree murder conviction of sixty-eight-year-old Fred Stroble, growing out of the brutal, sex-induced killing of a six-year-old girl in Los Angeles. Local newspapers gave sensationalistic descriptions of the crime and of the prime suspect, who was immediately implicated by strong circumstantial evidence. Several months prior to the crime, Stroble had been charged with molesting a small girl and had been released on bail. The murder occurred at the home of his daughter and son-in-law at a time when Stroble was supposedly alone in the house. Three days later in a local bar a private citizen recognized him from a newspaper photograph and notified the police. Arrested just before noon, Stroble was immediately taken to the nearby park foreman's office, where he was searched and briefly questioned. During the search, according to later testimony, an officer kicked the suspect and threatened him with a blackjack. It also appears that the park foreman slapped him just after he admitted his guilt. While en route to the district attorney's office, Stroble confessed to a police officer, but the voluntariness of this confession was not questioned. The challenged confession was made to an assistant district attorney some four hours after the arrest, and following a two-hour period of interrogation in the presence of nineteen other law enforcement officials.

At the trial five additional confessions were admitted into evidence and no question was raised concerning their voluntariness. Stroble was not promptly arraigned in accordance with California law, though the period of illegal detention was less than twenty-four hours. While a public defender was provided for him some ten hours after the arrest, a private attorney was refused permission to talk with the suspect shortly before his confession in the district attorney's office.[32] Newspapers were immediately pro-

---

[31] 343 U. S. 181 (1952).

[32] This attorney made no attempt to represent Stroble but was sent by his son-in-law to inquire directly about the suspect's guilt. 343 U. S., at 187–88.

vided with details of this confession, and the entire text was included in several evening editions. The subsequent testimony of four psychiatrists and one psychologist indicated that the accused was "sane" at the time of the murder. Other evidence suggested, however, that Stroble possessed a "weakened mentality," probably resulting from arteriosclerosis and heavy consumption of alcohol. His conviction and death sentence were unanimously affirmed by the California Supreme Court, despite its finding that the confession made in the district attorney's office was coerced. Writing for the state court, Justice B. Rey Schauer conceded that the investigating officers had been "guilty of flagrant misconduct" but insisted that "such misconduct, however reprehensible," apparently did not, "under the extraordinary circumstances of this case," materially affect the "regularity" of the trial. The presence of several voluntary confessions, as well as additional evidence of guilt, rendered the use of one admittedly coerced confession insignificant in the judgment of California's highest court. In an oblique criticism of earlier decisions of the federal Supreme Court, Justice Schauer asserted that the state court should not "reverse a judgment solely as a rebuke to 'law enforcement' officers for their own lawless acts . . . ."[33]

Although agreeing with this affirmance of conviction, the United States Supreme Court, in an opinion by Justice Clark, refused to accept the California court's conclusion that the disputed confession was coerced. In light of earlier decisions a finding of coercion would have demanded the Court's reversal of conviction, regardless of additional evidence of guilt.[34] In affirming the conviction, Clark could not avoid a serious dilemma: The state court's view of the confession, if accepted, meant that the conviction could not be sustained without the flat rejection of over-

[33] *People* v. *Stroble*, 227 P. 2d 330, 332 (1951).
[34] Announcing the judgment of the Court in *Malinski* v. *New York*, Justice Douglas stated that the introduction of a coerced confession at trial nullified the judgment of guilt, "even though the evidence apart from the confession might have been sufficient to sustain the jury's verdict." 324 U. S. 401, 404 (1945). The same view was expressed by Justice Reed in the following language: "The use of any confession obtained in violation of due process requires the reversal of a conviction even though unchallenged evidence, adequate to convict, remains." *Gallegos* v. *Nebraska*, 342 U. S. 55, 63 (1951).

whelming precedent. On the other hand, its finding of coercion could not be repudiated without at the same time disregarding principles of federalism and judicial self-restraint, under which great weight was given to state court decisions on the issue of coercion. In choosing the second of these difficult alternatives, the majority was compelled to play down the elements of physical force and psychological pressure plainly revealed by the record. Furthermore the "weakened" mental condition of the defendant was altogether disregarded. In like manner the Court rejected Stroble's contention that inflammatory publicity made it impossible for him to have a fair trial in the Los Angeles area. In newspaper reports he had been variously characterized as a "werewolf," "fiend," and "sex-mad killer." The district attorney was quoted as expressing his belief that Stroble was "guilty and sane." The Court pointed out that these accounts appeared six weeks before the trial began, implying that all adverse influences were somehow washed from the public's memory during this time span, and concluding that there was "no affirmative showing that any community prejudice ever existed or in any way affected the deliberation of the jury."[35]

Justice Frankfurter in dissent questioned the Court's authority to declare a confession voluntary in the face of a contrary finding by the state's highest court. Such a conclusion, "made in light of . . . intimate knowledge of local police and prosecutorial methods," should not be questioned.[36] Ironically, this was the identical position repeatedly taken in earlier cases by Reed, Jackson, Burton, and other members of the *Stroble* majority.[37] Douglas, in a dissenting opinion supported by Black, confined his remarks to the question of the challenged confession's admissibility, reasserting his position regarding interrogation prior to arraignment, which for him was by definition unconstitutional. "The practice

[35] *Stroble* v. *California*, 343 U. S., at 192, 195.

[36] *Ibid.*, at 203. Frankfurter also objected to the quality and tone of newspaper publicity attending the investigation of this case and to the district attorney's role in providing much of the inflammatory material.

[37] See, for example, Reed's majority opinion in *Lyons* v. *Oklahoma*, 322 U. S. 596 (1944); Burton's dissent, endorsed by Vinson, Reed, and Jackson, in *Haley* v. *Ohio*, 332 U. S. 596, 607 (1948); and Reed's opinion announcing the judgment of the Court in *Gallegos* v. *Nebraska*, 342 U. S. 55 (1951).

of obtaining confessions prior to arraignment breeds the third degree and the inquisition." As long as the police are allowed to hold suspects incommunicado for questioning, he asserted, "coerced confessions will infect criminal trials in violation of the commands of due process of law."[38]

The judicial retreat signaled by *Gallegos* and accelerated in *Stroble* turned into a near rout in *Stein v. New York*,[39] decided June 15, 1953. This decision constituted the final and most detailed pronouncement of the Vinson Court in the confession field. A majority of six justices led by Jackson further narrowed the "fair trial" requirement and accorded greater weight to the common-law test of "trustworthiness."

In addition to familiar questions of coercion, the Court examined, for the first time, the procedure under which a state trial court determined the admissibility of pretrial confessions.[40] After protracted incommunicado detention and questioning, Harry Stein and a codefendant, Calman Cooper, had confessed to the highly publicized murder of a *Reader's Digest* employee during the course of a robbery near the magazine's Pleasantville, New York, headquarters. These confessions also implicated a third defendant, Nathan Wissner who, like Stein and Cooper, had an extensive criminal record. Along with substantial additional ev-

---

[38] 343 U. S., at 203–204.

[39] 346 U. S. 156. In *Brown v. Allen*, 344 U. S. 443 (1953), decided four months prior to the *Stein* ruling, the Court reviewed a confession challenge in combination with several other questions enumerated in petitions for habeas corpus under the post-conviction procedure governing federal court review of state convictions, as outlined in 28 U. S. C. 2241 et seq. While recognizing that use of a coerced confession in a state trial could be challenged in a federal habeas corpus proceeding, Justice Reed, writing for the majority, rejected the petitioner's contention that his confession, obtained during an eighteen-day period of detention prior to arraignment, had been coerced. By contrast with most earlier cases the majority accorded no discernible importance to the fact that the petitioner was an uneducated Negro, tried in a southern state (North Carolina.) Reed simply restated the view that: "Mere detention and police examination in private of one in official state custody do not render involuntary the statements or confessions made by the person so detained." (344 U. S., at 476.)

[40] In connection with this aspect of the *Stein* ruling see Bernard D. Meltzer, "Involuntary Confessions: The Allocation of Responsibility between Judge and Jury," *University of Chicago Law Review* 21 (Spring 1954), 317–54. See generally, Warren L. Sevanson and Roger W. Eichmeier, "The Role of Judge and Jury in Determining a Confession's Voluntariness," *Journal of Criminal Law, Criminology and Police Science* 48 (May–June 1957), 59–65.

idence, the confessions were submitted to the jury which, under the procedure then followed in New York, exercised wide discretion in resolving the issue of voluntariness. Under this procedure the trial judge might exclude a confession on his own authority only if overwhelming evidence indicated that it was coerced. When evidence on this point was conflicting, as it was in the *Stein* case, he was required to "receive the confession and leave to the jury under proper instructions the ultimate determination of its voluntary character and also its truthfulness."[41] The jury's finding of coercion theoretically required exclusion of the confession from evidence. But because in all criminal cases juries deliberated privately and returned general verdicts of guilty or not guilty, it was impossible under this procedure to know whether and to what extent challenged confessions influenced decisions. Accordingly, the confessions of Stein and Cooper were submitted to the jury, which found the three defendants guilty of first-degree murder, resulting in sentences of death. But whether the jury accepted or rejected the confessions as evidence could not be ascertained. The Supreme Court in reviewing the convictions could be certain only that the jury had been apprised of the contents of the confessions during the trial. Because the New York Court of Appeals handed down its decision without opinion, it was also impossible to determine the grounds on which that tribunal affirmed the convictions.[42]

While acknowledging the uncertainties of the "New York method" for determining confession admissibility, Justice Jackson concluded that this procedure did not violate requirements of due process under the Fourteenth Amendment. The Court would not, he said, "strike down as unconstitutional procedures so long established and widely approved by state judiciaries," despite any justice's personal view "as to their wisdom." Jackson next considered the question of whether the two confessions had been coerced. Medical examinations conducted shortly after the interrogations revealed evidence of physical injuries, but it was im-

[41] *Stein v. New York*, 346 U. S. 156, 172.
[42] *People v. Cooper et al.*, 104 N. E. 2d 917 (1952). The decision of the New York Court of Appeals affirming the convictions was unanimous.

possible to determine whether these occurred at the hands of the police or prior to the defendants' arrest. Jackson therefore concluded that no evidence connected the "admitted injuries" with the period of incommunicado questioning. In like manner he rejected the allegations of psychological coercion as lacking support from the undisputed portions of the record. The defendants, he observed, "were not young, soft, innocent or timid." They were experienced criminals, familiar with the methods of crime detection and well aware of their procedural rights. They confessed only after they were convinced that further denial of guilt was pointless, in light of additional evidence against them. He thus concluded that the confessions were voluntary "in the only sense in which confessions to the police by one under arrest and suspicion ever are."[43]

The *Stein* ruling placed one further restriction on the Court's scope of review, and Jackson introduced this limitation by posing the following question: If the jury in fact rejected the confessions as involuntary, could it have constitutionally based the convictions "on other sufficient evidence"? In a number of earlier decisions the Court had held that the admission of a coerced confession into evidence rendered a conviction unconstitutional, regardless of additional evidence of guilt. The leading precedent here was *Malinski v. New York*,[44] a case tried under the same procedure as that followed in *Stein*. Jackson maintained that in New York and other states following the same procedure the common practice ran contrary to the holding in the *Malinski* decision. Juries in these states were allowed to reject confessions as involuntary and at the same time to base verdicts of guilt on other evidence. Moreover, because the *Malinski* decision did not clearly represent the views of a Court majority on this point, Jackson refused to regard it as a binding precedent. He also dismissed as "dicta" other Supreme Court pronouncements that agreed with the *Malinski* holding. Having thus attempted to minimize the departure from prior decisions, he ruled that a jury might find a

[43] 346 U. S., at 179, 183, 186.
[44] 324 U. S. 401 (1945).

confession to have been coerced but at the same time convict the defendant on "other sufficient evidence."

In attempting to buttress his position, Jackson urged that coerced confessions violated the due process requirement because they constituted "inherently untrustworthy evidence." He insisted that only if the Fourteenth Amendment were deemed to embody "a rigid exclusionary rule of evidence" would the presence of a coerced confession automatically render a conviction unconstitutional. And in his view the Fourteenth Amendment by no means embodied such a rule. On the point of "trustworthiness" he again departed from precedent:

> Reliance on a coerced confession vitiates a conviction because such a confession combines the persuasiveness of apparent conclusiveness with what judicial experience shows to be illusory and deceptive evidence.

Once again the almost certain guilt of the defendants apparently had a decisive influence on Jackson and other members of the majority. Nowhere is this more evident than in his closing remarks, which state in part: "We are not willing to discredit constitutional doctrines for the protection of the innocent by making of them mere technical loopholes for the escape of the guilty."[45]

In separate opinions each of the three dissenting justices excoriated the majority opinion. Far more was involved than a mere difference of views respecting the voluntariness of confessions. They denounced in unusually strong language what they saw as a repudiation of the Court's previous commitments in the confession field, charging the majority with unjustifiable departure from the most basic precedents, a position endorsed by most legal commentators and ultimately by a new Supreme Court majority.[46]

---

[45] 346 U. S., at 192, 196–97.

[46] See generally, Monrad G. Paulsen, "The Fourteenth Amendment and the 'Third Degree,' " *Stanford Law Review* 6 (May 1954), 411–37; Edmond L. Cohn, "Federal Constitutional Limitations on the Use of Coerced Confessions in the State Courts," *Journal of Criminal Law, Criminology and Police Science* 50 (Sept.–Oct. 1959), 265–73; Comment, "The Decade of Change Since the Ashcraft Case," *Texas Law Review* 32 (Apr. 1954), 429–40; "Note," *Kentucky Law Journal* 43 (Spring 1955), 392–407.

Aside from Justice Jackson, who took no part in later confession rulings, all members of the *Stein* majority subsequently retreated, in varying degrees, from the position there asserted. The tone of these dissents is suggested by a few excerpts. Frankfurter maintained that the issue of psychological coercion—which he regarded as crucial in this case—"must be decided without regard to the confirmation of details in the confession by reliable other evidence." He regarded as "irrelevant" the "feeling of certitude that the accused is guilty of the crime to which he confessed." He found it "painful to be compelled to say that the Court [was] taking a retrogressive step in the administration of criminal justice" and expressed the hope that it was "a temporary, perhaps an ad hoc, deviation from a long course of decisions." Justice Douglas warned that if the Court's opinion meant what it said, the country was "entering upon a new regime of constitutional law that should give every citizen pause."[47] In a similar vein, Justice Black asserted that "police wishing to seize and hold people incommunicado" were "given a green light."[48]

As it turned out, Jackson's adoption of the "other evidence" test in fact represented only the "ad hoc deviation" from precedent that Frankfurter had hoped it would be.[49] Likewise the rule of "trustworthiness" never again achieved majority status and was formally repudiated in 1961.[50] Finally in 1964 the "New York method" for determining confession admissibility was declared unconstitutional, thus overruling the one remaining aspect of the *Stein* decision.[51]

With this 1953 ruling the period of reaction in the confession field reached its culmination. The death of Chief Justice Vinson later in the same year and the appointment of Earl Warren as his successor heralded a new era in this, as in other fields of civil rights and liberties under the federal Constitution. The Court began in

[47] 346 U. S., at 200, 201, 203.
[48] *Ibid.*, at 197.
[49] It appears that the test was invoked in only one subsequent Supreme Court case—and then unsuccessfully in a dissenting opinion by Justice Clark. See *Payne* v. *Arkansas*, 356 U. S. 560, 569–70 (1958).
[50] *Rogers* v. *Richmond*, 365 U. S. 534.
[51] *Jackson* v. *Denno*, 378 U. S. 368.

1954 to move back toward the majority position of the late 1940s. It accorded increasing importance to such factors as a defendant's level of intelligence and psychological condition; and, through a weighing of the "totality of circumstances" revealed by each case, formulated a far more stringent due process requirement of confession admissibility.

The trend of the early fifties was reversed by the decision of *Leyra* v. *Denno* on June 1, 1954. By a five-three majority (Justice Jackson not participating) the Court reversed the defendant's conviction of the "hammer murders" of his parents. Justice Black spoke for the new majority which, in addition to Justices Frankfurter and Douglas, included Chief Justice Warren and one defector from the old majority, Justice Clark, the author of the *Stroble* opinion. Black's ruling was based in large part on the ground that a confession used against the defendant was made under hypnosis after an hour and a half of intensive questioning by a state-employed psychiatrist.[52] Beyond indicating a change of direction, the *Leyra* decision was important because it (1) required assessment of a form of coercion quite different from ordinary police interrogation, and (2) involved an effort to determine the mental and emotional state of the suspect at the time of confession. While the Court had made passing reference to the men-

---

[52] Black summarized the controlling circumstances as follows: "First, an already physically and emotionally exhausted suspect's ability to resist interrogation was broken to almost trance-like submission by the use of the arts of a highly skilled psychiatrist. Then the confession [the] petitioner began making to the psychiatrist was filled in and perfected by additional statements given in rapid succession to a police officer, a trusted friend, and two state prosecutors. We hold that use of confessions extracted in such a manner from a lone defendant unprotected by counsel is not consistent with due process of law as required by our Constitution." 347 U. S. 556, 561. Reference to the absence of counsel suggests the high priority that Black consistently accorded that right. But in this case it was cited in combination with other factors as a single element contributing to the denial of due process.

Justice Minton, in a dissenting opinion supported by Reed and Burton, adhered in part to the *Stein* decision, minimizing the legitimate scope of Supreme Court review of state criminal convictions. He made a sharp distinction between the confession made to the psychiatrist and confessions repeated immediately thereafter: "I cannot say here that the subsequent confessions as a matter of law were so completely under the influence of the first confession that to let a jury pass upon that influence as it affected the voluntariness of the later confessions amounts to a denial of due process of law." *Ibid.*, at 588.

tal condition of a defendant in at least one previous confession case arising under the Fourteenth Amendment,[53] the *Leyra* decision marked the first occasion on which this factor was accorded great weight.

As additional cases fell into the pattern set by the *Leyra* decision, it became increasingly clear that with some modifications the Court was reasserting values stressed in such earlier rulings as *Ashcraft* v. *Tennessee* and *Haley* v. *Ohio*. Once again attention was directed to methods of law enforcement that most of the justices regarded as irreconcilable with guarantees of due process. If anything, the trend toward individualization of cases became stronger, although the growing list of variables tended in general to offer greater support for allegations of coercion—especially coercion of a more sophisticated psychological kind. Parallels between the development of due process requirements in the confession and right-to-counsel field have been suggested previously. From the mid-fifties forward this parallel was closer than ever, the case-by-case approach, with its emphasis on discrete "totalities" of facts and circumstances resulting in the extension of constitutional rights in both fields.[54] Moreover, in the late 1950s, Justice Douglas, with the consistent support of Justice Black and the frequent endorsement of Chief Justice Warren and Justice Brennan, began to insist on a constitutional right to requested counsel during police interrogation, thus anticipating the position ultimately taken in the *Escobedo* and *Miranda* cases.[55] Sharp differences continued to exist within the Court throughout this period. The expansion of procedural rights did not go unchallenged and did not follow a smooth unbroken course. While it is unnecessary to comment on each ruling, the general outlines of constitutional development may be traced with reference to several representative decisions.

[53] In *Lyons* v. *Oklahoma* the Court found "no indication" that the defendant was "of a sub-normal intelligence." 322 U. S. 596, 599 (1944).

[54] In the right-to-counsel area see, for example, *Reece* v. *Georgia*, 350 U. S. 85 (1955); *Moore* v. *Michigan*, 355 U. S. 155 (1957); *Cash* v. *Culver*, 358 U. S. 633 (1959).

[55] See, for example, Douglas' dissenting opinion in *Crooker* v. *California*, 357 U.S. 433, 442–48 (1958).

In *Fikes* v. *Alabama* the Court by a six-three majority reversed the conviction of a Negro defendant on the principal ground that his mental abnormality in combination with incommunicado detention and intermittent questioning for over one week rendered his confession involuntary. William Earl Fikes, who had a third-grade education, was described by psychiatrists as "schizophrenic and highly suggestible." Writing his first opinion in the confession field, Chief Justice Warren concluded that "the circumstances of pressure applied against the power of resistance of this petitioner, who cannot be deemed other than weak of will or mind, deprived him of due process of law."[56] A similar result was reached by a seven-two margin in the 1958 case of *Payne* v. *Arkansas*. Here the circumstances of coercion were more conspicuous than in the *Fikes* case, perhaps explaining Justice Harlan's shift to the majority position.[57] By contrast, on the day of the *Payne* decision the Court affirmed the murder conviction of a Negro defendant from Arizona. The confession under review was made to a justice of the peace some twenty hours after the defendant's arrest by a sheriff and his posse. At the time of the arrest a rancher, apparently not connected with the posse, had lassoed the suspect and dragged him a few steps in the direction of some nearby trees. The sheriff's immediate admonition did not dissuade a second rancher from a similar attempt at "frontier justice." Again the sheriff intervened successfully and later stopped still another such effort. Rejecting the contention that the subsequent confession was "coerced by fear of lynching," Justice Clark, speaking for five members of the Court, took the position that although "these ropings" were "deplorable," the "undisputed facts" failed

[56] 352 U. S. 191, 193, 198 (1957).
[57] Payne, a nineteen-year-old Negro described as "mentally dull" was suspected of the murder of his white employer, a retail lumber dealer in Pine Bluff, Arkansas. Arrested without a warrant and held incommunicado for more than forty-eight hours, Payne ultimately confessed after the chief of police told him that thirty or forty people were outside the jail and wanted to "get to him." The record also reveals that during his detention Payne was given very little food. Justice Charles E. Whittaker for the majority found that "from the totality of this course of conduct, and particularly the culminating threat of mob violence, . . . the confession was coerced" and that its use as evidence violated due process of law. 356 U. S. 560, 567.

to "show that petitioner's oral statement was a product of fear engendered by them." [58] Even though the defendant was said to be of normal intelligence and was apparently not subjected to long relays of questioning, it is difficult to square the result in this case with the decisions just noted. The problem is compounded by the failure of the four dissenters—Warren, Black, Douglas, and Brennan—to file an opinion setting forth their views on the question of coercion. The case simply furnished one more example of the highly uncertain character of constitutional restrictions under the due process requirement.

Six weeks later, in *Crooker v. California,* another five-four decision, the Court rejected a defendant's contention that his confession was inadmissible under the Fourteenth Amendment because it was made in the absence of requested counsel. Once again the majority refused to invoke an automatic exclusionary rule similar to requirements at the federal level, but, as previously noted, Justice Douglas in dissent stated the view that later replaced the traditional approach in this field. Referring to the interrogation stage he said that:

> The mischief and abuse of the third degree will continue as long as an accused can be denied the right to counsel at this the most critical period of his ordeal. For what takes place in the secret confines of the police station may be more critical than what takes place at the trial.

Specifically, he urged that the Due Process Clause be more broadly interpreted to "require that the accused who wants a counsel should have one at any time after the moment of arrest." [59]

The *Crooker* decision and two related holdings handed down on the same day[60] marked the Court's last affirmances of conviction under the pre-*Escobedo* approach to confession admissibility. From 1959 to 1963 an unbroken line of decisions further sharpened the due process standard of voluntariness.[61] It was during this

[58] *Thomas v. Arizona,* 356 U. S. 390, 400 (1958).
[59] 357 U. S. 433, 444–45, 448 (1958).
[60] *Cicenia v. Lagay,* 356 U. S. 504 (1958) and *Ashdown v. Utah,* 357 U. S. 426 (1958).
[61] In chronological order these decisions are: *Spano v. New York,* 360 U. S. 315

period that the Court officially repudiated the rule of "trustworthiness" as an element of due process. Although this test had been ignored by the majority in every decision since *Stein v. New York*, its status had remained somewhat uncertain. Justice Frankfurter put at rest any lingering doubts on the subject. Holding that the correct constitutional standard had not been applied in the case under review, he said:

> Our decisions under that [the Fourteenth] amendment have made clear that convictions following the admission into evidence of confessions which are involuntary, i.e., the product of coercion, either physical or psychological, cannot stand. This is so not because such confessions are unlikely to be true but because the methods used to extract them offend an underlying principle in the enforcement of our criminal law: that ours is an accusatorial and not an inquisitorial system—a system in which the state must establish guilt by evidence independently and freely secured and may not by coercion prove its charge against an accused out of his own mouth.[62]

Not only did Frankfurter's remarks sound the death knell of the rule of "trustworthiness," they aroused once more the nagging question of the philosophical connection between the restrictions on coerced confessions and the constitutional right against compulsory self-incrimination. Ironically, Frankfurter himself acknowledged no formal kinship between these requirements, and was especially vehement in denying that the Due Process Clause of the Fourteenth Amendment "incorporated" the Fifth Amendment's Self-incrimination Clause.[63] Nevertheless, his recognition that a state "may not by coercion prove its charge against an ac-

---

(1959); *Blackburn v. Alabama*, 361 U. S. 199 (1960); *Rogers v. Richmond*, 365 U. S. 534 (1961); *Reck v. Pate*, 367 U. S. 433 (1961); *Culombe v. Connecticut*, 367 U. S. 568 (1961); *Gallegos v. Colorado*, 370 U. S. 49 (1962); *Townsend v. Sain*, 372 U. S. 293 (1963); *Lynumn v. Illinois*, 372 U. S. 528 (1963); *Haynes v. Washington*, 373 U. S. 503 (1963).

[62] *Rogers v. Richmond*, 365 U. S. 534, 540–41 (1961).

[63] See his concurring opinion in *Adamson v. California*, 332 U. S. 46, 59–68 (1947). For further discussion of Justice Frankfurter's "due process" approach, as contrasted with the "full incorporation" approach of Justice Black, see Wallace Mendelson, *Justices Black and Frankfurter: Conflict in the Court*, 2d ed. (Chicago: Univ. of Chicago Press, 1966), 49, 66, 118–31.

cused out of his own mouth" brought him very close to a restatement of the Fifth Amendment guarantee. What Frankfurter implied, perhaps unintentionally, Douglas strongly suggested in a 1962 decision. Writing for a four-three majority, Frankfurter and White not participating, he stated that Fourteenth Amendment restrictions on coerced confessions resulted from a "compound of two influences." These he summarized as (1) basic procedural guarantees as set forth in several early decisions, notably *Chambers* v. *Florida*; and (2) "the element of compulsion . . . condemned by the Fifth Amendment."[64] His attempt to square the second of these "influences" with precedent did little to dispel the confusion long surrounding the relationship between the Self-incrimination and Due Process clauses in this field. Moreover, Douglas reemphasized, in traditional fashion, the importance of considering the "totality of circumstances" reflected by each confession. Finally, the views that he expressed regarding the Self-incrimination Clause were not those of an absolute Court majority. These limitations aside, however, the fact remains that within roughly two years from the date of this decision the Court "incorporated" the privilege against self-incrimination into the Fourteenth Amendment, fully accepting Douglas' analogy between self-incrimination and due process standards in the confession field.[65]

Although the Court's exclusive reliance on a due process standard of state confession admissibility ended in 1963,[66] its invalidation of the New York procedure under which juries were given wide discretion in determining the admissibility of confessions did not come until the following year. In *Jackson* v. *Denno*, decided June 22, 1964, the day of the *Escobedo* ruling, a five-four majority, speaking through Justice Byron White, held that this procedure "did not adequately protect Jackson's right to be free of a conviction based upon a coerced confession" and thus could not "with-

[64] *Gallegos* v. *Colorado*, 370 U. S. 49, 51.
[65] *Malloy* v. *Hogan*, 378 U. S. 1 (1964). For a perceptive analysis of the implications of *Gallegos* v. *Colorado* in the context of expanding constitutional requirements, see Donald B. King, "Developing a Future Constitutional Standard for Confessions," *Wayne Law Review* 8 (Summer 1962), 481–496.
[66] *Haynes* v. *Washington*, 373 U. S. 503.

stand constitutional attack under the Due Process Clause of the Fourteenth Amendment." This final step in the total emasculation of *Stein* v. *New York* brought a sharp dissent from Justice Black, who had dissented from the *Stein* ruling itself. He insisted that his opinion in that case "went to other points" and that he "most assuredly did not dissent because of any doubts about a state's constitutional power in a criminal case to let the jury . . . decide the question of a confession's voluntariness."[67] Four activist members of the Court—Warren, Douglas, Brennan, and Goldberg—agreed with Justice White in restricting the jury's independence; while the three remaining advocates of judicial restraint—Clark, Harlan, and Stewart—supported Justice Black, whose libertarian voting record in the confession field is unsurpassed. This variation in alignment indicates no necessary inconsistency, but serves to underscore the breadth and complexity of issues and values associated with the broad question of the use of pretrial confessions as evidence of guilt. The Court by no means exhausted all the possibilities in over thirty full-opinion decisions arising under the Fourteenth Amendment between 1936 and 1964 —as developments beginning with the *Escobedo* ruling amply revealed.[68]

[67] 378 U. S. 368, 377, 401.

[68] For further commentary on the Court's development of confession standards under the Fourteenth Amendment prior to *Escobedo* v. *Illinois*, see Wilfred J. Ritz, "Twenty-five Years of State Criminal Confession Cases in the United States Supreme Court," *Washington and Lee Law Review* 19 (Spring 1962), 35–70; J. A. Spanogle, "The Use of Coerced Confessions in State Courts," *Vanderbilt Law Review* 17 (Mar. 1964), 421–61; Otis H. Stephens, Jr., "The Fourteenth Amendment and Confessions of Guilt: Role of the Supreme Court," *Mercer Law Review* 15 (Spring 1964), 309–34.

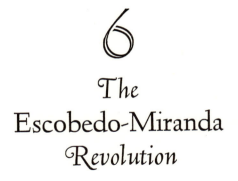

6

The
Escobedo-Miranda
Revolution

DESPITE FAR-REACHING and sometimes abrupt shifts of emphasis, the Supreme Court from 1936 through 1963 relied on standards of voluntariness in determining the admissibility of state confessions under the Due Process Clause of the Fourteenth Amendment. Sometimes *voluntariness* was closely identified with certain methods of interrogation alone, but more often it assumed form and meaning from what was loosely termed the "totality of circumstances" bearing on the question of admissibility. This flexible approach made it possible for a changing Court majority to equate due process requirements with diverse objectives of public policy, ranging all the way from denunciation of various types of police pressure to endorsement of the same or similar conduct when the demands of effective law enforcement took priority. In other words, the due process approach, with its emphasis on the voluntariness of confessions as judged by separate sets of circumstances, allowed ample room for judicial response to a wide variety of social demands, some of which appeared to be diametrically opposed to each other. The upshot of all this activity was that under the due process rationale no single policy commitment achieved more than momentary dominance. It is true that between 1959 and 1963 the Court's dissatisfaction with certain methods of police interrogation was increasingly evident, but even during this period the justices usually tried to assess the coercive effect of a given form of pressure in combination with the suspect's relative vulnerability to coercion.

The conflicting objectives underlying Supreme Court review of state cases contrasted sharply with its articulation of a confession standard for federal prosecutions. Here the emphasis was, for the most part, placed on what the Court regarded as objectionable police methods—specifically, the investigative technique of private interrogation. The Court sought to minimize, if not eliminate, any form of private questioning conducted under the exclusive control of federal law enforcement officers. As always, it approached the problem indirectly through formulation of a rule of evidence that simply barred the admission of any confession or other statement obtained during a period of "unnecessary delay" in bringing the suspect before a United States commissioner for a preliminary examination. But this indirect mode of restricting the police by no means obscured the main thrust of the Court's objective: that of removing the conditions under which confessions might be forcibly extracted from persons suspected of crime. One important result of decisions analyzed in the following pages was that the Court gave definite priority to this objective as applied to state and local law enforcement processes.

The separate lines of state and federal development in the confession field merged in the *Miranda* ruling, and this important development was greatly facilitated, if not foreordained by the application of procedural guarantees of the Bill of Rights to the states via the Fourteenth Amendment. This revolution in criminal procedure began with the search-and-seizure decision of *Mapp* v. *Ohio* in 1961[1] and soon extended to the right-to-counsel and self-incrimination provisions. By the close of the Warren era in June, 1969, almost all procedural rights contained in Amendments Four, Five, Six, and Eight had been either fully "incorporated" into the Fourteenth Amendment or accorded broader protection than in earlier years under the rubric of due process of law.[2] The sweeping changes in constitutional requirements affecting confessions and police interrogation should be identified with

[1] 367 U. S. 643.
[2] For analysis of this sequence of developments in broad perspective, see Henry J. Abraham, *Freedom and the Court,* 2d ed. (New York: Oxford Univ. Press, 1972), Chs. 3 and 4.

this broad revolution in procedural rights. By the same token, the revolution in criminal procedure was only one dimension (albeit a major dimension) of the Warren Court's effort to expand the scope of constitutional rights along a wide spectrum that included the many facets of freedom of expression, the condemnation of various forms of racial discrimination, and the implementation of principles of equality in voting for officials at all levels of government. An appreciation of the variety and depth of constitutional change during this era of judicial activism should not, however, minimize awareness of the importance of links with the past. The term "revolution" may be accurately applied to developments in the confession field as well as in the broader areas just noted, without suggesting that the major outlines of change were altogether unprecedented or unforeseen. In one form or another most of the new confession requirements of the mid-1960s had been urged previously, either in dissenting or concurring opinions, or in majority decisions restricted to particular sets of circumstances. Moreover, the chief elements of legislative and popular criticism so prominent in the late 1960s were foreshadowed by congressional reaction first to the *McNabb* case of 1943, then to the *Mallory* decision fourteen years later.

With the 1964 ruling in *Escobedo* v. *Illinois*,[3] the Court abandoned the test of voluntariness in its traditional form, rejecting alleged admissions to the police, not because they were coerced, but because they were obtained in the absence of requested counsel and effective warning of the suspect's constitutional right to remain silent. The new standard of admissibility, while at variance with traditional confession rules, simply represented one aspect of the Warren Court's general expansion of procedural safeguards in state prosecutions. As we have seen, a minority of justices led by Black and Douglas, had urged at various times during the preceding twenty years that explicit reliance be placed on either a self-

---

[3] 378 U. S. 478. Portions of the material presented in this chapter are adapted from two of my previously published articles: "Police Interrogation and the Supreme Court: an Inquiry into the Limits of Judicial Policy-Making," *Journal of Public Law* 17, no. 2 (1968), 241–57; and "The Assistance of Counsel and the Warren Court: Post-*Gideon* Developments in Perspective," *Dickinson Law Review* 74 (Winter 1970), 193–217.

incrimination or a right-to-counsel rationale in state confession cases.[4] During the late fifties and early sixties, they were particularly insistent on the exclusion of all challenged confessions secured in the absence of requested counsel, and on occasion Chief Justice Warren and Justice Brennan endorsed this position.[5] Adoption of the new standard for police interrogation was facilitated by an important change in Court membership; namely, the retirement of Justice Frankfurter in 1962 and the appointment of Arthur J. Goldberg as his successor. Frankfurter was the principal architect of the due process rationale with which the test of voluntariness was so closely identified. Justice Goldberg, on the other hand, soon adopted the constitutional philosophy of Black and Douglas with respect to confession admissibility and served as the initial spokesman of the new majority, which also included Warren and Brennan.

The new standard was in fact suggested by *Haynes* v. *Washington,* the last of the state confession cases decided prior to *Escobedo* in accordance with due process requirements.[6] There Justice Goldberg recognized a close relation between the due process requirement and a suspect's right to contact his attorney at some point during the interrogation process. Doubtless this decision, like those of *Escobedo* and *Miranda,* was rendered easier

---

[4] See, for example, Black's dissenting opinion in *Stein* v. *New York,* 346 U. S. 156, 197–99 (1953). In his concurring opinion in *Reck* v. *Pate,* Justice Douglas urged the exclusion of "any confession obtained by the police while the defendant is under detention . . . unless there is prompt arraignment and unless the accused is informed of his right to silence and accorded an opportunity to consult counsel." 367 U. S. 433, 448 (1961). Cf. his concurring opinion, joined by Black and Brennan, in *Spano* v. *New York,* 360 U. S. 315, 325 (1959).

[5] Referring to the interrogation stage, Douglas, in a dissenting opinion endorsed by Warren, Black, and Brennan, said: "The mischief and abuse of the third degree will continue as long as an accused can be denied the right to counsel at the most critical period of his ordeal. For what takes place in the secret confines of the police station may be more critical than what takes place at the trial." *Crooker* v. *California,* 357 U. S. 433, 444–45 (1958). It is apparent from this and similar statements in other opinions that Douglas had adopted the essence of the *Miranda* rationale long before it achieved majority status and that three other members of the Court were willing to accept at least the right-to-counsel aspect of that rationale as early as 1958. The four dissenters in the *Crooker* case were joined by Justice Fortas to form the majority in *Miranda* v. *Arizona,* 384 U. S. 436 (1966), which explicitly overruled the *Crooker* decision and the companion case of *Cicenia* v. *Lagay,* 357 U. S. 504 (1958).

[6] 373 U. S. 503 (1963).

by the landmark ruling two months earlier in *Gideon* v. *Wainwright,* in which the Court extended the indigent defendant's right to appointed counsel under the Fourteenth Amendment to all but the most minor criminal cases.[7] Raymond L. Haynes, unlike most previously successful petitioners in the confession field, suffered from no conspicuous disadvantage resulting from limited intelligence, psychological abnormality, youth, inexperience, or the like. Moreover, the record revealed no indication of excessive police pressure, either physical or psychological—no threats of violence, no protracted questioning, no deprivation of sleep or other basic necessities. The Court reversed Haynes' robbery conviction on the ground that a signed confession was made only after he was told that he could not telephone his wife, for purposes of contacting a lawyer, unless he "cooperated and gave . . . a statement . . . ."[8] Goldberg viewed this refusal by the police as an "express threat of continued incommunicado detention" which, along with "the promise of communication with and access to family," easily explained the decision "to make and sign the damning written statement . . . ." The choice was made in "an unfair and inherently coercive context" and was not "the voluntary product of a free and unconstrained will, as required by the Fourteenth Amendment."[9] Thus for the first time in almost twenty years, the Court unequivocally reasserted Justice Black's standard of "inherent coerciveness," this time, however, condemning a far milder form of pressure than the thirty-six hours of continuous questioning disclosed in the *Ashcraft* case. Once again the emphasis was on the private interrogation process itself rather than on a suspect's presumed capacity to withstand pressure. True, in reaching its conclusion, the Court reaffirmed the "totality of circumstances" rationale followed in earlier cases; but accent was clearly on police methods presumably capable of undermining the free will of *any* suspect. To cite but one illustration from Goldberg's opinion:

[7] 372 U. S. 335 (1963). For the Court's subsequent expansion of the *Gideon* Rule to any criminal case in which a defendant is subject to imprisonment, see *Argersinger* v. *Hamlin,* 32 L. Ed. 2d 530 (1972).
[8] For details, see 373 U. S., at 507–11.
[9] *Ibid.,* at 514.

We cannot blind ourselves to what experience unmistakably teaches: that even apart from the express threat, the basic techniques present here—the secret and incommunicado detention and interrogation—are devices adapted and used to extort confessions from suspects.[10]

Writing also for the *Escobedo* majority, Goldberg stressed the importance of a lawyer's presence during police interrogation, expressing serious doubts about the constitutionality of a process that accorded great weight to confessions and admissions privately secured. "The right to counsel," he asserted, "would indeed be hollow if it began at a period when few confessions were obtained. There is necessarily a direct relationship between the importance of a stage to the police in their quest for a confession and the criticalness of that stage to the accused in his need for legal advice."[11] Without formally condemning the use of all confessions elicited by the police, Goldberg sharply criticized reliance on this type of evidence and the customary methods used in obtaining it:

> We have learned the lesson of history, ancient and modern, that a system of criminal law enforcement which comes to depend on the "confession" will, in the long run, be less reliable and more subject to abuses than a system which depends on extrinsic evidence independently secured through skillful investigation . . . .
>
> We have also learned the companion lesson of history that no system of criminal justice can, or should, survive if it comes to depend for its continued effectiveness on the citizens' abdication through unawareness of their constitutional rights. No system

[10] Recognizing the great difficulties accompanying the "detection and solution of crime," and denying any intention of condemning "all interrogation of witnesses and suspects," Goldberg was nevertheless "impelled to the conclusion, from all of the facts presented," that due process was violated. *Ibid.*, at 514–15.

[11] 378 U. S. 478, 488 (1964). It should also be noted that, one month prior to announcement of the *Escobedo* decision, the Supreme Court held that a defendant was deprived of his right to counsel by the admission into evidence of incriminating statements made in the absence of his attorney. These statements were made during a conversation with an alleged confederate who had consented to install a radio transmitter in the defendant's automobile, thereby enabling a federal narcotics agent to overhear everything that was said. Unlike the situation in *Escobedo*, this incident occurred after indictment, while the defendant was free on bail. Nevertheless, it dealt with the same broad question: the admissibility of statements elicited from the accused in the absence of his attorney. *Massiah* v. *United States*, 337 U. S. 201 (1964).

worth preserving should have to fear that if an accused is permitted to consult with a lawyer, he will become aware of, and exercise, these rights. If the exercise of constitutional rights will thwart the effectiveness of a system of law enforcement, then there is something very wrong with that system.[12]

Despite its sweeping language, Goldberg's opinion left several persistent questions unanswered. As in earlier cases, the Court confined its attention to the particular set of circumstances revealed by the record. Danny Escobedo's brother-in-law was murdered on the night of January 19, 1960. A few hours later, in the course of a general investigation, Escobedo was arrested, questioned, and released on a writ of habeas corpus obtained by his attorney. On January 30 a suspect, later indicted for the murder along with Escobedo, informed the police that the latter had fired the fatal shots. On the basis of this allegation, Escobedo was arrested and questioned a second time. Shortly after he reached headquarters his lawyer arrived and made repeated but unsuccessful attempts to see his client. Escobedo caught a glimpse of his attorney at the station house but was denied requests to talk with him. It was in this atmosphere that he made the admissions and exculpatory statements introduced and subsequently challenged in court.

These circumstances limited the Supreme Court's decision to the qualified holding that:

> where . . . the investigation is no longer a general inquiry into an unsolved crime but has begun to focus on a particular suspect, the suspect has been taken into police custody, the police carry out a process of interrogations that lends itself to eliciting incriminating statements, the suspect has requested and been denied an opportunity to consult with his lawyer, and the police have not effectively warned him of his absolute constitutional right to remain silent, the accused has been denied "the Assistance of Counsel" in violation of the Sixth Amendment to the Constitution, as "made obligatory upon the states by the Fourteenth Amendment," . . .

[12] 378 U. S., at 488–89.

and . . . no statement elicited by the police during the investigation may be used against him at a criminal trial . . . .[13]

The Court failed to determine any precise point at which the "general inquiry" begins to "focus on a particular suspect." While roundly criticizing interrogation procedures disclosed by the record, the majority did not impose a general exclusionary rule governing the private questioning of suspects. Under the traditional test of voluntariness the Court might have found ample justification for reaching an identical decision of reversal. In applying this rationale, it had rejected confessions obtained under circumstances perhaps less objectionable than those revealed here.[14] Yet without direct explanation it chose to disregard a standard used repeatedly in similar cases.[15] Perhaps its previous enlargement of the right to counsel and its "incorporation" of the Self-incrimination Clause into the Fourteenth Amendment only one week before announcement of the *Escobedo* decision were explanation enough.[16]

The dissenting opinions of Justices Potter Stewart and Byron White sharply assailed the indefiniteness of the majority ruling and raised several other objections. But the dissents were hardly free of the imprecision and subjectivity imputed to the majority. Stewart concluded his remarks with the following blunt appraisal:

[13] *Ibid.,* at 490–91.

[14] See, for example, *Haynes* v. *Washington,* 373 U. S. 503 (1963).

[15] For a thorough analysis of the *Escobedo* rationale and its relation to traditional confession standards applied by the Supreme Court, see Lawrence Herman, "The Supreme Court and Restrictions on Police Interrogation," 449–500. A detailed discussion of the historical antecedents of the *Escobedo* decision is found in "Comment," *Yale Law Journal* 73 (May 1964), 1000–57. Cf. Arnold N. Enker and Sheldon H. Elsen, "Counsel for the Suspect: *Massiah* v. *United States* and *Escobedo* v. *Illinois*," *Minnesota Law Review* 49 (1964), 47–91. See generally Arthur E. Sutherland, "Crime and Confession," 21–41; and Yale Kamisar, "Equal Justice in the Gatehouses and Mansions of American Criminal Procedure," in *Criminal Justice in Our Time,* ed. by A. E. Howard (Charlottesville: Univ. of Virginia Press, 1965), 1–96.

[16] For expansion of the right to counsel see, in addition to *Gideon* v. *Wainwright,* 372 U. S. 335 (1963), *Hamilton* v. *Alabama,* 368 U. S. 52 (1961); *White* v. *Maryland,* 373 U. S. 59 (1963); *Douglas* v. *California,* 372 U. S. 353 (1963). The Fifth Amendment restriction on self-incrimination was applied to the states through the Fourteenth Amendment in *Malloy* v. *Hogan,* 378 U. S. 1 (1964).

Supported by no stronger authority than its own rhetoric, the Court today converts a routine police investigation of an unsolved murder into a distorted analogy of a judicial trial. It imports into this investigation constitutional concepts historically applicable only after the onset of formal prosecutorial proceedings. In doing so, I think the Court perverts those previous constitutional guarantees, and frustrates the vital interests of society in preserving the legitimate and proper function of honest and purposeful police investigation.[17]

White maintained that the ruling of the Court reflected "a deep-seated distrust of law enforcement officers everywhere, unsupported by relevant data or current material based upon our own experience." Whatever one might think of the merits of the *Escobedo* approach to confession admissibility or the alternative test of voluntariness that White wished the Court to continue applying, his criticism of the absence of empirical support for assumptions about police illegality was well taken. It must be added, however, that his own conclusion that law enforcement would be "crippled" by the decision was equally lacking in support.[18]

The *Escobedo* decision evoked considerable public criticism, much of it echoing, in substance, if not in tone, the objections raised by the dissenting justices. Negative reaction focused on the alleged "handcuffing" of police during a period of rising crime and emphasized the inexactness of the new interrogation requirements.[19] It was clear that the Court had gone far toward repudiating traditional confession standards in state cases. At an early point in the process of questioning, the suspect was entitled under the Fourteenth Amendment (although without specific reference to the Due Process Clause) to the assistance of counsel. But when was this point reached? Did the new requirements preclude private interrogation generally, or could the police still make limited use of this basic investigative technique?

17 378 U. S., at 494.
18 *Ibid.*, at 499.
19 See *New York Times*, Nov. 29, 1964, Sec. 6 (Magazine), at 36; and Fred E. Inbau, "Law Enforcement, the Courts, and Individual Liberties," in *Criminal Justice in Our Times*, ed. by A. E. Howard (Charlottesville: Univ. of Virginia Press, 1965), 97–136.

Some of the confusion and uncertainty produced in state courts and police departments by the *Escobedo* decision was dispelled two years later by the landmark ruling in *Miranda v. Arizona*.[20] Once again the Court expanded constitutional restrictions on police interrogation, but this time—perhaps in response to criticism—it specified the new requirements in far more explicit terms. The *Miranda* ruling covered four cases, three of them coming from state courts and the other originating in a United States district court.[21] These cases uniformly involved the admissibility of statements obtained during periods of private interrogation characterized either by failure to advise the suspects of their constitutional rights or by the absence of "knowing and intelligent" waiver of those rights.

By contrast with most of its earlier confession decisions, the Court gave only nominal attention to the particular circumstances out of which each case arose. Thus, for example, the drama surrounding the alleged kidnapping and rape of an eighteen-year-old girl by an emotionally unstable Mexican-American youth named Ernesto Miranda is totally overshadowed by the Court's preoccupation with the establishment of inflexible constitutional prerequisites, applicable at least in theory to police interrogation throughout the country.[22]

By reviewing state and federal convictions in a single decision, the Court officially erased differences between interrogation requirements at these separate levels of government. Accordingly, considerations of federalism, so crucial to a majority of the justices only a few years earlier, gave way to the new objective of uniform minimum standards of interrogation for all law enforcement agencies. While the *Miranda* decision did not disturb the

[20] 384 U. S. 436 (1966).

[21] In the order of their appearance in the reported record of the Court, these cases are: *Miranda v. Arizona, Vignera v. New York, Westover v. United States, California v. Stewart.*

[22] An interesting and comprehensive presentation of the factual circumstances out of which the *Miranda* case developed is found in Richard C. Cortner and Clifford M. Lytle, *Modern Constitutional Law* (New York: The Free Press, 1971), 158–200. For analysis of all aspects of this decision, see Richard Medalie, *From Escobedo to Miranda: The Anatomy of a Supreme Court Decision* (Washington, D. C.: Lerner Law Book Company, 1966). See also B. James George, ed., *A New Look at Confessions.*

McNabb-Mallory Rule, the new array of constitutional protections in effect overshadowed the extraconstitutional procedure
required by the latter.

A bare majority of five,[23] speaking through Chief Justice Warren, held, in an elaborate opinion, that "the prosecution may not
use statements whether exculpatory or inculpatory, stemming
from custodial interrogation of the defendant unless it demon-
strates the use of procedural safeguards effective to secure the
privilege against self-incrimination."[24] These safeguards may be
summarized as follows: (1) the suspect must be warned prior to
questioning that he has a right to remain silent; (2) this warning
must be accompanied by the explanation that anything he says
may be used as evidence against him; (3) he "must be clearly informed that he has the right to consult with a lawyer and to have
the lawyer with him during the interrogation"; (4) because the
suspect's financial status has nothing to do with "the scope of the
rights involved here," he must be told "that if he is indigent a
lawyer will be appointed to represent him"; (5) the suspect may
waive these rights and submit to questioning, but "a heavy burden
rests on the government to demonstrate" that he did so "knowingly and intelligently;" (6) even if the suspect initially waives his
rights, he may stop the interrogation at any time by asserting his
right to remain silent or requesting the assistance of counsel.[25]

This ruling struck directly at established forms of police interrogation. While the familiar pattern of private questioning
might seldom be accompanied by outright violence, the interrogation atmosphere, with its emphasis on privacy, was viewed as
psychologically coercive. The Court maintained that the element of secrecy implicit in private interrogation made it impossible to know "what in fact goes on in the interrogation rooms."[26]
Citing techniques of deception and psychological persuasion
recommended in leading police interrogation manuals, Warren

[23] Justice Goldberg, the author of the *Escobedo* decision, resigned from the
Court in 1965, but the judicial alignment remained unchanged in the interrogation
area with the appointment of Justice Fortas as his successor.

[24] 384 U. S., at 444.

[25] *Ibid.*, at 47, 472, 475.

[26] *Ibid.*, at 448.

concluded that the atmosphere in which questioning typically occurred completely undermined the suspect's privilege against self-incrimination. From a technical standpoint the emphasis of the *Miranda* decision differed from that of *Escobedo* v. *Illinois.* The latter ruling was based largely on the Sixth Amendment right to the assistance of counsel, while the former relied principally on the Fifth Amendment immunity against self-incrimination. Despite this apparent shift in constitutional emphasis, the *Miranda* majority regarded the "presence of counsel" as the "adequate protective device" by which police interrogation could be brought into conformity with requirements of the Fifth Amendment.[27] Of course the significance accorded to the presence of a lawyer during police questioning underscored the Court's expression of distrust about what took place at private sessions of station house interrogation. Apart from the Court's long-standing concern about the "third degree" and less blatant methods of coercion, a majority of the justices in both *Escobedo* and *Miranda* were raising questions about the very existence of a system that permitted exertion of official pressure on a suspect to obtain evidence in a manner that would be totally unacceptable if conducted in open court.[28] This scepticism was reflected in Warren's reference to the "interrogation atmosphere and the evils it can bring."[29] The *Miranda* requirements rested squarely on the assumption that deficiencies in the interrogation process could be remedied by the conversion of that process into something more closely resembling the adversary system. To most judges and lawyers this assumption of the corrective quality of the adversary system might seem altogether reasonable.[30] Members of the law enforcement profession, how-

[27] *Ibid.,* at 446.

[28] This aspect of the problem of law enforcement within a constitutional framework is examined by Yale Kamisar, "Equal Justice in the Gatehouses and Mansions of American Criminal Procedure," 1–96. For a more critical view of the court-related aspects of the criminal justice system, see generally Abraham S. Blumberg, *Criminal Justice* (Chicago: Quadrangle Books, 1967). See also, Tigar, "Waiver of Constitutional Rights," 1–29.

[29] *Miranda* v. *Arizona,* 384 U. S., at 456.

[30] For a perceptive inquiry into the utility and limitations of the adversary system in the judicial formulation of public policy, with particular emphasis on the work of the Supreme Court, see Carl Brent Swisher, "The Supreme Court and 'The Moment of Truth,'" *American Political Science Review* 54 (Dec. 1960), 879–86.

ever, could hardly be expected to concede that police methods are so deficient as to require surveillance by the legal profession.

As in the *Escobedo* case, the departure from a more flexible due process standard drew fire from the four dissenting justices. For example, Harlan, in an opinion supported by Stewart and White, expressed strong preference for the "elaborate, sophisticated, and sensitive approach" developed during more than one-quarter of a century for determining the "admissibility of confessions." This standard had proved adaptable to individual cases and to "the endless mutations of fact presented." Such adaptability had made it possible for the Court on occasion to recognize what Harlan called "society's interest in suspect questioning as an instrument of law enforcement."[31] He seriously doubted whether, under the *Miranda* rules, this broad social interest could be protected. Sounding the same theme, Justice Clark expressed preference for the "more pliable dictates" of due process "which we are accustomed to administering and which we know from our cases" to be effective "in protecting persons in police custody."[32] He was uneasy about the "almost total lack of empirical knowledge on the practical operation of requirements, truly comparable to those announced by the majority . . . ." By retaining the due process approach, the Court could avoid "acting in the dark" and "in one full sweep changing the traditional rules of custodial interrogation . . . so long recognized as a justifiable and proper tool in balancing individual rights against the rights of society."[33]

On the other hand, Warren insisted that the interests of the community were not endangered by the new requirements, that they "should not constitute an undue interference with a proper system of law enforcement," and that the decision in no way precluded law enforcement officers from "carrying out their traditional investigatory functions."[34] Conceding that confessions might be of some importance as evidence of guilt, he strongly suggested, nevertheless, that police and prosecutors tended to overestimate the value of such evidence in obtaining convictions.

[31] 384 U. S., at 508–509.
[32] *Ibid.*, at 503.
[33] *Ibid.*, at 503.
[34] *Ibid.*, at 481.

He pointed out that in each of the cases under review substantial evidence was introduced apart from the confession. Warren was unwilling, however, to accept the contention, advanced by many critics of the ruling, that advising a suspect of his rights prior to questioning or even the presence of an attorney during interrogation would necessarily make it impossible for the police to obtain confessions.

In support of his contention that the effectiveness of law enforcement would not be impaired by the new restrictions on interrogation, Warren cited the "exemplary record" of the Federal Bureau of Investigation in advising suspects of their rights. By comparison he also noted safeguards contained in the English Judges' Rules and procedures followed in Scotland, India, and Ceylon.[35] Apparently there had been "no marked detrimental effect on criminal law enforcement in these jurisdictions as a result of these rules." He contended that sufficient similarity existed between conditions of law enforcement in the United States and the countries compared "to permit reference to this experience as assurance that lawlessness will not result from warning an individual of his rights or allowing him to exercise them."[36] The dissenting justices took sharp issue with this reliance upon comparative data. Justices Clark and Harlan maintained that procedures followed by the FBI in warning suspects of their rights to silence and the assistance of counsel were less detailed and exacting than the *Miranda* requirements. They further insisted that Warren's discussion of interrogation rules in England and elsewhere overlooked counterbalancing prosecutorial advantages.[37] Harlan pointed out, for example, that English police were instructed by the Judges' Rules to "caution" suspects about their right to remain silent, but that no affirmative advice of the right to counsel was included in this preinterrogation warning. Moreover, in the discretion of English courts "confessions can be and apparently quite frequently are admitted in evidence despite disregard of the Judges' Rules so long as they are found voluntary

[35] *Ibid.,* at 483–90.
[36] *Ibid.,* at 489.
[37] *Ibid.,* at 500 n. 3, 521–23.

under the common-law test."[38] Harlan's criticism exposed a serious weakness in Warren's analysis. While it might be argued that the Judges' Rules and the *Miranda* requirements shared the same lofty values of human dignity and a common commitment to civilized standards of law enforcement, the sharp differences between their respective sanctions rendered any direct comparison highly dubious. The *Miranda* requirements, after all, had the immediate and formal authority of an exclusionary rule, automatically binding, at least in theory, on every trial judge in the United States. The English Judges' Rules, by contrast, were originally devised and have continued to serve only as broad policy guidelines for police interrogation. While their violation has often (perhaps more often than not) resulted in the exclusion of evidence, they have had no more legal force than individual judges, at their own discretion, have chosen to give them. Ironically, the *Miranda* requirements and the Judges' Rules may be more accurately compared from the standpoint of the continuing public controversy surrounding them. Critics in both countries have seriously questioned their deterrent effect upon police malpractice. They are alike in their susceptibility to reevaluation and possible repudiation in the face of changing criminal justice priorities that accord greater importance to the goal of effective law enforcement administration and relatively less weight to procedural safeguards of the accused.[39]

Although the *Miranda* ruling was more specific in detailing formal requirements than earlier Supreme Court decisions on police interrogation, it left several questions unanswered and raised some new problems. One difficulty stemmed from the Court's implicit assumption concerning the presence of counsel as a "pro-

[38] *Ibid.*, at 522.

[39] After eight years of study, England's Criminal Revision Committee published a report on June 27, 1972, recommending the easing of restrictions on the admissibility of certain kinds of evidence. The fourteen prominent judges and jurists comprising this government-appointed committee were pointedly critical of several safeguards in the Judges' Rules. One principal recommendation was, in fact, abolition of the "caution" contained in Rule II, under which police interrogators advise suspects of their right to remain silent. See *The Criminal Law Revision Committee, Eleventh Report, Evidence (General)* (London: Her Majesty's Stationery Office, 1972).

tective device" at the interrogation stage. Can this "critical stage" be sharply separated from the earlier period in which the suspect is given his warnings and required to decide whether he wants a lawyer? In other words, can an uncounseled suspect "knowingly and intelligently" waive his right to counsel during interrogation?[40] Furthermore, the Court failed to indicate the manner in which counsel for indigent suspects should be selected. Apparently the suspect would have some choice in the matter, but if he expressed no preference, who should then designate the attorney and in accordance with what criteria? The basic question raised by the decision is whether the objectionable features of private police questioning are significantly modified by the constitutional requirements of warnings and waiver. As Justice Harlan aptly remarked, "Those who use third degree tactics and deny them in court are equally able and destined to lie as skillfully about warnings and waivers."[41] The Court did, of course, stipulate that "unless and until . . . warnings and waiver are demonstrated by the prosecution at trial, no evidence obtained as a result of interrogation" is admissible.[42] Precisely how the prosecution might accomplish this task remained unclear. Presumably the Court would consider a variety of factors in ascertaining in a given case whether a suspect voluntarily waived his rights. These circumstances would include the length of detention prior to any statement made to the police and the question of whether the suspect was "threatened, tricked or cajoled into a waiver . . . ."[43] Thus the Court applied to the question of waiver something very close to the flexible due process standard—a "totality of circumstances" test much like that which it expressly rejected as an inadequate protection against the undue pressure of private interrogation.[44]

Most of the criticisms voiced in dissenting opinions focused on two basic questions: (1) the scope historically accorded the im-

[40] See generally Sheldon H. Elsen and Arthur Rosett, "Protections for the Suspect under *Miranda* v. *Arizona*," *Columbia Law Review* 67 (Apr. 1967), 645–70.
[41] 384 U. S., at 505.
[42] *Ibid.*, at 479.
[43] *Ibid.*, at 476.
[44] For discussion, see Nathan R. Sobel, *The New Confession Standards: Miranda v. Arizona, a Legal Perspective, a Practical Perspective* (New York: Gould Publications, 1966), 6, 10.

munity against self-incrimination and the majority's selection and interpretation of precedents: (2) the wisdom or practicality of the decision as a statement of public policy. Mr. Justice Harlan was explicit in his objections on both these grounds. In his view, Warren's opinion revealed "no adequate basis for extending the Fifth Amendment's privilege against self-incrimination to the police station." Of far greater importance, however, was its failure "to show that the Court's new rules are well supported, let alone compelled, by Fifth Amendment precedents."[45] He also called attention to the separate historical origins of the privilege against self-incrimination and restrictions on out-of-court confessions. Conceding that these arguments standing alone might not be conclusive, that the Constitution had proved capable of flexibility in response to changing needs and circumstances, and that a philosophical relation existed between the confession rules and the Self-incrimination Clause, he nevertheless insisted that the *Miranda* requirements represented unwise and potentially harmful policy choices. While admitting the difficulty of predicting the effect that the decision would have on law enforcement, he left no doubt about his own estimate of its impact: "We . . . know that some crimes cannot be solved without confessions, that ample expert testimony attests to their importance in crime control, and that the Court is taking a real risk with society's welfare in imposing its new regime on the country. The social costs of crime are too great to call the new rules anything but hazardous experimentation."[46]

In his strongly worded dissent, Justice White contended that many of the precedents cited by the majority specifically recognized the legality and appropriateness of private interrogation. In determining the voluntariness of a confession, even under a self-incrimination standard, the Court had, he contended, always considered private police interrogation as only one of many relevant and potentially important factors. On the other hand, departure from precedent and history did not, in and of itself, "prove either that the Court [had] exceeded its powers" or that it was "wrong

[45] 384 U. S., at 510.
[46] *Ibid.*, at 517.

or unwise" in its new interpretation of the Self-incrimination Clause. Far from discovering the law or deriving it "from some irrefutable sources," the Court had made "new law and new public policy," as it had done over the years in "interpreting other great clauses of the Constitution." White frankly acknowledged that in the absence of "some fundamental change in the constitutional distribution of governmental powers,"[47] this policy-making role of the Supreme Court would remain essential. New policy considerations should be as fully supported as possible, not only by constitutional provisions, but also by strong practical considerations.

Having stated his objections to the decision on the first of these grounds, White went on to contend with even greater insistence that the second prerequisite was also lacking. He was certain that the decision rested on the premise that it was "inherently wrong for the police to gather evidence from the accused himself," that confessions in general constituted a dubious form of evidence. The factual basis of the Court's premise was in his view totally unsupported "by any of the standards for empirical investigation utilized in the social sciences . . . ."[48] White's reference to knowledge in the social sciences did not lead, however, to his own reliance on empirical data for conclusions respecting the practical consequences that would result from adoption of the new rules. Without further support than the citation of statistics on recidivism and related matters having no direct bearing on police interrogation, he bluntly asserted that the *Miranda* requirements would "measurably weaken the ability of the criminal law" to prosecute and ultimately to rehabilitate criminals. Without reservation he flatly predicted that:

> In some unknown number of cases the Court's rule will return a killer, a rapist or other criminal to the streets and to the environment which produced him, to repeat his crime whenever it pleases him. As a consequence, there will not be a gain, but a loss, in human dignity. The real concern is not the unfortunate consequences of this new decision on the criminal law as an abstract,

[47] *Ibid.*, at 531.
[48] *Ibid.*, at 533.

137

disembodied series of authoritative proscriptions, but the impact on those who rely on the public authority for protection and who without it can only engage in violent self-help with guns, knives and the help of their neighbors similarly inclined. There is, of course, a saving factor: the next victims are uncertain, unnamed and unrepresented in this case.[49]

Aside from revealing the intensity and bitterness of his disagreement with the majority, this statement merely underscored White's policy preference on the question of police interrogation and confessions—a preference probably as unsupported by empirical findings as the position that he so freely attacked. In the light of subsequent studies aimed at assessing the impact of the *Miranda* requirements on the routine process of interrogation, it appears that his conclusions were premature.[50]

Sharp differences in constitutional interpretation and in the choice of policy alternatives tend to obscure the one important point on which the justices apparently agreed: their belief that the *Miranda* rules would—for better or for worse—greatly alter traditional police interrogation practices. This belief was implicit not only in strong objections by the dissenters to what they regarded as a dangerous experiment, but also in the majority's careful listing and detailed explanation of the new requirements.[51] It was further reflected in subsequent decisions in which the Court declared that the *Escobedo* and *Miranda* requirements would not be given retroactive application.[52] Although dissatisfied with the voluntariness test as an effective restriction on objectionable interrogation practices, the Court majority was unwilling to scrap the older standard entirely. Its reluctance was influenced perhaps

---

49 *Ibid.*, at 542–43.
50 See "Interrogations in New Haven: The Impact of *Miranda*," *Yale Law Journal* 76 (July 1967), 1521–1648; Seeburger and Wettick, "*Miranda* in Pittsburgh," 1–26; Medalie, Zeitz, and Alexander, "Custodial Police Interrogation in Our Nation's Capital, 1347–1422; Neal A. Milner, "Comparative Analysis of Patterns of Compliance with Supreme Court Decisions: *Miranda* and the Police in Four Communities," *Law and Society Review* 5 (Aug. 1970), 119–34.
51 In *United States* v. *Tempia*, 16 U.S.C.M.A. 629, 37 C.M.R. 249 (1967), the United States Court of Military Appeals extended the *Miranda* protections to persons within the jurisdiction of military tribunals.
52 See *Johnson* v. *New Jersey*, 384 U. S. 719 (1966), and *Davis* v. *North Carolina*, 384 U. S. 737 (1966).

as much by awareness of the hostility with which law enforcement officers would receive the *Miranda* decision as by the sharp division among the justices. In short, the majority recognized that no matter how forceful or how often it invoked constitutional provisions, the effectiveness of this ruling would depend largely on its acceptance by the very officials whose conduct it sought to regulate.

In outlining the *Miranda* requirements, Chief Justice Warren recognized that Congress or the states might develop equally effective alternatives for the protection of a suspect's rights:

> Our decision in no way creates a constitutional straitjacket which will handicap sound efforts at reform, nor is it intended to have this effect. We encourage Congress and the states to continue their laudable search for increasingly effective ways of protecting the rights of the individual while promoting efficient enforcement of our criminal law.[53]

While the Court might have had some basis for expecting legislative efforts at reform in this area, there was little reason to believe that Congress or the states would seriously propose anything approaching the explicit and far-reaching *Miranda* requirements. Indeed, it soon became clear that Congress was more inclined to challenge the new procedural requirements than to consider legislation aimed at implementing them.

Although the decision drew praise from Senator Wayne Morse (D., Ore.) in remarks made on the Senate floor two days after its announcement,[54] the preponderance of congressional reaction was negative. Georgia's junior senator, Herman Talmadge, sounded what came to be a familiar note when he asserted one week later that the ruling virtually banned "effective police interrogation" and would "very likely make questioning a thing of the past."[55] Typical of the free-swinging attacks leveled at the Court was a Florida congressman's lament that, while the justices prior to their Supreme Court appointments were "intelligent and respected

[53] 384 U. S., at 467.
[54] 112 *Cong. Rec.* 13261 (June 15, 1966).
[55] *Ibid.*, at 13861.

lawyers and jurists," some of them had apparently become "lost in a liberal daydream with no conception of down-to-earth reality."[56] The decision also produced partisan criticism aimed at individual members of the Court and even at the President himself, as the following allegation reveals:

> The Supreme Court ruling [*Miranda*] carried by one vote. The deciding vote on this issue was cast by Abe Fortas, the Johnson appointee, who only a few days before his appointment, said that he believed in the right of the police to question criminal suspects . . . . The full weight of this decisive one vote rests squarely on the new justice—Abe Fortas—and on the man who appointed him—President Lyndon B. Johnson.[57]

A Senate Judiciary Subcommittee on Constitutional Amendments held hearings on the *Miranda* decision in mid-July, and Senator Sam Ervin took this occasion to link his persistent and determined opposition to the *McNabb-Mallory* Rule with a renewed effort to restrict the Court's interrogation requirements. In a detailed statement to the subcommittee he reiterated his belief that the Court had "stressed individual rights" at the expense of public safety and to the serious detriment of the administration of criminal justice. Echoing Justice White's dissenting views, Ervin concluded that the *Miranda* majority had "not only practically eliminated confessions from trial court consideration," but had also "probably made impossible the ordinary practice of police interrogation itself, a result which surely entails harmful consequences for the country at large."[58] Consistent with his far-reaching criticism, Ervin introduced a constitutional amendment on July 29, 1966, designed, among other things, to overrule the *Miranda* decision and to withdraw from Supreme Court review all rulings of trial judges, state and federal, admitting confessions

[56] *Ibid.*, at 14975 (remarks of Congressman Robert L. Sikes [D., Fla.], July 11, 1966).
[57] *Ibid.*, at 13945–46 (remarks of Congressman Durward G. Hall [R., Mo.], June 22, 1966). It should be remembered that Justice Fortas took a position fully consistent with that of his predecessor Justice Goldberg regarding standards applicable to police interrogation and confessions. In this context his vote was no more "decisive" than that of any other member of the *Miranda* majority.
[58] Quoted in 112 *Cong. Rec.* 16778 (July 22, 1966).

into evidence on grounds of voluntariness provided such rulings were supported by competent evidence.[59] This marked the formal beginning of a two-year effort to nullify *Miranda, Mallory,* and related Supreme Court restrictions on police investigation procedures—an effort that apparently achieved partial success with passage of Title II of the Omnibus Crime Control and Safe Streets Act of 1968.[60]

Senator Ervin reintroduced the anti-*Miranda* amendment on January 23, 1967, this time with the cosponsorship of fifteen colleagues.[61] During the same session of Congress several bills were proposed in an effort to achieve the identical objective via the less cumbersome route of ordinary legislation.[62] Under the chairmanship of Senator John L. McClellan (D., Ark.) the Judiciary Subcommittee on Criminal Laws and Procedures held extensive hearings on a variety of legislative measures in the field of law enforcement, including restrictions on the *Miranda* ruling and related cases. These hearings revealed inflexible, at times bitter, opposition to the Court's interrogation guidelines. Often in emotion-charged language, the familiar claims of a direct connection between the enlargement of procedural requirements and a rising crime rate were repeated by a parade of district attorneys, police chiefs, and other representatives of what might be called the "law enforcement lobby." For example, one witness contended that the *Escobedo* and *Miranda* decisions had not only led to and encouraged "crime in the streets," but had also spawned the formation of "criminal syndicates and organizations." Commenting on the decline in police morale allegedly produced by these rulings, another critic charged that an "opaque curtain of judicial protection" cloaked "the activities of the criminal" with the result that many officers were "becoming understandably reluctant" even to attempt "to part this curtain."[63] Some witnesses adopted

[59] *Ibid.,* at 17626.
[60] Act of June 19, 1968, Pub. L. No. 90–351, 82 Stat. 210.
[61] S. J. Res. 22, 90 Cong., 1 sess. (1967), reprinted in 113 *Cong. Rec.* 1173.
[62] See S. 674, S. 1194, and S. 1333, 90 Cong., 1 sess. (1967).
[63] *Controlling Crime Through More Effective Law Enforcement,* statements of James T. Wilkinson, Commonwealth's attorney for the city of Richmond, Virginia, 246, and Quinn Tamm, executive director, International Association of Chiefs of Police, Washington, D. C., 329.

a more moderate view of the Court's impact on law enforcement. Sounding a note of caution, Chief Judge J. Edward Lumbard of the United States Court of Appeals for the Second Circuit reminded the subcommittee that since the *Miranda* decision rested on constitutional grounds, Congress could validly modify the new rules only by initiating the process of constitutional amendment.[64] Although generally recognized as preferable from a theoretical standpoint, this method, with its dual requirement of an affirmative two-thirds vote by both Houses of Congress and favorable action by three-fourths of the states, was ultimately dropped in favor of regular statutory enactment. It was generally recognized that Congress had full authority to revise the *McNabb-Mallory* Rule in this manner. In fact, its opponents late in 1967 finally pushed through a measure, applicable only to the District of Columbia, permitting police to question suspects for a period of three hours prior to a hearing before a United States commissioner.[65] Scholarly opinion was fairly well united, however, in condemning the effort to overturn the Court's interpretation of the Self-incrimination Clause as applicable to interrogation. Nevertheless, when it came to a choice between a constitutionally acceptable method of legislative response and the practical demands of actually passing an anti-Court measure, a sizable majority of senators and congressmen chose the latter course. This result appears particularly ironic in view of the professed "strict constructionist" views of several leading proponents of the "court-curbing" effort.

It is true that a Court majority, on the very day that *Miranda* was decided, had recognized independent congressional authority to interpret the scope of Fourteenth Amendment rights, even if, under certain circumstances, such interpretation ran counter to the Court's own prior decisions.[66] Thus it upheld Section 4(e) of the 1965 Voting Rights Act which had the effect of nullifying the English literacy requirement then operating in New York and presumably consistent with an earlier Supreme Court decision

[64] *Ibid.*, at 184.
[65] Act of Dec. 27, 1967, Pub. L. No. 90–226.
[66] *Katzenbach* v. *Morgan*, 384 U. S. 641 (1966).

sustaining an English literacy test in North Carolina.[67] Proponents of anti-*Miranda* legislation made an oblique and highly inconclusive effort to draw an analogy between this development and the congressional resurrection of the voluntariness test of confession admissibility. They contended that the Court's expansion of the right against self-incrimination in *Miranda* rested squarely on the assumption, drawn largely from "police manuals and tests," that custodial interrogation was "inherently coercive." They then proceeded to the questionable conclusion that, if interrogation were not, "*in fact*," inherently coercive, "the Court would be compelled to retreat" to the earlier standard of voluntariness and "that congressional legislation" based on "a finding of fact" would be an appropriate means by which to achieve this end.[68] But no such factual basis for anti-*Miranda* legislation was ever established. While the Court might be expected to accept some congressional modification of the *Miranda* requirements, it would have no easy time in sustaining a measure that sought to reinstate the very test that a majority of the justices had deliberately repudiated.[69]

Out of congressional activity in 1967 and growing public concern with urban violence, assassination, mounting racial tension, and related problems, emerged the Omnibus Crime Control and Safe Streets Act of 1968. As previously indicated, one of the most controversial provisions of this many-sided enactment was a section of Title II purporting to overturn the *Miranda* requirements as applied to "criminal prosecutions brought by the United States or the District of Columbia."[70] In addition, the act expanded the earlier anti-*Mallory* restriction by authorizing in federal prosecutions a six-hour period of delay between a suspect's arrest and his appearance before a United States commissioner. It also sought to overrule lineup identification decisions as applied to federal crim-

[67] *Lassiter v. North Hampton County Board of Election*, 360 U. S. 45 (1959). For sec. 4(e) of the Voting Rights Act, see 42 USC 1973B, (e).
[68] U. S., Congress, Senate, *Report 1097*, 90 Cong., 2 sess., 1968, pp. 60–61.
[69] For analysis of the possible constitutional status of anti-*Miranda* legislation in light of *Katzenbach* v. *Morgan*, see Robert A. Burt, "*Miranda* and Title II: A Morganatic Marriage." In Philip B. Kurland, ed., *Supreme Court Review* (1969), 81–134.
[70] Pub. L. No. 90–351, Title II, Sec. 3501 (June 19, 1968), 82 Stat. 210.

inal investigations.[71] Deleted from the original Senate version of the bill were much broader restrictions on federal judicial power. One of these was aimed at abolishing the jurisdiction of the Supreme Court and lower federal courts to review decisions of the highest state appellate courts admitting confessions into evidence on grounds of voluntariness.[72] Although Congress stopped somewhat short of a serious confrontation with the Supreme Court—a confrontation virtually assured by the Senate bill prior to this deletion—the reaction to judicial interpretation of interrogation requirements and related matters underscored deep and long-smouldering hostility toward the Warren Court. Hearings and floor debate are replete with assertions by Senators Ervin, McClellan, and others that Supreme Court decisions had not only impeded effective law enforcement but had also contributed greatly to a dramatic increase in the crime rate. The following excerpt from one of McClellan's Senate speeches is representative of this attitude:

> Gangsters, racketeers, and habitual criminals are increasingly defying the law and flouting duly constituted authority and getting away with it. As a consequence, public confidence in the ability of the Courts to administer justice is being undermined and gravely impaired. Until the courts, and particularly the United States Supreme Court, become cognizant of this damaging trend and begin to administer justice with greater emphasis on truth and a deeper concern for the protection of the public, the crime rate will continue its upward spiral and the quality of justice will further deteriorate.[73]

Such charges evoked sharp counterattacks in the floor debate over Title II. Strongly opposing the measure, Senator Edward M. Kennedy maintained that "keystones" in the tradition of ordered

---

[71] *United States* v. *Wade*, 388 U.S. 218 (1967). In *Gilbert* v. *California*, 388 U.S. 263, decided on the same day as the *Wade* case, the Court applied identical lineup identification restrictions to the states through the Fourteenth Amendment.

[72] Also struck from the bill was a provision intended to divest the federal courts of authority to review state convictions in *habeas corpus* proceedings. See Title II of S. 917, 90 Cong., 1 sess., as reported by the Committee on the Judiciary, Apr. 29, 1968, 90 Cong., 2 sess.

[73] 114 *Cong. Rec.* 11201 (May 1, 1968).

liberty were "threatened because some Americans [had] panicked about crime and [wanted] scapegoats to flay and panaceas to grasp at." "It is ironic," he asserted, "that those who rail the loudest about obedience to law as an unshakable absolute, those who inveigh against civil disobedience in all its forms, should be in the forefront of an effort to violate the Constitution, and rob the Supreme Court of its power."[74] But in terms of the Supreme Court's role in American government and politics, the important question is not the inaccuracy or exaggeration of hostile sentiment, but the widespread appeal that such arguments have had in Congress and, we may reasonably assume, throughout the country.

Questions of constitutionality aside, the legislative curbs on *Miranda, Mallory,* and related decisions might have been intended to signal a warning to the Court majority that its own scale of activity, not traditional methods of law enforcement, could inflame the reforming zeal of legislative leaders. Whatever the motives behind Title II, the Warren Court showed no immediate inclination to ease the new requirements. To the contrary, on May 6, 1968, amid Senate debate on this measure, the Court added a new dimension to the scope of the *Miranda* ruling. In *Mathis* v. *United States*[75] the original *Miranda* majority, speaking this time through Justice Black, applied the controversial requirements to a form of questioning quite different from station house interrogation. While Mathis was in jail serving a state sentence, he was questioned by a federal agent of the Internal

[74] *Ibid.,* at 14147 (May 21, 1968). Pointing to several "paradoxes" in the bill, Senator Joseph D. Tydings (D., Md.) noted that the provisions seeking to overrule the *Miranda* and *Wade* decisions applied "only to trials in federal courts." The measure did not even purport to extend to state jurisdictions where, paradoxically, *Miranda's* impact was "alleged to have been most severe." 114 *Cong. Rec.* 14082 (May 20, 1968). At several points during the debate, Senator Tydings entered in the record numerous letters from deans and professors at major law schools throughout the country uniformly opposing Title II on constitutional or policy grounds. See, e.g., 114 *Cong. Rec.* 13850–67 (May 17, 1968). For additional criticism of Senate restrictions on the Court, see Fred P. Graham, "Congress Still Battling the Court," *New York Times,* May 26, 1968, at E–15. For a comprehensive account of congressional reaction to *Miranda* and related decisions, see Adam Carlyle Breckenridge, *Congress Against the Court* (Lincoln: Univ. of Nebraska Press, 1970).
[75] 391 U. S. 1 (1968).

Revenue Service and made statements that were used later as part of the evidence on which he was convicted of income tax fraud. The government contended that the *Miranda* warnings were not required (1) because the questioning was conducted merely as part of a routine tax investigation which might or might not result in a criminal prosecution and (2) because Mathis had not been arrested by the officer who questioned him but was serving a sentence for a separate offense. Rejecting these contentions, Black stated that such differences were "too minor and shadowy to justify a departure from the well considered conclusions of *Miranda* with reference to warnings to be given to a person held in custody."[76] The *Mathis* case in no way changed the substance of the *Miranda* warnings and should not be regarded as an effort on the part of the Court to respond to criticisms respecting the clarity of those warnings. Rather, the importance of the decision resulted from its recognition that the *Miranda* requirements might operate outside the ordinary setting of station house interrogation. This point was underscored by the Court's decision the following year in *Orozco v. Texas*.[77] Here the *Miranda* requirements were held to apply to statements made by a suspect in his own bedroom immediately after he was taken into custody by the police.[78]

On the other hand, as previously noted, the Court limited the scope of the new interrogation rules by refusing to apply them retroactively. Writing for a majority of seven in *Johnson v. New Jersey*,[79] a case argued along with *Miranda* but decided one week after announcement of that decision, Chief Justice Warren made it clear that "the choice between retroactivity and nonretroactiv-

[76] *Ibid.*, at 4.

[77] 394 U. S. 324 (1969).

[78] Mr. Justice Harlan, who strongly dissented from the *Miranda* and *Mathis* rulings, concurred in *Orozco* "purely out of respect for *stare decisis* . . . ." He added, however, that "the constitutional condemnation of this perfectly understandable, sensible, proper, and indeed commendable piece of police work highlights the unsoundness of *Miranda*." *Ibid.*, at 328.

[79] 384 U. S. 719 (1966). The Warren Court has been sharply criticized for what some commentators regard as obvious inconsistencies in applying or refusing to apply various criminal procedure requirements retroactively. See, for example, Alexander M. Bickel, *The Supreme Court and the Idea of Progress* (New York: Harper, 1970), 54–58.

ity" did not turn on "the value of the constitutional guarantee involved."[80] Attempting to differentiate between this ruling and others in which the Court had given retroactive application to procedural guarantees, he pointed to the well developed safeguards long recognized under the voluntariness test. Among the many components of that flexible standard were the weighing of any failure to advise a suspect of his right to remain silent and refusal "to allow him access to outside assistance." While adhering to the view that coerced confessions are inadmissible irrespective of their trustworthiness, the Court seemed reluctant to disturb convictions based on reliable evidence, provided they met previously existing constitutional standards. Warren made specific reference to this element of reliability by asserting that "retroactive application of *Escobedo* and *Miranda* would seriously disrupt the administration of our criminal laws."[81] He used the same rationale three years later in holding that the *Miranda* requirements did not apply "to any retrial of a defendant whose first trial commenced prior to June 13, 1966."[82] These expressions of sensitivity toward the practical problems of criminal prosecution clash sharply with the image of a sentimental, misguided group of activist judges blithely releasing criminals to prey on the innocent and defenseless public—a collective portrait of the Court so often provided by its most ardent critics during the late 1960s.

As if to underscore the continuing utility of the test of voluntariness, the Court, on the very day of the *Johnson* decision, reversed the rape-murder conviction of a Negro defendant in a North Carolina court.[83] A majority of six, speaking again through Chief Justice Warren, found that the defendant "went through a prolonged period in which substantial coercive influences were brought to bear upon him to extort the confessions that marked the culmination of police efforts." In traditional pre-*Miranda* fashion, the Court took account of a variety of circumstances, in-

---

[80] 384 U. S., at 728.
[81] *Ibid.*, at 731.
[82] *Jenkins v. Delaware*, 395 U. S. 213 (1969).
[83] *Davis v. North Carolina*, 384 U. S. 737 (1966).

cluding intermittent private questioning of the accused during a sixteen-day period, concluding that his confessions "were the involuntary end product of coercive influences" and were thus inadmissible.[84] In a similar case decided almost one year later, the Court reversed the murder conviction of Marvin Clewis, a Negro defendant with a fifth-grade education, placing importance on the circumstances of his nine-day interrogation and on the failure of police officers to advise him of his right to remain silent and to have the assistance of counsel.[85] Once more attention focused on the combination of factors surrounding the challenged confession. Violations of Fifth and Sixth Amendment guarantees were considered only as elements of coercion, not as independent grounds for reversal.[86]

On the other hand, a sharply divided Court held in *Boulden* v. *Holman*[87] that a Negro defendant's second confession had been properly admitted into evidence under the voluntariness test at his Alabama murder trial. Vacating a lower court judgment and remanding the case on other grounds,[88] Justice Stewart concluded without elaboration that "although the issue" was "a relatively close one" a finding of voluntariness was justified. In a cogent dissenting opinion, Justice Harlan, joined by Warren and Thurgood Marshall, criticized what he saw as an unjustified refusal on the part of the lower courts and the Supreme Court majority to give due attention to Boulden's argument that his confession was the product of coercion. It appeared from the trial transcript that Boulden admitted his guilt at the arrest scene after a "pretty good-sized crowd" had gathered, and that he made his first confession later that night shortly after his removal "to a jail in another county as a precautionary measure." Harlan insisted that attention should have been given to the question of coercion on the afternoon of Boulden's arrest and the possible effect that "the events of

[84] *Ibid.*, at 752. Black concurred in the result but did not join the opinion of the Court. Clark, joined by Harlan, dissented, finding ample support for the conclusion that under the traditional test this confession was voluntary.
[85] *Clewis* v. *Texas*, 386 U. S. 707 (1967).
[86] See also *Darwin* v. *Connecticut*, 391 U. S. 346 (1968).
[87] 394 U. S. 478 (1969).
[88] *Ibid.*, at 481.

that afternoon had on the voluntariness of the [second] confession" obtained some five days later and introduced at his trial.[89] The majority's failure to emphasize this aspect of the case is particularly difficult to understand in view of Harlan's uncontroverted description of the petitioner as "a slight, sickly youth, with an I.Q. of eighty-three."[90] This part of the decision stands in sharp contrast with a host of state confession rulings decided under the due process requirement[91] and reemphasizes the extreme uncertainty and elusiveness of the voluntariness test.

Although these rulings followed logically from the refusal to apply *Escobedo* and *Miranda* retroactively, it is interesting that the Court chose, through grants of the discretionary writ of certiorari, to restate in some detail the familiar due process requirements of voluntariness. More intriguing and perhaps more important from the standpoint of constitutional development was the apparent unwillingness to depart from the traditional approach even in cases tried after *Escobedo* but prior to *Miranda*. For example, in *Beecher* v. *Alabama*[92] the Court divided five-four, not on the question of reversal, but on the proper standard to be applied in reaching that result. Two challenged confessions to the murder of a white woman were obtained by Alabama investigators on June 22, 1964,[93] five days after an oral confession had been extracted at gunpoint as Johnny Daniel Beecher, an escaped Negro prisoner, lay bleeding from a serious bullet wound in the leg. According to the undisputed record, his written confessions were obtained during a ninety-minute "conversation" in the hospital, while he was under the influence of a morphine injection for pain. From its "realistic appraisal of the circumstances of *this* case" the majority, in a *per curiam* opinion, concluded that the "confessions were the product of gross coercion" and held that under the due process requirement "no conviction tainted by a confession so obtained

---

[89] *Ibid.*, at 488.
[90] *Ibid.*, at 486.
[91] Cf. *Chambers* v. *Florida*, 309 U.S. 227 (1940); *Harris* v. *South Carolina*, 338 U.S. 68 (1949); *Fikes* v. *Alabama*, 352 U.S. 191 (1957); *Payne* v. *Arkansas*, 356 U.S. 560 (1958); *Beecher* v. *Alabama*, 389 U.S. 35 (1967).
[92] 389 U.S. 35 (1967).
[93] This was the day on which the Supreme Court decided the *Escobedo* case.

can stand." [94] Black, in a brief separate statement, and Brennan, joined by Warren and Douglas, also voted for reversal, but solely on the ground that the confessions had been obtained in violation of the immunity against self-incrimination. Avoiding any reference to the *Escobedo* case, they relied explicitly on *Malloy* v. *Hogan*[95] which applied this guarantee to the states through the Fourteenth Amendment.[96] In *Brooks* v. *Florida*[97] the Court, again through a *per curiam* opinion, held inadmissible on due process grounds a confession elicited from a participant in a prison riot that occurred on May 27, 1965, almost one year after the *Escobedo* decision. Bennie Brooks confessed to authorities immediately after being removed from what was described as a "windowless sweatbox" where he had been confined for fourteen days with two other prisoners. Clearly aroused by the "shocking display of barbarism" revealed in the record, the Court explicitly reaffirmed the standard of voluntariness in condemning the confession.[98] While it is true that the petitioners in these cases did not rely on the *Escobedo* rationale, the Court might have given at least passing notice to the question of its relation (or, for that matter, its irrelevance) to these decisions. Certainly the majority might have been expected, in light of *Malloy* v. *Hogan*, to explain its nonre-

---

[94] 389 U. S., at 38. Italics added. Three months after the Supreme Court's reversal of his first conviction, Beecher was reindicted and retried on the same charge of first-degree murder. This time the state introduced an oral confession made to a doctor one hour after Beecher's arrest and while he was under the influence of a heavy dose of morphine administered to alleviate the extreme pain of a gun shot wound "that had blown most of the bone out of one leg." Beecher was again convicted and sentenced to death. Reversing the Alabama Supreme Court's affirmance of this second conviction, a unanimous Court emphatically reiterated the original rationale: "The oral confession, made only an hour after the arrest and upon which the state now relies, was surely a part of the same 'stream of events' " that rendered the other confessions involuntary. *Beecher* v. *Alabama*, 33 L. Ed. 2d 317, 320 (1972).

[95] 378 U. S. 1 (1964).

[96] In *Murphy* v. *Waterfront Commission*, 378 U. S. 52 (1964), the Court extended the *Malloy* principle by barring from a federal case testimony compelled under a state grant of immunity. For additional refinement of the self-incrimination requirement under the Fourteenth Amendment, see *Griffin* v. *California*, 380 U. S. 609 (1965). See generally George W. Spicer, *The Supreme Court and Fundamental Freedoms*, 2d ed. (New York: Appleton, 1967), 37; Henry J. Abraham, *Freedom and the Court*, 67–68, 83, 132.

[97] 389 U. S. 413 (1967).

[98] *Ibid.*, at 415.

liance on the Self-incrimination Clause in holding the confessions inadmissible.[99]

Even when petitioners have relied squarely on the *Escobedo* ruling, the Court has shown marked reluctance to apply its restrictions independently, in the absence of the *Miranda* requirements. Thus it was held, without a dissenting vote, that the following remarks made by a suspect during a tape-recorded interrogation session did not require rejection of his confession as a violation of the *Escobedo* rationale: "I think I had better get a lawyer before I talk any more. I am going to get into trouble more than I am in now."[100] Conceding that the *Miranda* requirements might have compelled immediate termination of questioning after such a comment, Justice Marshall, the author of the Court's opinion, pointed out that the "statement about seeing a lawyer was neither as clear nor as unambiguous as the request Escobedo made." There the police "were unmistakably informed of their suspect's wishes; in fact Escobedo's attorney was present and repeatedly requested permission to see his client." By contrast, the questioning officer in the case under review might have interpreted the suspect's remark "not as a request that the interrogation cease but merely as a passing comment." Such a view seemed to be supported, according to Marshall, by the suspect's failure to "pursue the matter," and his continued willingness to answer questions.[101] The highly individualized character of the *Escobedo* ruling has thus limited its explicit application. Nevertheless, it was this decision that marked the sharp break with traditional due process interpretation and provided a theoretical basis for the formulation of custodial interrogation requirements, broadly applicable to police practice at all levels of government.

[99] This view is further supported by the Court's application of the Self-incrimination Clause to proceedings in which public officials were required to testify, under threat of removal from office, about allegedly illegal conduct. Ironically, the individuals protected by the Court's ruling were police officers suspected of "fixing" traffic tickets. *Garrity* v. *New Jersey*, 385 U. S. 493 (1967). For another illustration of the Court's post-*Miranda* application of the voluntariness test, see *Greenwald* v. *Wisconsin*, 390 U. S. 519 (1968).

[100] *Frazier* v. *Cupp*, 394 U. S. 731, 738 (1969).

[101] "In this context," Marshall concluded, "we cannot find the denial of the right to counsel which was found so crucial in *Escobedo*." *Ibid.*, at 739.

Despite indications that Attorney General John Mitchell would seek an early test of the constitutionality of Title II,[102] the Court during 1969–72 undertook no direct revaluation of its controversial interrogation guidelines.[103] Several of the cases noted in preceding paragraphs suggest an inclination during 1968–69 to tighten and sharpen the *Miranda* requirements, without changing their form and content. Other cases, however, reflected the Court's reluctance to disregard the old test of voluntariness in determining the admissibility of confessions introduced into evidence before announcement of the *Miranda* decision. Moreover, in the principal "stop-and-frisk" case of 1968, the Court, through Chief Justice Warren, recognized "a narrowly drawn authority to permit a reasonable search for weapons for the protection of the police officer where he has reason to believe that he is dealing with an armed and dangerous individual, regardless of whether he has probable cause to arrest the individual for a crime."[104] While indicating some hesitancy to enlarge restrictions on police procedures, it is important for purposes of comparison with decisions on interrogation and confessions that the stop-and-frisk cases were decided under the Fourth Amendment and have no direct bearing on the scope of the Fifth Amendment immunity against self-incrimination or the Sixth Amendment right to counsel. At the same time it has long been recognized that the "probable cause" requirement of the Fourth Amendment has at least an indirect bearing on questions of confession admissibility. This connection was explicitly noted in one of the early decisions of the Burger Court. Vacating a judgment of the New York Court of Appeals, the Supreme Court, on December 8, 1969, held that although the petitioner's confessions met the voluntariness test, further proceedings should be conducted on the issue of whether the confessions were the inadmissible fruits of illegal detention.[105] The

---

[102] For discussion, see *infra*, 164.

[103] But cf. *Harris* v. *New York*, 401 U. S. 222 (1971), discussed *infra*, 159–63.

[104] *Terry* v. *Ohio*, 392 U. S. 127 (1968). The Burger Court further relaxed constitutional restrictions on the "stop and frisk" procedure in *Adams* v. *Williams*, 32 L. Ed. 2d 612 (1972).

[105] *Morales* v. *New York*, 396 U. S. 102. For an incisive analysis of several related problems of judicial interpretation in this area, see Joseph G. Cook, "Probable

Court did not, however, elaborate on the far-reaching implications of the Fourth Amendment for standards of confession admissibility in this context.

Miranda v. *Arizona*, along with such decisions as *Mallory, Mapp, Wade,* and *Chimel,*[106] clearly represented the Warren Court's inclination to initiate major reform of law enforcement policy. In the wake of sharp congressional reaction and the intense political controversy surrounding the Court during 1968 and 1969, some alteration of judicial goals was hardly surprising. Principal elements contributing to this embroilment included President Johnson's abortive effort to elevate Justice Fortas to the chief justiceship as Earl Warren's successor; Fortas' subsequent resignation amid allegations of financial improprieties; and, more generally, attacks leveled at the Court during the 1968 presidential campaign. The first clear indications of a change in judicial mood came in the area of guilty pleas and appeared to have important implications for interrogation standards. In a series of complex decisions beginning late in the Warren era, the justices grappled with questions of the extent to which constitutional considerations may affect the use of a defendant's plea of guilty.[107] Since a preponderance of criminal convictions rests on such pleas,[108] the practical importance of procedural safeguards is read-

---

Cause to Arrest," *Vanderbilt Law Review* 24 (Mar. 1971), 317–39; Cook, "Subjective Attitudes of Arrestee and Arrestor as Affecting Occurrence of Arrest," *Kansas Law Review* 19 (Winter 1971), 173–83.

[106] *Mallory* v. *United States,* 354 U. S. 449 (1957); *Mapp* v. *Ohio,* 367 U. S. 643 (1961); *United States* v. *Wade,* 388 U. S. 218 (1967); and the companion case of *Gilbert* v. *California,* 388 U. S. 263 (1967); *Chimel* v. *California,* 395 U. S. 752 (1969).

[107] The following analysis of Court performance regarding guilty pleas was previously published in slightly modified form in my article: "The Burger Court: New Dimensions in Criminal Justice," *Georgetown Law Journal* 60 (Nov. 1971), 249–78.

[108] It has been estimated that "up to nine out of ten convictions on serious charges are based on the defendant's admission of his guilt by a plea in court." Arthur Rosett, "The Negotiated Guilty Plea," *Annals of the Academy of Political and Social Science* 374 (Nov. 1967), 70–82, at 71. See also *The Challenge of Crime in a Free Society.* A Report by the President's Commission on Law Enforcement and Administration of Justice, 1967, pp. 134–37; and Donald J. Newman, *Conviction: The Determination of Guilt or Innocence Without Trial* (Boston-Little, 1966), 3, 8. Blumberg's data, drawn from a large metropolitan area, indi-

ily seen. Yet the Court was late in entering the field, and its decisions thus far have reflected the uncertainty and confusion so often produced by conflicting social values, in the absence of clear-cut constitutional provisions.

The Court approached this complex area with its 1968 decision in *United States* v. *Jackson*,[109] striking down the death penalty provision of the Federal Kidnapping Act[110] because it imposed an unnecessary burden on the exercise of constitutional rights to plead not guilty and to demand a jury trial. This part of the famous "Lindbergh Law" was presumably designed to narrow the possibility of the death penalty by authorizing only the trial jury to impose it. Since a plea of guilty resulted in waiver of jury trial, it automatically insulated a defendant from the possibility of execution. Without criticizing the implicit objectives of Congress in establishing this procedure, Mr. Justice Stewart concluded for a Court majority that these ends could not "be pursued by means that needlessly chill the exercise of basic constitutional rights." He found the procedure objectionable not because it necessarily coerced guilty pleas but because it "needlessly *encourages* them."[111] Pointing out that a defendant has no constitutional right either to waive a jury trial or to have his guilty plea accepted by the trial court, Stewart nevertheless maintained that the *Jackson* ruling was not aimed at undermining the use of guilty pleas. Apparently, it sought to remove improper influences from the defendant's choice of whether to exercise or waive procedures to which he is entitled. Whatever its intent or objective, this ruling was set forth in ambiguous terms. The exercise of constitutional rights had been unnecessarily penalized; guilty pleas had been needlessly encouraged. Yet the Court acknowledged that the criminal justice

---

cate that defendants plead guilty in over 90 percent of felony cases decided from 1950 through 1964, with a high point of 95.19 percent in 1960. Blumberg, *Criminal Justice*, at 29. A broader survey, based on a nationwide sample of state criminal jurisdictions, placed the median percentage for felony cases at 69. Lee Silverstein, *Defense of the Poor in Criminal Cases in State Courts* (Chicago: American Bar Foundation, 1965), 90.

[109] 390 U. S. 720.

[110] 18 u.s.c. Sec. 1201 (a) (1964).

[111] 390 U. S., at 583.

system depends heavily on the use of such pleas, and conceded that it would be out of the question to require every defendant "to submit to a full-dress jury trial as a matter of course."[112] Just where the line should be drawn between needless and permissible encouragement of guilty pleas, and exactly what constitutional standard should govern, remained unclear.

The Burger Court gave its first indication of a changing attitude toward guilty pleas in three decisions announced on May 4, 1970.[113] With Justice White, a dissenter from the *Jackson* ruling, serving as spokesman for the Court, a majority of five refused in each case to disturb convictions based on negotiated guilty pleas. As one commentator saw it: "The Court went out of its way and off the record to validate a number of aspects of present-day plea bargaining, approving the practice of granting lighter sentences or reducing charges in exchange for pleas of guilty, and putting its imprimatur upon the litany of the plea as it is performed in almost every court in the land."[114] Without formally overruling the *Jackson* decision, Justice White stressed a new set of priorities reflecting the practical demands of an overburdened criminal justice system, thus taking a position in sharp contrast with the Warren Court's earlier commitments to the articulation and development of constitutional safeguards applicable to individuals accused of crime.

The new priorities were apparent in *McMann* v. *Richardson*, where it was held that counseled defendants who pled guilty to preclude the state from introducing prior confessions were not entitled to federal habeas corpus hearings on allegations that their confessions had been coerced. Hearings would be justified only if the defendants could "demonstrate gross error" or "serious dere-

---

[112] *Ibid.*, at 584. In *Boykin* v. *Alabama*, the Court, through Justice Douglas, held that under the due process requirement a trial judge erred in accepting a "guilty plea without an affirmative showing that it was intelligent and voluntary." 395 U. S. 238, 242 (1969). This ruling did little, however, to clarify the meaning of constitutional standards applicable to such pleas.

[113] *Parker* v. *North Carolina*, 397 U. S. 790; *McMann* v. *Richardson*, 397 U. S. 759; *Brady* v. *United States*, 397 U. S. 742 (1970).

[114] Tigar, foreword to "The Supreme Court: 1969 Term," *Harvard Law Review* 84 (Nov. 1970), at 4.

lictions on the part of counsel," thereby indicating that the pleas were not made intelligently.[115] A lawyer could not be presumed incapable simply because he "may have misjudged" the admissibility of a confession.[116] Moreover, the Court in *Parker* v. *North Carolina* held that the guilty plea of a fifteen-year-old Negro defendant charged with burglary and rape was not rendered involuntary by a confession made one month earlier, even if that confession had been coerced by the police. Once again the issue turned upon the competence of counsel, and the Court reiterated its view that a mistake in assessing the admissibility of a confession did not necessarily mean that the guilty plea was made unintelligently. The advice that Parker received was, in White's words, "well within the range of competence required of attorneys representing defendants in criminal cases."[117]

In *Brady* v. *United States*, the Court observed that the *Jackson* ruling had not, after all, "fashioned a new standard for judging the validity of guilty pleas."[118] All relevant circumstances should continue to be considered in determining the voluntariness of a guilty plea; the possibility of avoiding the death sentence would not, in and of itself, render a guilty plea invalid. White compared this aspect of the plea bargain with promises of leniency so frequently made by the police in obtaining confessions and so often condemned by the Court as violations of suspects' constitutional rights. In his view, the possibility of coercion in negotiations for a reduced sentence would be "dissipated by the presence and advice of counsel" just as the "possibly coercive atmosphere of the police station" might be "counteracted by the presence of counsel or other safeguards."[119]

The thrust of these decisions was accentuated by a ruling six months later that a defendant's plea of guilty, made with the advice of counsel and supported by substantial evidence, was not invalidated even by his accompanying protestations of inno-

[115] 397 U. S. 759, 772 (1970).
[116] *Ibid.*, at 770.
[117] 397 U. S. 790, 797–798 (1970).
[118] *Ibid.*, at 742, 747.
[119] *Ibid.*, at 754.

cence.[120] Writing this time for a majority of six,[121] Justice White declared that a defendant could "voluntarily, knowingly, and understandingly consent to the imposition of a prison sentence even if . . . unwilling or unable to admit his participation in the acts constituting the crime."[122] Taken together, these decisions might warrant Justice Brennan's assertion that the majority was deliberately attempting "to insulate all guilty pleas from subsequent attack no matter what influences induced them."[123] The Court has indeed shown marked reluctance to take a critical look beneath the surface of the plea-bargaining process. It has apparently assumed that constitutional rights are adequately protected by the advice of reasonably competent counsel; but, despite earlier affirmations of the right to effective representation,[124] the Court has failed to state anything approaching clear, systematic criteria for assessing a defense attorney's competence or his client's ability to waive constitutional rights intelligently. Whether or not the justices fully appreciate "the real-life events which daily occur in our criminal courts," it would not be surprising, in light of mounting concern with the administration of criminal justice, if they "have decided that some problems of process are simply too cumbersome to manage by means of decree, and should therefore be ignored."[125]

The hesitancy to challenge prevailing modes of plea-bargaining has an important bearing on the *Miranda* requirements and on the exclusionary rule designed to give effect to Fourth Amendment guarantees.[126] As currently interpreted by most trial judges,

[120] *North Carolina* v. *Alford*, 400 U. S. 25 (1970).
[121] Justice Blackmun, who came to the Court after the *Brady, Parker,* and *McMann* decisions, joined the majority in *North Carolina* v. *Alford.*
[122] 400 U. S., at 37.
[123] This statement appears in an opinion by Justice Brennan, endorsed by Justices Douglas and Marshall, dissenting in *Parker* v. *North Carolina* and concurring in *Brady* v. *United States*, 397 U. S., at 800.
[124] Cf. *Powell* v. *Alabama*, 287 U. S. 45 (1932); *Anders* v. *California*, 386 U. S. 738 (1967).
[125] Tigar, foreword, at 4, 7. For an indication of Chief Justice Burger's endorsement of plea-bargaining in the context of expediting the criminal process, see *Williams* v. *Florida*, 399 U. S. 78, 105–106 (1970). (Concurring opinion.)
[126] See *Weeks* v. *United States*, 232 U. S. 383 (1914); *Mapp* v. *Ohio*, 367 U. S. 643 (1961); cf. *Ker* v. *California*, 374 U. S. 23 (1963).

a guilty plea amounts to the relinquishment of such constitutional rights as immunity against self-incrimination, trial by jury, confrontation of witnesses, and a host of safeguards covered by the concept of due process of law. The interrogation requirements are limited to confessions, admissions, or other statements made to the police and later used as evidence; but if the defendant pleads guilty, such evidence is not formally introduced. Constitutional restrictions on unreasonable searches and seizures have generally the same kind of limited application. As long as the Supreme Court refuses to disrupt the plea-bargaining mechanism, the practical influence of exclusionary rules can be expected to remain slight, regardless of the lofty ideals underlying them and the prolonged controversy that they have aroused.[127] In effect, those rules come into play only in the small percentage of cases in which defendants choose to plead not guilty. Thus police and prosecutors are left largely free of vaunted constitutional restrictions in the vast majority of their investigations. This limitation on the practical importance of the exclusionary rules has, of course, always been present. The Court's refusal to become enmeshed in the plea-bargaining phenomenon, with its confused and contradictory implications for a wide range of constitutional rights and liberties, has simply made the problem more conspicuous. A negotiated guilty plea, unlike a coerced confession later challenged at trial, could have the effect of shielding a defendant from the imposition of "cruel punishment" and other excesses of an unfair trial that might go unchallenged in subsequent proceedings. The point is that, despite its procedural shortcomings, plea-bargaining is not always inconsistent with the protection of constitutional rights. The most serious objection to Supreme Court decisions

---

[127] Recent empirical studies suggest that Supreme Court efforts to deter police misconduct via the exclusion of evidence have had little impact on law enforcement practices. See, for example, Neal A. Milner, *The Court and Local Law Enforcement: The Impact of Miranda* (Beverly Hills: Sage Publications, 1971); Wasby, *The Impact of the United States Supreme Court*, Ch. 5; Medalie, Zeitz, and Alexander, "Custodial Police Interrogation in Our Nation's Capital," 1347–1422; Dallin H. Oaks, "Studying the Exclusionary Rule in Search and Seizure," *University of Chicago Law Review* 37 (Summer 1970), 665–757; Note, "Effect of *Mapp v. Ohio* on Police Search and Seizure Practices in Narcotics Cases," *Columbia Journal of Law and Social Problems* 4 (Mar. 1968), 87–104.

in this area is not that they recognized the legitimacy of plea-bargaining per se, but that they avoided critical examination of specifically alleged abuses of that practice. This posture of aloof-ness contrasts not only with the broad policy objectives of *Mapp* and *Miranda* but also with the Court's older due process approach in safeguarding the rights of the accused.[128]

Growing limitations on the scope of the exclusionary rules—implicit in the 1970 plea-bargaining decisions—became even more apparent in early 1971. Without touching the core of police inter-rogation requirements or reexamining their constitutional ration-ale, a majority of five in *Harris* v. *New York*[129] placed what may be regarded as a significant limitation on the breadth of the *Miranda* ruling. The contrasting approaches taken by majority opinion authors Warren in *Miranda* and Burger in *Harris* underscore the Court's changing priorities in the criminal justice field as well as differences between the chief justices as legal theorists. The *Harris* majority included Justice Harry A. Blackmun and three members of the dissenting bloc in *Miranda*—Justices Harlan, Stewart, and White. At issue was the question of whether, under *Miranda*, statements concededly inadmissible in the prosecution's case-in-chief might still be introduced to impeach the credibility of a de-fendant whose testimony at trial was inconsistent with such statements. Viven Harris had been taken into custody and ques-tioned about his alleged sale of heroin to an undercover agent. In violation of one of the *Miranda* requirements, however, he had not been warned of his right to the presence of appointed counsel during interrogation. Acknowledging that the statements subse-quently obtained by the police were inadmissible as direct ev-idence of guilt, the prosecution nevertheless introduced them to impeach testimony in which Harris explicitly denied having made the sales in question.

Warren's majority opinion in *Miranda* states that "the privilege against self-incrimination protects the individual from being com-

---

[128] Cf. *Moore* v. *Dempsey*, 261 U.S. 86 (1923); *Chambers* v. *Florida*, 309 U.S. 227 (1940); *Rochin* v. *California*, 342 U.S. 165 (1952); *Culombe* v. *Connecticut*, 367 U.S. 528 (1961).

[129] 401 U.S. 222.

pelled to incriminate himself in any manner." In holding that the requirements applied to exculpatory statements, he pointed out that prosecutors "often used" the former to impeach a defendant's testimony at trial or "to demonstrate untruths in the statement given under interrogation and thus to prove guilt by implication." Chief Justice Warren regarded such statements as "incrimination in any meaningful sense of the word" and thus inadmissible without the "full warnings and effective waiver required for any other statement."[130]

While acknowledging that *Miranda* contains language that could be read to bar the "use of an uncounselled statement for any purpose," Chief Justice Burger maintained that "discussion of that issue was not at all necessary to the Court's holding and could not be regarded as controlling." According to this narrow interpretation: "*Miranda* barred the prosecution from making its case with statements of an accused while in custody prior to having or effectively waiving counsel. It does not follow from *Miranda* that evidence inadmissible against an accused in the prosecution's case in chief is barred for all purposes, provided of course that the trustworthiness of the evidence satisfies legal standards."[131] He went on to limit *Miranda* to statements of the accused that the state might introduce for the purpose of establishing guilt. On the other hand, he did not question the presumption that, if Harris' statements to the police had been coerced or involuntary, they would have been inadmissible for impeachment purposes.

Burger based this ruling on the 1954 decision of *Walder* v. *United States*,[132] in which the court, speaking through Justice Frankfurter, had recognized a limited exception in applying the Fourth Amendment Exclusionary Rule. On direct examination at his trial, Sam Walder denied ever having sold or possessed narcotics. It was held that this assertion in effect permitted the government, in attacking his credibility, to introduce evidence seized illegally in connection with an earlier proceeding. Although

[130] 384 U. S. 436, 476–77 (1966).
[131] 401 U. S., at 224.
[132] 347 U. S. 62.

Harris' testimony dealt directly with the charge against him, while that of Walder concerned collateral matters, Chief Justice Burger drew no distinction in determining the admissibility of evidence for impeachment purposes. He spoke in terms of the utility of the impeachment process—its value to the jury in assessing the defendant's credibility—insisting that "the benefits of this process should not be lost because of the speculative possibility that impermissible police conduct will be encouraged thereby." Confining the question solely to the context of the trial, he thus concluded that "the shield provided by *Miranda* cannot be perverted into a license to use perjury by way of a defense, free from the risk of confrontation with prior inconsistent utterances."[133]

In a strongly worded dissenting opinion, Justice Brennan, joined by Justices Douglas and Marshall,[134] contended that the ruling seriously inhibited the exercise of the privilege against self-incrimination. He thought it "monstrous that courts should aid or abet the law-breaking police officer." Reflecting the belief that *Miranda's* deterrent effect had been substantial, he concluded that the *Harris* decision went "far toward undoing much of the progress made in conforming police methods to the Constitution."[135] If the tangible impact of *Miranda* on the interrogation process is as nominal as most empirical studies indicate, Brennan's estimate might be regarded as excessive. On the other hand, if the ultimate significance of *Miranda* is seen as symbolic—as representing through constitutional interpretation, the highest ideals of the criminal justice system—the *Harris* decision might well foreshadow a full reappraisal of judicial goals in the field of police interrogation.

It is difficult to assess the importance of this case because it focused on a question of admissibility beyond the main thrust of *Miranda*. While Warren's opinion touched upon the question of admissibility in the impeachment context, it did not fully resolve the ambiguity created by the *Walder* exception, as subsequent disagreement of interpretation among state and lower federal courts

---

[133] 401 U. S., at 425–26.
[134] Justice Black dissented separately without opinion.
[135] 401 U. S., at 232.

indicated.[136] Although Burger held that the standard used to impeach a defendant's credibility should be governed by considerations of trustworthiness based on a determination of whether the statements of the accused were voluntary, it would be premature to conclude that he prefers the voluntariness test over the *Miranda* requirements in ascertaining the admissibility of such statements as direct evidence of guilt. Shortly before leaving the District of Columbia Circuit to assume his duties as chief justice, Burger filed an opinion, criticizing among other things the voluntariness approach to confession admissibility.[137] He accurately portrayed this rationale as a counterpart of the "special circumstances" approach of *Betts* v. *Brady*[138] and expressed the belief that *Miranda*'s "essentially objective mode of analysis" furnished "courts with a more workable method of evaluating the reasonableness of police conduct." [139] Of course this opinion does not indicate approval of the basic policy objectives of *Miranda* or of the appropriateness of pursuing those objectives by means of constitutional adjudication. The Chief Justice is on record as opposing the Exclusionary Rule of the Fourth Amendment,[140] and the possible analogy with its Fifth Amendment counterpart, as contained in *Miranda*, should not be disregarded. His dissatisfaction with the Court's approach in expanding certain procedural rights of the accused could have an important bearing on the Court's policy regarding police interrogation.[141] At the very least *Harris* v. *New York* resolved one tangential issue of *Miranda*'s coverage in favor of the prosecution. This result might presage a process of attrition by which the substance of the interrogation rules could be undermined without openly overturning such a recent landmark precedent.[142] But even

136 For a partial list of cases illustrating this disagreement, see Justice Brennan's dissenting opinion, *ibid.*, at 231 n. 4.

137 *Frazier* v. *United States*, 419 F 2d 1161, 1171 (1969).

138 316 U. S. 455 (1942).

139 419 F 2d, at 1174–75.

140 See, for example, *Bivens* v. *Six Unknown Named Agents*, 403 U. S. 388 (1971).

141 The same, of course, may be said with regard to Justice Blackmun, who appears to share the views of the Chief Justice in this field.

142 For a trenchant criticism of Burger's opinion in *Harris*, see Alan M. Dershowitz and John Hart Ely, Comment, "*Harris* v. *New York*: Some Anxious Ob-

this result—which *Harris* by no means dictates—would not necessarily mean a return to the pre-*Escobedo–Miranda* approach. Burger's reliance on Frankfurter's opinion in the *Walder* case should be viewed in the context of his sharp criticism of Frankfurter's due process rationale,[143] and any speculation about a renaissance of Frankfurter's version of judicial self-restraint in the criminal justice field should not overlook Burger's essentially pragmatic criticism.

Harris v. *New York*, together with the plea-bargaining decisions and other manifestations of change in the Court's criminal justice priorities,[144] tend to overshadow the practical significance of the constitutional status of anti-*Miranda* legislation. From a theoretical and symbolic standpoint, however, the question remains fundamentally important. The traditional view shared by most authorities has been that, short of the formal amending process, the Supreme Court's interpretation of a constitutional provision is final and thus binding upon coordinate branches of government. At the same time it is important to recognize that these branches too have considerable latitude in interpreting the Constitution and that the Court in recent years has broadened this authority, as exercised by Congress, for example, in implementing civil rights guarantees of the Fourteenth Amendment.[145] Yet Congress explicitly rejected the Court's interpretation of Fifth Amendment

---

servations on the Candor and Logic of the Emerging Nixon Majority," *Yale Law Journal* 80 (May 1971), 1198–1227.

[143] See, for example, *Quicksall* v. *Michigan*, 339 U. S. 660 (1950).

[144] See, for example, the recent five-four decision in *Milton* v. *Wainwright*, 33 L. Ed. 2d 1 (1972). Here the majority, through Chief Justice Burger, concluded that Milton was not entitled to a writ of habeas corpus, even assuming for the sake of argument that a challenged post-indictment confession of murder made to a cell mate, who turned out to be a police officer in disguise, should have been excluded from evidence. Burger reasoned that the existence of three other confessions and extensive corroborative evidence of guilt rendered the admission of the jail cell confession "harmless beyond a reasonable doubt." In a blistering dissent, Stewart, joined by Douglas, Brennan, and Marshall, contended that, since the post-indictment confession was made some two weeks after Milton retained an attorney, its admission into evidence flagrantly violated the right to assistance of counsel as guaranteed by *Powell* v. *Alabama*. Stewart asserted that "under the guise of finding 'harmless error,' " the majority was turning its back on this "landmark constitutional precedent" of forty years' standing. *Ibid.*, at 7.

[145] See *Katzenbach* v. *Morgan*, 384 U. S. 641 (1966).

requirements applicable to custodial police interrogation. In so doing, it sought to reinstate a constitutional standard that a Court majority had deliberately abandoned. In the very act of signing the broad crime control bill, of which this anti-*Miranda* measure was but a small part, President Johnson expressed misgivings on the matter of constitutionality, views that were apparently shared by his attorney general, Ramsey Clark.[146] On the other hand, Clark's successor, Attorney General John Mitchell, relied heavily on the controversial legislation in seeking a new Supreme Court test of the *Miranda* rules. With his authorization a memorandum dated June 11, 1969, was circulated among Justice Department attorneys, advising them to introduce confessions into evidence even if unaccompanied by all of the *Miranda* warnings. Mitchell explained that, although federal officers were instructed to continue giving the warnings, their inadvertent failure to do so would not, in his judgment, render an otherwise voluntary confession inadmissible. This memorandum, reflecting the conclusion that *Miranda* was no longer fully binding, was consistent with President Nixon's frequent criticism of Warren Court decisions on interrogation and related aspects of police procedure.[147]

Irrespective of the formal status of the *Miranda* requirements in federal jurisdictions, their effectiveness at all levels of law enforcement may be seriously doubted from a strictly practical standpoint. Empirical studies examined in the following chapter provide substantial, albeit inconclusive, support for this generalization. Moreover, the Supreme Court has already demonstrated its willingness to stress the values of administrative regularity at the expense of procedural rights without disavowing the individualistic constitutional ideals underlying interrogation decisions of the 1960s.

[146] See *New York Times*, June 20, 1968, p. 223, cols. 2–7.
[147] *New York Times*, Aug. 1, 1969, p. 38, col. 1.

7

Miranda, the Police, and the Interrogation *Process*

IN THE AFTERMATH OF *Miranda* v. *Arizona*,[1] an array of Supreme Court critics, in and out of Congress, insisted on linking the new interrogation requirements with what they described as an unparalleled national crisis in crime control and law enforcement. Perhaps unwittingly they attributed at least as much immediate influence to this decision as would the most optimistic proponent of judicial policy-making in this area—though for diametrically opposite reasons. It is, of course, possible that the extravagant estimates of *Miranda*'s negative impact amounted to nothing more than self-serving rhetoric aimed at a visible and vulnerable target, all the more attractive because of its inability to retaliate in kind. Whatever the motivation, the "activist" Warren Court was charged in campaign speeches, legislative debates, and newspaper editorials, with "coddling criminals," "handcuffing police," and otherwise undermining "law and order" at the very time when police faced their most perilous and overwhelming challenge.[2]

Responding to such charges, Senator Joseph Tydings (D., Md.), a leading opponent of the anti-*Miranda* legislation enacted

[1] 384 U. S. 436 (1966).

[2] On May 1, 1968, for example, Senator John L. McClellan, urging his colleagues to support Title II of the Omnibus Crime Bill, alleged that *Miranda* and related decisions had brought "confusion and disarray . . . into law enforcement" with results that were "deplorable and demoralizing." These rules had "weakened intolerably the force and effect of our criminal laws," had "set free many dangerous criminals," and were "daily preventing the conviction of others," including "known, admitted, and confessed murderers, robbers and rapists . . . ." 114 *Cong. Rec.* 11201 (90 Cong., 2 sess.).

in 1968,[3] called attention to three empirical studies designed to assess various dimensions of *Miranda*'s impact on police attitudes and practices in New Haven, Connecticut, Pittsburgh, Pennsylvania, and Washington, D. C. While differing in approach and emphasis, these studies shared the central conclusion that little, if any, change in traditional interrogation patterns could be attributed to *Miranda*.[4] Senator John L. McClellan (D., Ark.), obviously unimpressed by such findings, claimed that "three out of four" judges would say "in private conversation" that *Miranda*'s effect had been "devastating to law and order."[5]

The assumption that great practical consequences are automatically produced by Supreme Court decisions served the immediate interests of *Miranda*'s critics but was by no means confined to persons sharing their point of view. Many supporters of the decision, including members of the original Court majority, apparently took it for granted that the new interrogation rules would assure major changes in law enforcement practices. Thus, almost five years after announcement of the *Miranda* decision, Justice Brennan spoke of its effectiveness in "deterring" objectionable police conduct, expressing fear that the majority in *Harris* v. *New York*[6] "was undoing much of the progress made in conforming police methods to the Constitution."[7] Broad estimates of the Court's impact, whether positive or negative, should, however, be tempered by recollection that a constitutional ruling, no matter how sweeping or emphatic, represents only one segment of a highly complex process, with far-reaching social and political dimensions well beyond even the remote control of appellate

---

[3] Title II of the Omnibus Crime Control and Safe Streets Act of 1968, 82 Stat. 210, 18 U.S.C. Secs. 3501, 3502. For discussion, see Ch. 6, *supra*.

[4] "Interrogations in New Haven: The Impact of *Miranda*," *Yale Law Journal* 76 (July 1967), 1521–1648; Seeburger and Wettick, "*Miranda* in Pittsburgh," 1–26; Medalie, Zeitz, and Alexander, "Custodial Police Interrogation in Our Nation's Capital," 1347–1422.

[5] 114 *Cong. Rec.* 14036 (90 Cong., 2 sess., May 20, 1968). Senator Sam Ervin, one of the most persistent critics of *Miranda*, stated flatly but without explanation that the studies cited "to show that Miranda had no adverse impact on the enforcement of criminal law" actually proved "exactly the contrary." *Ibid.*, at 14141 (May 21, 1968).

[6] 401 U. S. 222 (1971).

[7] *Ibid.*, at 232.

judges.[8] This factor alone poses enormous difficulties for any thorough appraisal of the impact of *Miranda* on even a single police department, not to mention the hundreds of local, state, and federal law enforcement agencies throughout the country.

An equally difficult problem of analysis is that of dealing precisely with the very concept of *impact* itself, and with such related terms as *implementation* and *compliance*. Nothing is gained by defining terms through the mere substitution of others, that, on close examination, turn out to be equally vague. Yet the inaccuracy and ambiguity of language cannot remove the writer's responsibility for attempting clear, consistent use of descriptive words. Accordingly, in the following discussion the term *impact* will refer to changes in police perceptions, attitudes, and practices that can be attributed to the *Miranda* requirements. *Implementation* will denote the process by which these requirements have been put into formal operation as a part of the routine preceding interrogation. Thus *implementation*, while related to *impact*, is used as a narrower concept focusing on the establishment of necessary constitutional prerequisites to police questioning. *Compliance*, on the other hand, will include police adherence to the "spirit" as well as the "letter" of *Miranda*. Obviously, mere perfunctory recitation of the *Miranda* warnings, however elaborate or technically correct, falls far short of the broad policy objectives emphasized in Chief Justice Warren's majority opinion. Broadly speaking, he sought to remove what the Court regarded as "inherent pressures of the interrogation atmosphere." It was assumed that this goal could be attained by making certain that the suspect was fully aware of his right to remain silent and that his option to exercise that right at any time was kept open to him. Thus the Court emphasized not only the applicability of the Self-incrimination Clause to custodial interrogation, but also "the right to have counsel present at the interrogation" as an "indispensable" means of protecting this immunity. Conceding that confessions might "play an important role in some convictions,"

[8] For an analysis of this practical limitation on Supreme Court power in another impact area, see Thomas Barth, "Perceptions and Acceptance of Supreme Court Decisions at the State and Local Level," *Journal of Public Law* 17, no. 2 (1968), 308–50.

Warren perceived a tendency in police circles to overstate the "need" for this form of evidence. Presumably, the *Miranda* requirements were announced with a view toward reducing the incidence of private interrogation and thereby encouraging greater reliance on investigative techniques used to obtain extrinsic evidence.[9]

Admittedly, the terms *impact, implementation,* and *compliance* have overlapping meanings; and their exclusive application to one among several important elements comprising the aftermath of a major judicial pronouncement further distorts reality.[10] Nevertheless, such selectivity permits more systematic and detailed examination of a given phenomenon—in this instance police reaction to a Supreme Court decision as an instrument of law enforcement reform. Data summarized in the latter part of this chapter generally support the conclusions of other empirical studies in this area. Beyond confirming the impression that the *Miranda* rules have had little tangible effect on criminal investigation, findings reported here underscore the existence of a wide gulf between police perceptions of the import of the decision—its scope and underlying objectives—and their own recognition that, after all, the questioning of suspects continues to follow a familiar pattern not significantly affected by *Miranda*.

The material for this study is drawn from interviews with fifty city and county law enforcement officers holding the rank of detective or above in Knoxville, Tennessee, and Macon, Georgia.[11] Before turning to the results of this survey, however, an examination of other *Miranda* impact studies is in order. For the most

[9] 384 U. S., at 468, 469, 481. For a summary of goals underlying the *Miranda* decision, see Milner, "Comparative Analysis of Patterns of Compliance with Supreme Court Decisions," 119–34.

[10] See generally Wasby, *The Impact of the United States Supreme Court.* On the phenomenon of compliance, see Samuel Krislov, *The Supreme Court in the Political Process* (New York: Macmillan, 1965), Ch. 6. For discussion of such related terms as "output," "outcome," and "consequences," see David Easton, *A Systems Analysis of Political Life* (New York: Wiley, 1965), 351–52.

[11] The principal findings of this survey were originally published in article form. See Otis H. Stephens, Robert L. Flanders, and J. Lewis Cannon, "Law Enforcement and the Supreme Court: Police Perceptions of the *Miranda* Requirements," *Tennessee Law Review* 39 (Spring 1972), 407–31.

part these analyses also focus on limited numbers of jurisdictions (usually a single city) and do not attempt systematic evaluation of *Miranda's* nationwide impact.[12] Apart from this basic similarity, however, they reflect a variety of methodological and conceptual differences. What follows is not a comprehensive review but an effort to highlight the principal findings in order to provide a more adequate background for analysis of the Knoxville and Macon interviews.

One of the most comprehensive studies of the impact of *Miranda v. Arizona* was conducted by Yale University law students during the summer of 1966.[13] For 11 weeks, on an around-the-clock basis, researchers witnessed the interrogations of 127 suspects in 90 cases and closely observed station-house procedures followed by the New Haven police department. Supplementary data included detailed interviews with 21 New Haven detectives and 55 local attorneys. From this multidimensional perspective the authors were able to draw conclusions about the nature of the interrogation process and to assess its relative importance as a crime-solving technique. This study also analyzed the question of *Miranda's* effect on a suspect's willingness to talk to police, the decision's impact on officer morale, and the consequences of a lawyer's presence during interrogation. It appeared that warnings seldom prompted suspects either to refuse to answer questions or to request counsel; that "substantial pressure to confess" probably continued; and "that the *Miranda* warnings, as given, did not alleviate the pressure."[14] The New Haven study produced additional support for the mounting, if still inconclusive, evidence[15]

---

[12] An exception to this generalization is Cyril D. Robinson, "Police and Prosecutor Practices and Attitudes Relating to Interrogation as Revealed by Pre- and Post-*Miranda* Questionnaires: A Construct of Police Capacity to Comply," *Duke Law Journal* (June 1968), 425–524.

[13] "Interrogations in New Haven," 1521–1648.

[14] *Ibid.*, at 1523. Observers noted that the detectives did not fully implement even the formal *Miranda* warnings, especially during the weeks immediately following the decision. Doubt was also expressed about whether they understood the meaning and implications of the requirements, even after they "were told of the decision by their superiors . . . ." *Ibid.*, at 1551.

[15] Survey data gathered by Evelle J. Younger, former district attorney for Los

that police interrogation might not be as crucial to criminal investigation as many *Miranda* critics had alleged. Analysts estimated that it was "necessary" to question suspects in only 13 percent of the observed cases, and the detectives themselves placed this figure at just 21 percent.[16]

Findings also disclosed a sharp disparity between *Miranda's* effect on police morale and its discernible impact on the daily routine of law enforcement. The detectives viewed *Miranda* as a "slap at policemen everywhere" and, perhaps more significantly, "as a personal rebuke by a Court that, in their eyes, [knew] very little about local police and their problems." These feelings of resentment were "intensified by a basic distrust of courts and lawyers, who just [made] more difficult an already thankless job."[17] By contrast with such attitudes, the central conclusion of this study was that *Miranda* had produced little change. "Despite the dark predictions by the critics of the decision, the impact on law enforcement" in New Haven had been "small."[18] Two reasons were given for this result: (1) interrogations played only "a secondary role in solving the crimes of this middle-sized city . . ." and (2) "the *Miranda* rules, when followed, [seemed] to affect interrogations but slightly." While the warnings could not be dismissed as altogether useless, neither could they be relied on to eliminate the "inherently coercive atmosphere" that the police station might convey to the suspect. Mere warnings, often given reluctantly by the very officers intent on questioning suspected

---

Angeles County, indicated that confessions were "essential to . . . successful prosecution in only a small percentage of criminal cases." Evelle J. Younger, "Results of a Survey Conducted in the District Attorney's Office of Los Angeles County Regarding the Effect of the *Miranda* Decision upon the Prosecution of Felony Cases," *American Criminal Law Quarterly* 5 (Fall 1966), 32–39, at 33. In another summary of these findings he pointed out that "confessions or admissions . . . were considered necessary in only 40 percent of the cases resulting in conviction after trial." Moreover, in just 10 percent of the total number of "cases decided after trial or on pleas of guilty" were the confessions or admissions deemed necessary. "Interrogations of Criminal Defendants—Some Views on *Miranda v. Arizona*," *Fordham Law Review* 35 (Dec. 1966), 169–262, at 262. See also Nathan R. Sobel, *The New Confession Standards: Miranda v. Arizona, a Legal Perspective, a Practical Perspective* (New York: Gould Publications, 1966), 143–44.

[16] "Interrogations in New Haven," 1585, 1592.
[17] *Ibid.*, at 1611.
[18] *Ibid.*, at 1613.

criminals, hardly ensured understanding, not to mention intelligent exercise, of constitutional rights—a conclusion calling for "fresh examination of the goals which prompted *Miranda*."[19]

The ineffectiveness of warnings prior to interrogation was underscored by the results of a second and quite different Yale study.[20] In October, 1967, consistent with growing opposition to the war in Vietnam, a small number of Yale faculty members and students organized a "draft card return campaign." Twenty-one participants were subsequently questioned by FBI agents and were later interviewed by authors of the study in an effort to determine their responses to this quasi-interrogation experience. It was found that despite "their superior education, few of the suspects knew their rights in even the grossest outline." Neither the extensive publicity given *Miranda* nor the formal "grudging" adherence accorded the requirements made the suspects fully aware of what was at stake for them.[21] Although waiver forms conveyed some meaning to them, they nevertheless yielded, in most instances, to what they apparently regarded as a social obligation or moral responsibility to answer questions. Subtle pressure was present, even though agents conducted questioning in university offices or dormitory rooms, far removed from the typical station-house setting. Moreover, the sessions were not lengthy or particularly intensive. Clearly, the achievement of *Miranda*'s objectives required more than a summary statement of procedural rights—more, in short, than even an FBI agent could provide, in the absence of "a capacity for schizophrenia as a qualification for the job."[22]

Results of a major attempt to give effect to the *Miranda* ruling in Washington, D. C., also minimized changes produced by the decision and cast further doubt on assumptions underlying it. The Institute of Criminal Law and Procedure of the Georgetown University Law Center conducted a systematic study of the Precinct Representation Project, a large-scale effort to provide volunteer attorneys to suspects on a continuous basis, twenty-four hours a

[19] *Ibid.*, at 1613–14.
[20] John Griffith and Richard E. Ayres, "A Post-script to the *Miranda* Project: Interrogation of Draft Protesters," *Yale Law Journal* 77 (Dec. 1967), 300–19.
[21] *Ibid.*, at 305–308.
[22] *Ibid.*, at 310.

day, seven days a week, from June 28, 1966, to June 27, 1967.[23] Relying on records of telephoned requests, Volunteer Attorney Reports, and defendant interviews, the authors found that "an astonishingly small number" of suspects availed themselves of the free legal assistance provided by the project. Only 7 percent of those arrested for felonies or serious misdemeanors sought such assistance, and the rate of requests dropped sharply during the single year of the project's duration.[24] Half of those requesting attorneys "maintained that they had been interrogated before the attorneys arrived at the police station." In addition, many suspects claimed that they had been given either incomplete warnings of their rights prior to questioning or no warnings at all.[25] Recognizing the hazards of placing heavy reliance on such assertions and on the perceptions of attorneys who quickly became disenchanted with the Representation Project, the authors still produced strong support for their contention that the basic premises underlying *Miranda* were open to serious doubt. These premises were identified as: (1) the police would "give adequate and effective warnings of legal rights" and would "honor" their exercise; (2) a suspect would understand the significance of the warnings as applied to him and would "thereby have sufficient basis to decide in his own best interest whether or not to remain silent and whether or not to request counsel"; and (3) an attorney's presence in the police station would "protect the accused's Fifth Amendment privilege."[26] With particular reference to the last of these premises, it was recognized that, in the absence of an attorney during questioning, a suspect would be likely to make incriminating statements; but that, since interrogation was required in "only a limited number of cases," the provision of counsel for every person requesting it made the lawyer feel that he was "wasting his time."[27]

---

[23] See Medalie, Zeitz, and Alexander, "Custodial Police Interrogation in Our Nation's Capital," 1347–1422.

[24] *Ibid.*, at 1352, 1383.

[25] *Ibid.*, at 1365–1366.

[26] *Ibid.*, at 1348.

[27] *Ibid.*, at 1391.

Besides the New Haven and Washington, D. C., studies, non-comparative analyses of *Miranda's* impact were also made in Pittsburgh and Denver. The Pittsburgh study relied primarily on statistical data drawn from the files of the Detective Branch of the city's Police Bureau.[28] Figures revealed a decline of 17 percent in the proportion of cases in which confessions were obtained during the year following *Miranda* but showed no significant change in the conviction rate.[29] In spite of their more limited use, confessions were still being obtained in over one third of the cases examined. Yet confessions appeared to be essential for conviction in only about 20 percent of the cases—a figure slightly higher than the New Haven estimate but still indicative of the limited support for sweeping claims about the indispensability of this form of evidence. A small increase in the percentage of guilty pleas and a slight drop in the "clearance rate"[30] followed the *Miranda* decision, but these changes furnished nothing more than a suggestion of causal influences. Beyond formal compliance with the requirement of warnings, no important innovations in the investigative procedures followed in Pittsburgh could be attributed to *Miranda*.

The Denver findings were generally consistent with those of other studies, but a few interesting variations emerged.[31] This study centered chiefly on the perceptions and attitudes of suspects some three years after announcement of the decision.[32] By the summer of 1969, Denver police officers were regularly advising suspects of their rights before attempting to question them, a practice apparently not uniformly followed in New Haven and

---

[28] Seeburger and Wettick, "*Miranda* in Pittsburgh, 1–26.

[29] *Ibid.*, at 11–13, 19.

[30] This has been defined broadly as "the percentage of crimes known to the police which the police believe have been 'solved.'" Jerome H. Skolnick, *Justice Without Trial: Law Enforcement in Democratic Society* (New York: Wiley, 1966), at 168. According to Seeburger and Wettick, "a case is considered cleared once the police have apprehended the persons they believe to be responsible for the crime regardless of whether the persons eventually are convicted." "*Miranda* in Pittsburgh," at 20.

[31] Lawrence S. Leiken, "Police Interrogation in Colorado: The Implementation of *Miranda*," *Denver Law Journal* 47, no. 1 (1970), 1–53.

[32] Specifically, the suspects were interviewed in the Denver County Jail during July and Aug. 1969. For details see *ibid.*, at 11.

173

the District of Columbia in the immediate aftermath of *Miranda*.[33] Officers relied exclusively on the standard advisement and waiver forms ultimately adopted by most departments in attempting to satisfy Supreme Court requirements. This development suggests at least formal institutionalization of the constitutional mandate, a factor also apparent in the Knoxville and Macon surveys. Interviews with fifty suspects, each of whom had submitted to police questioning, indicated that despite a high level of formal implementation by the Denver detectives, Fifth and Sixth Amendment rights, as outlined, were by no means fully understood. Almost one-third of those interviewed could remember neither the right to remain silent nor the right to counsel. While 40 percent professed knowledge of these rights, 45 percent mistakenly believed that oral statements could not be used against them; and about 60 percent "thought that under no circumstances" could their signing of waiver forms "have any legal effect."[34] Such responses cast serious doubt on the very meaning of a judicial ideal of "knowing and intelligent waiver." In addition, the Denver study revealed that the "*Miranda* hearing," a preliminary judicial determination of the admissibility of statements obtained through interrogation, was frequently confined to *pro forma* examination of the signed waiver and nothing more. Thus it was tentatively concluded that "one of the latent functions of *Miranda*" might have been "to aid the police in overcoming their evidentiary burden with respect to proving the suspect's knowledge and waiver of his constitutional rights."[35]

Evaluation of the impact of *Miranda* in a single city is difficult enough, as even a brief look at the foregoing studies should suggest. Comparative impact analysis poses still greater problems for the researcher. Beyond virtually endless variations, large and small, overt and subtle, from one local law enforcement jurisdiction to another, he is faced with staggering problems of quantity, expense, and time. These difficulties are formidable even for teams of scholars, but they present far more serious challenges for

[33] Cf. "Interrogations in New Haven," at 1551; and Medalie, Zeitz, and Alexander, "Custodial Police Interrogation in Our Nation's Capital," at 1365–66.
[34] Leiken, at 15–16, 33.
[35] *Ibid.*, at 48.

the individual who is working alone. Accordingly, it is hardly surprising that few comparative studies have been completed and that the most highly detailed analysis of this kind was restricted to four cities within a single state. This extensive research effort by Neal A. Milner furnished material for a doctoral dissertation in political science at the University of Wisconsin, subsequently published in 1971.[36] While acknowledging the absence of fully reliable indicators of police compliance and the resulting difficulty of assessing impact, Milner nevertheless undertook a systematic analysis of police response to the policy goals underlying *Miranda.* These goals called for the establishment of procedures aimed at eliminating the "inherently coercive" atmosphere presumed to characterize private interrogation. A suspect's clear understanding of his right to remain silent and to have a lawyer with him during questioning could be accomplished through a series of warnings by the police, and could provide the desired shield against coercive interrogation sessions. Within limits, interrogation might still be used legitimately and effectively, but the Court implicitly stressed what Milner described as "the goal of developing police officers who relied on techniques other than interrogation."[37] For purposes of analysis, Milner identified the "policy output" of Warren's majority opinion as the independent variable; the "impact of policy output as the dependent variable; and designated as intervening variables the degree of police professionalization, and extent of group participation in their decision-making process.[38]

Relying on such criteria as general education, recruit and in-service training, specialization, and salary, he constructed an index of professionalization for the police departments of Madison, Racine, Kenosha, and Green Bay. Not surprisingly, some relationship was found to exist between the degree of professionalization within a department and "the level of group participation surrounding its activities . . . ." Yet even in Madison, which had the

[36] Milner, *The Court and Local Law Enforcement.* For a summary of the findings, see Milner, "Comparative Analysis of Patterns of Compliance with Supreme Court Decisions," 119–34.
[37] Milner, *The Court and Local Law Enforcement,* at 41.
[38] *Ibid.,* at 18–19.

most highly professionalized of the four departments, it appeared that "internal sources of information were paramount."[39] Milner discovered that, even though some positive relationship existed between professionalization and approval of the *Miranda* ruling, an overwhelming majority of officers in all departments disapproved the decision.[40] Level of formal education turned out to be an unreliable indicator of attitudes toward *Miranda*. Officers with some college education were more likely to approve the decision, but high school graduates were more inclined to disapprove it than those who had not completed high school. Despite this ambiguous relationship, it appeared that those who approved *Miranda* were likely to know more about the decision than those who disapproved.[41]

Milner was unwilling to attribute much importance to the differences in perception and attitude that seemed to accompany variations in degree of professionalization. Questionnaires might probe such differences, but the answers of respondents could by no means serve as objective criteria for the measurement of impact. Whatever the difference in stated outlook from one department to another, he found evidence of very little change in actual interrogation behavior, irrespective of professionalization and the capacity for innovation commonly identified with it:

> The more professionalized departments did seem more likely to make their formal procedures consistent with *Miranda*, but in their informal procedures they were much like their less professional counterparts. They were not more likely to refrain from the use of interrogation, and their interrogation techniques were not only similar in all departments but also similarly reflected practices somewhat contrary to the goals of *Miranda*.[42]

[39] *Ibid.*, at 224. Despite its reliance on internal sources, the Madison department still had relatively greater access to outside sources of information, including material provided by the Wisconsin attorney general, a prominent advocate of the *Miranda* reform. This suggested at least the possibility of kinship between professionalization and participation in the state capital. *Ibid.*, at 204.

[40] This finding was based on questionnaire responses to the following inquiry: "What is your personal opinion of the *Miranda* rule?" Only fifty-three officers, 19.6 percent of the total, expressed approval, while 213, or 78.9 percent, disapproved. Four officers, 1.5 percent, remained undecided. *Ibid.*, at 197.

[41] *Ibid.*, at 199.

[42] *Ibid.*, at 220.

The goals of the police were clearly not the "due process" goals of *Miranda*. Still, given their wide discretion in implementing the *Miranda* requirements, the officers could artificially adhere to the decision while perpetuating objectives that placed far greater importance on practical considerations such as clearance rates, rather than on the procedural rights of suspects. Consequently, from the standpoint of altering behavior patterns of the police, *Miranda* was far off target. Milner attributed this result largely to the Court's alleged failure to rely heavily on empirical knowledge of police practices, thus echoing a criticism made by Justice White in his *Miranda* dissent.[43] The Court, in Milner's view, paid little attention to the wide differences between its own goals and those of its policy implementers.

Reiss and Black, writing in 1967, saw the problem as one of sharp disparity between the fundamental organizational objectives of appellate courts and law enforcement agencies:

> The judicial system, especially its higher courts, is organized to articulate a moral order—a system of values and norms—rather than an order of behavior in public and private places. By contrast, the police are organized to articulate a behavior system—to maintain law and order .... The justices of our highest courts and the police officer on patrol represent almost opposite poles in their processing of people and information.[44]

A nationwide survey of law enforcement officers via sets of questionnaires mailed before and after the *Miranda* ruling also revealed the wide gulf between respective goals of the judiciary and the police: "It is of little use to speak to the police of the individual in a democratic society if the goals that are set for him [*sic*] are inconsistent with the preservation of such rights."[45]

As previously indicated, the *Miranda* requirements have not been confined to station-house interrogation but have been applied to various stages of custodial questioning, including field in-

---

[43] 384 U. S., at 532–37.
[44] Albert J. Reiss, Jr., and Donald J. Black, "Interrogation and the Criminal Process," *Annals of the American Academy of Political and Social Science* 374 (Nov. 1967), at 48.
[45] Robinson, "Police and Prosecutor Practices and Attitudes, 498.

terrogation immediately after arrest.[46] Thus, while *Miranda* has focused principally on those detectives responsible for conducting interrogation, it has also applied directly to patrolmen. *Miranda's* impact on the latter has received relatively little attention from most scholars, but its importance should not be overlooked. R. C. Schaefer's study of Minneapolis patrolmen, published in 1971, went far toward filling this gap in the literature. Sixteen patrolmen who joined the force in 1968 were interviewed once every two months during a one-year period. In addition, Schaefer, relying heavily on a format developed by Milner, administered a fourteen-question test designed to ascertain the officers' general knowledge of "the main tenets of *Miranda*." He found wide variations in their levels of information about the decision and concluded that these were closely linked to differences of role perception among the officers. "Law enforcers," those who viewed their role as that of "crime control," appeared "to be aware of the procedural guarantees that should be extended" to suspects covered by the decision. Conversely, "officers with the lowest level of information about the correct application of the *Miranda* ruling turned out to be relatively unconcerned with the law enforcement aspect of their profession."[47] Finally, this study cast further doubt upon any clear connection between such variables as social class, age, and education and the officers' perceptions of and probability of compliance with *Miranda*.

In general the studies discussed in the preceding paragraphs found widespread adherence to the letter but not the spirit of the *Miranda* ruling. They discovered little indication of tangible change in the standard investigatory procedures characterizing the questioning of suspects. The mere recitation of constitutional rights, under circumstances that obviously encourage the signing of a waiver form could hardly assure the "voluntary, knowing and intelligent waiver" of those rights. Viewed in this light, *Miranda* represented a modest effort toward interrogation reform—a fact

[46] *Orozco v. Texas,* 394 U. S. 324 (1969).
[47] R. C. Schaefer, "Patrolman Perspectives on *Miranda*," *Law and the Social Order* (1971), 81–101, at 98.

probably recognized by most law enforcement officers, despite their well-known penchant for blasting the decision and the tribunal that rendered it.

The setting and methodology of the Knoxville-Macon survey can be described in brief outline. The findings are based on responses to a questionnaire administered to officers in person by one or more members of a research team consisting of two graduate students, one undergraduate assistant, and the author.[48] Knoxville officers were interviewed in June and July, 1969; Macon and Bibb County officers in August and September, 1969; and Knox County officers in June, 1970.

The Knoxville and Macon areas were chosen for study primarily because of geographical convenience and personal entrée to the four local police agencies included in the survey. Although Knoxville is the larger and reports a somewhat lower crime rate, these two medium-sized southern metropolitan centers do not differ markedly in either respect or in *per capita* income and forms of government.[49] On the other hand, distinct differences are apparent in racial composition as well as in political and social traditions. The Knoxville area has a comparatively small Negro population: 12.2 percent for the city and only 1.5 percent for that part of Knox County located outside the corporate limits, according to the 1970 census. Corresponding figures for Macon and Bibb County are 37.7 percent and 23.5 percent. Macon is closely identified with the Deep South, and until the recent past strongly sup-

[48] J. Lewis Cannon and Robert L. Flanders, graduate students in the Department of Political Science, University of Tennessee, Knoxville, collaborated with me in preparing the questionnaire uniformly administered in all interviews. At least one of these three persons participated in all interviews of Knoxville city detectives. Roger G. Brown, an undergraduate assistant in the same department, conducted all Knox County interviews. Mr. Flanders conducted all interviews in Macon and Bibb County. I gratefully acknowledge the invaluable assistance thus provided in completing this survey.

[49] The 1970 census placed Knoxville's population at 174,587. The population of Knox County, including the city of Knoxville, was 276,293. Macon had a 1970 population of 122,423; and Bibb County which includes most of the city, had 143,418. For comparative data on levels of reported crime in the two metropolitan areas during the period of our suvey, see F.B.I. *Uniform Crime Reports* (Washington, D. C.: United States Government Printing Office, 1969), 80–81.

179

ported the Democratic Party.[50] Knoxville, while geographically inside the "old Confederacy," has a strong Republican tradition more readily identified with the Appalachian "border states."[51]

The original intention of interviewing all city and county officers regularly assigned custodial interrogation duties soon yielded to factors that limit most surveys—"time, money, and personnel."[52] It was possible, however, to include a large sample of the total "universe" chosen for study. It was assumed that the four law enforcement agencies surveyed were composed of a fairly homogeneous "population," thereby permitting reliance on a somewhat smaller sample than might otherwise be required for purposes of statistical analysis.[53] The Macon–Bibb County sample consisted of twenty respondents. The county's Bureau of Criminal Investigation had an eight-man professional staff, and seven of these officers were interviewed. By contrast with this nearly total coverage, we were able to obtain interviews with only thirteen of the thirty-five city detectives to whom interrogation duties were assigned. In Knoxville and Knox County we interviewed thirty officers—eight of a possible ten at the county level, and twenty-two of thirty-seven city detectives. The total sample of fifty included the chief of detectives from each of the four jurisdictions. But beyond an effort to include these key officers we did not attempt to interview detectives on the basis of rank.

We received full cooperation from administrative officials in the four departments, thus facilitating completion of the survey.[54]

[50] In the mid-1960s the Republican party began to make substantial organizational efforts in many parts of Georgia, including the Macon–Bibb County area. Barry Goldwater carried Bibb County in the 1964 presidential election, with 25,641 to Lyndon Johnson's 17,831. George Wallace and his American Independent party carried Bibb County in the 1968 election, with the Republicans running second, and the Democrats third. The three totals were 17,328, 13,490, and 10,579, respectively.

[51] See generally John H. Fenton, *Politics in the Border States* (New Orleans: Hauser Press, 1957).

[52] For discussion of this problem and some of its implications, see Charles H. Backstrom and Gerold D. Hursh, *Survey Research* (Evanston: Northwestern Univ. Press, 1963).

[53] Backstrom and Hursh define homogeniety, ". . . as the degree to which people are alike with respect to the particular characteristics of the community being studied, such as their political attitudes." *Ibid.*, at 25.

[54] In particular we gratefully acknowledge the assistance provided by: H. C.

To broaden the setting of the study, a limited number of interviews were conducted with individuals participating in other aspects of the law enforcement process. These included prosecuting attorneys, trial judges, and private attorneys who had served either as retained or appointed counsel during police interrogation. Although valuable as peripheral information, this material is excluded from data summarized in the tables below. The principal purpose of the survey was to probe the attitudes and perceptions of police interrogators in an effort to determine: (1) the extent to which the *Miranda* requirements had become absorbed into the institutionalized routine of law enforcement several years after announcement of the decision; (2) the officers' understanding of the policy objectives of *Miranda*; and (3) their views of the interrogation process in the aftermath of the ruling. Such an inquiry, of course, falls short of a systematic assessment of *Miranda's* impact on the law enforcement process. The significance of such a survey rests squarely on the assumption that stated opinions of professional interrogators adequately reflect their perceptions of policy changes initiated by the Supreme Court. Given the closed aspect pervading criminal investigation, such an assumption is, at best, difficult to test in any rigorous or systematic fashion.[55]

In developing the questionnaire administered in all interviews, we placed principal reliance on open-ended questions, as opposed to those with limited or specified alternatives. This technique al-

---

Huskisson, former chief of police, Knoxville; Joe C. Fowler, former assistant chief and currently chief of police, Knoxville; Bernard Wagner, sheriff, Knox County; Jimmy E. Bloodworth, sheriff, Bibb County; and W. H. Bargeron, chief of detectives, Macon.

[55] As previously indicated, some attempts have been made to observe the interrogation process. See, for example, "Interrogations in New Haven," 1521; and Leiken, "Police Interrogation in Colorado," 1. The presence of an observer, if known to the interrogator, obviously introduces a factor that could have incalculable effect on the questioning process itself. Moreover, given the close-knit organization of most interrogation bureaus, it is highly unlikely that arrangements could be made to observe interrogation without disclosing this fact to the interrogating officers. In our study the possibility of direct observation was considered but proved to be unfeasible. Differences in the record-keeping procedures of the four departments further minimized the already doubtful utility of attempting to measure the impact of the *Miranda* decision by reference to statistics on clearance rates, conviction rates, and the incidence of confession. For a comment on the nature and limited reliability of clearance rate data, see Skolnick, *Justice Without Trial*, at 168–69.

lowed the respondent "to answer in his own terms and in his own frame of reference."[56] Furthermore, since a major objective of the survey was to obtain detailed descriptions of the interrogation process, use of the open-ended questionnaire was deemed essential. This decision was made despite careful consideration of the obvious disadvantages inherent in such questions. The difficulty of analyzing, classifying, and evaluating numerous rambling, discursive answers was believed to be outweighed by the advantages of detailed and presumably more faithful reflection of the respondents' attitudes, perceptions, and general understanding of the *Miranda* requirements and their implications for the interrogation process.

Prior to administering the questionnaire the interviewers informed each respondent of the general nature of the study. We pointed out that our purpose was neither to defend nor attack Supreme Court decisions affecting law enforcement practices. We attempted to make it clear that our questions implied no necessary criticism of law enforcement methods. Assurances of anonymity were given the respondents; and although each questionnaire was numbered to facilitate computation of the findings, the names of officers were not recorded. We proceeded on the assumption that the officers would be more likely to give open, candid, and critical answers than if faced with the possibility of having to answer to their superiors for statements attributed to them.[57]

The format of the interview may be briefly described as follows: It began with seven questions designed to obtain demographic data, including the officer's age, general education, years of experience, and amount of professional training in police work. Questions 8, 9, and 10 elicited his impressions of community attitudes toward his department, possible changes in the crime

[56] Claire Selltiz *et al.*, *Research Methods in Social Relations*, rev. ed. (New York: Holt, 1959), 257.

[57] This assumption is of course open to question, as the following observations by James P. Levine make clear: "Assurances of confidentiality made to respondents hardly eliminate apprehension that confessions of impropriety will be disclosed, resulting in censure or sanction of various kinds. Even if anonymity is preserved in research reports, public attention brought to non-compliance could threaten those who are trying to resist change." Levine, "Methodological Concerns in Studying Supreme Court Efficacy," *Law and Society Review* 4 (1970), 583–611.

rate during recent years, and his estimate of whether recent court decisions (in general and with no specific reference to *Miranda*) had affected his work. Questions 11 through 28 focused on various aspects of the interrogation process—the officer's estimate of its importance; the content of the *Miranda* rules; changes, if any, that their introduction had brought to the traditional role and form of interrogation; any changes he might wish to see in existing procedures; his ranking of preferred interrogation methods; the physical surroundings in which interrogation typically occurred; and the usual number and duration of interrogation sessions. Questions 29 through 37 dealt with various aspects of the right to counsel during interrogation, including the officer's estimate of the frequency with which suspects requested legal assistance and the effect of a lawyer's presence on the conduct of police questioning. A final question gave the officer an opportunity to make any additional comments about interrogation or other points raised in the preceding interview. Interviews ranged in length from an hour to an hour and a half. Answers and comments were copied in the fullest possible detail and, whenever feasible, the interviews were tape recorded.

Despite the apparent openness and candor of most of the respondents, it should not be assumed that the data reported in this study necessarily accord with actual interrogation practices. Our inquiry was directed not at the interrogation process per se but at the attitudes and perceptions of law enforcement officers chiefly responsible for putting into operation a major policy pronouncement of the Supreme Court. Inevitably respondent bias and error are reflected in the data, although such distortion is probably unintended and unrecognized by the officer.[58] Other equally unavoidable limitations are inherent in the phrasing and presentation of the questions themselves. Nevertheless it seems reasonable to view these data as broadly representative of actual perceptions and assessments of the *Miranda* decision. Often such perceptions

---

[58] As Stephen L. Wasby has pointed out: "Not all events are remembered with equal accuracy; displeasing events may be retained less well than events which were pleasing at the time they occurred or which had beneficial effects for the respondent." Wasby, *Political Science: The Discipline and Its Dimensions* (New York: Scribners, 1970), 177–80.

are of questionable accuracy, especially with regard to the objectives emphasized by the Court majority. These objectives were, of course, aimed at a major transformation of the interrogation process from what the Court saw as a private and often sinister confrontation of suspects by police interrogators into a far more open proceeding readily accessible to defense counsel. It is hardly surprising that interrogating officers have, for the most part, rejected the Warren Court's negative impression of the traditional interrogation process, thus resisting acknowledgment of the premise on which *Miranda* was based.

This factor does not necessarily reflect merely a negative attitude on the part of the police toward all efforts to alter interrogation procedure. A substantial part of the misunderstanding no doubt results from the Court's own failure to communicate clearly with those responsible for carrying out its decision. While *Miranda* is far more explicit than many of the Court's search-and-seizure decisions also aimed at police standards,[59] its exact scope and implications continue to arouse dispute even among judges.[60] In considering the impact of such a decision, it is important to go beyond the commonplace fact that it is partially misunderstood by those at whom it is directed. More important is the question of *why* this misunderstanding arises. Does it result simply from hostility, or is it also attributable to the awkwardness, excessive formalism—in short, the possible inappropriateness—of a massive judicial opinion as an instrument of police reform? That question should be kept in mind when examining the following data.

Before examining responses to questions regarding *Miranda's* perceived effect on interrogation, it seems appropriate to consider the officers' views on a few broader, but not unrelated, questions. Almost all the respondents (48 of 50, or 96 percent) maintained that changes in public attitudes toward the police had occurred since the date of their employment. Twenty-eight of these officers, approximately 60 percent, indicated that the change had been

[59] See, e.g., *Chimel* v. *California,* 395 U.S. 752 (1969); *Coolidge* v. *New Hampshire,* 403 U.S. 443 (1971); *United States* v. *Harris,* 403 U.S. 573 (1971).
[60] See, e.g., the majority opinion of Chief Justice Burger and the dissenting opinion of Justice Brennan in *Harris* v. *New York,* 401 U.S. 222 (1971).

negative, and 18 (37.5 percent) thought that it had been positive. Almost three-fourths of the respondents agreed that the "crime problem" had become more serious within their jurisdictions during the preceding five years.[61] Table 1 summarizes this information and includes stated reasons for perceived changes. Tables 2 and 3 organize the same data by jurisdiction.

As Tables 2 and 3 indicate, the Macon detectives were more inclined than respondents in the other three jurisdictions to view the crime problem as increasingly serious and to attribute this change to court-related factors. The Macon detectives were also more likely to attribute negative effects to *Miranda*—to view it as an obstacle to effective police work. Although more than 70 percent of the total sample felt that the crime problem had become more serious, no more than 30 percent concurred in designating any single dominant factor as having contributed to this trend. The officers were, of course, aware of the general nature of the survey. They knew that we were interested in their views regarding controversial criminal justice decisions in general and the *Miranda* ruling in particular. Yet less than one third of them identified the rising crime rate with court decisions. While far from conclusive as a measurement of impact, this response casts further doubt on the validity of equating the reactions of typical police investigators with the highly publicized views of law enforcement spokesmen, within and outside Congress, who led Court-curbing efforts in the late 1960s.

The remaining tables summarize principal results of this survey. The presentation is selective, omitting, for the most part, responses to questions concerning the officers' familiarity with the *Miranda* warnings, their estimates of suspects' capacity to understand them, and the length and frequency of interrogation sessions. Detectives in each of the four jurisdictions were making regular use of the "*Miranda* cards" distributed to departments throughout the country in the months immediately following the decision. When asked to describe the procedure they followed before

[61] The full question, as posed to the detectives, was as follows: "Do you think the crime problem in Knoxville (or appropriate jurisdiction) is more or less serious than five years ago (or when you joined the force, if less than five years)? What do you think accounts for this? (ask with either *yes* or *no* answer.) Explain."

Table 1.
PERCEPTIONS OF CHANGE IN THE RATE OF CRIME[1]

Seriousness of Crime	Percentage	Number
More serious than 5 years ago	72	36
Less serious than 5 years ago	10	5
No change	18	9
N–50	100	50

Reasons for Change in the Rate of Crime		
Court related factors	30	15
Population growth	24	12
Limited police personnel and equipment	14	7
Up-grading of law enforcement	6	3
No response or do not know	26	13
N–50	100	50

[1] Tables 1, 2, and 3 are based upon responses to the following questions: Do you think the crime problem in (Knoxville, Knox County, Macon, or Bibb County) is more or less serious than 5 years ago (or when you joined the force, if less than 5 years)? What do you think accounts for this? (Only first priorities are accounted for in the tables.)

Table 2.
PERCEPTIONS OF CHANGE IN THE RATE OF CRIME BY JURISDICTION

Jurisdiction	Rate of Crime					
	More		Less		No Change	
	%	No.	%	No.	%	No.
Knoxville	68	15	9	2	23	5
Knox County	50	4	38	3	12	1
Macon	92	12	0	0	8	1
Bibb County	71	5	0	0	29	2
N–50		36		5		9

questioning suspects, the officers almost invariably produced such cards and read the brief restatement of warnings printed on them. We noted, however, that in addition to the familiar four-item ennumeration of rights,[62] the card used by Tennessee officers con-

[62] The following is a reproduction of the warnings as they appeared on the card used by the officers at the time of our survey:

186

Table 3.
Reasons for Change in the Rate of Crime by Jurisdiction

Reasons Given	Jurisdiction			
	Knoxville	Knox Co.	Macon	Bibb Co.
	Number of Respondents			
	22	8	13	7
	Percentage			
Population growth	18	12	31	43
Court related	27	25	38	29
Limited personnel and equipment	9	12	23	14
Up-grading of law enforcement	5	25	0	0
Do not know	23	13	0	14
No response	18	13	8	0
	100	100	100	100

tained the following advice: "If you decide to answer questions without a lawyer present, you will have the right to stop answering at any time. You also have the right to stop answering at any time until you talk to a lawyer." [63] Although not explicitly designated as

---

MIRANDA WARNING CARD
Side One: 1. You have the right to remain silent.
2. Anything you say can and will be used against you in a court of law.
3. You have the right to talk to a lawyer and have him present with you while you are being questioned.
4. If you cannot afford to hire a lawyer, one will be appointed to represent you before any questioning, if you wish one.

WAIVER
Side Two: After the warning and in order to secure a waiver, the following questions should be asked and an affirmative reply secured to each question:
1. Do you understand each of these rights I have explained to you?
2. Having these rights in mind, do you wish to talk to us now?

[63] This statement appears as point 5 on the card used by Knoxville officers. The first four items are exactly the same as those used by Macon and Bibb County officers. It appears that officers in Davidson County (Nashville) were using the five-point card at least as early as Dec. 1966. See *Floyd* v. *State*, 430 S. W. 2d 888, 891 (Tenn. 1968). FBI's Advice Waiver Form includes basically the same warning, although in language that differs in minor detail from that appearing on the Tennessee card. This part of the FBI form reads as follows: "If you decide to answer questions now without a lawyer present, you will still have the right to stop answer-

one of the pre-interrogation warnings, this admonition follows logically from the Court's emphatic command that, if a suspect "indicates in any manner, at any time prior to or during questioning, that he wishes to remain silent, the interrogation must cease."[64] Although two-thirds of the respondents indicated that they did not, in fact, persist in trying to question a suspect in this situation,[65] the Georgia detectives recognized no obligation to specify this point in advance. Moreover, even the Tennessee officers regarded it as far less crucial than the first four warnings. Such views underscore the limited, formalistic basis on which the *Miranda* decision has been implemented.

While only 30 percent of the respondents identified court decisions with a rising crime rate, over 90 percent maintained that court decisions had adversely affected their work, and 58 percent attributed this negative influence primarily to *Miranda*. Table 4 summarizes these findings, and Table 5 provides a breakdown of views on *Miranda*'s negative effects by age and experience of officers.

As indicated in Table 4, 20 percent of the officers ascribed negative influences chiefly to search-and-seizure decisions. This figure consists almost entirely of responses by Macon and Bibb County officers, interviewed in August and September, 1969, shortly after circulation of a memorandum on the new requirements set forth in *Chimel* v. *California*,[66] narrowing the permissible scope of a warrantless search incident to a valid arrest. Eighteen of these officers maintained that court decisions had adversely affected their work. Eleven made some general reference to search-and-seizure restrictions, and twelve explicitly referred to *Miranda*. To the Knoxville detectives, interviewed just prior to or immediately after announcement of *Chimel* and before circula-

---

ing at any time until you talk to a lawyer." It is possible that the warning procedure followed in Knoxville is based on this form. However, the discrepancy between practices in the two states suggests that, while local police might rely heavily on the FBI for explanation and interpretation of judicial requirements, no uniform system of communication can be presumed to exist in this area.

[64] *Miranda* v. *Arizona*, 384 U. S. 436, 473–74 (1966).

[65] See Table 10, *infra.*, p. 196.

[66] 395 U. S. 752 (1969).

tion of a memorandum on the decision,[67] search-and-seizure requirements appeared far less crucial. Moreover, the Knox County officers, canvassed one year later, were virtually silent on Fourth Amendment issues. If they had received information on *Chimel*, it apparently made no lasting impression.

Police interrogation serves a variety of purposes in addition to that of obtaining confessions and admissions of guilt. As if to emphasize this point, 96 percent of the officers agreed that interrogation continued to be an essential phase of their work, while 74 percent asserted that confessions were becoming less important in the successful prosecution of cases.[68] In stating their reasons for regarding interrogation as essential, the officers were conspicuously reluctant to make direct references to the obtaining of confessions. They tended to prefer such ambiguous substitutes as "the filling of information gaps" or "the implication of other suspects." Clearly, much of what they said implied the obtaining of incriminating statements, but we noted a tendency to explain the purposes of interrogation in terms that deemphasized the direct confrontation of the arrested person by officers presumably inclined to regard him as guilty.

Table 6 enumerates stated reasons for designating interrogation as an essential part of police work. Table 7 indicates, with reference to education and jurisdiction, the officers' assessments of the importance of confessions at the time of our interviews by comparison with the situation five years previously. Although about three-fourths of the respondents stated that confessions were being accorded less reliance in the investigative process, four of the six officers with less than a high school education acknowledged no change. On the other hand, each of the sixteen officers with more than a high school education said that confessions were of diminishing importance. Differences among the jurisdictions were far less striking than those reflecting the education variable.

Most of the officers expressed the belief that investigation was

[67] A majority of these interviews were conducted in mid-June 1969. The *Chimel* decision was announced on June 23, 1969.

[68] Other studies have challenged traditional police views regarding the importance of confessions as evidence of guilt. For discussion and citations, see n. 15 *supra*.

Table 4.
EFFECTS OF COURT DECISIONS ON POLICE WORK[1]

Have Court Decisions Affected Police Work?	Percentage	Number
Yes	94	47
No	2	1
Cannot say	2	1
No response	2	1
	100	50
Perceived Negative Effects		
Miranda v. *Arizona*	58	29
Search and seizure decisions	20	10
Legal technicalities	12	6
Decline of capital punishment	2	1
No response	8	4
	100	50

1 Tables 4 and 5 are based on responses to the following question: Do you think that any recent Court decisions have affected your work? Yes, no, explain. (Individuals could suggest several items. The tables employ the first given.)

hampered by giving the *Miranda* warnings, but they did not reach consensus on the question of whether any warning in particular was most likely to interfere with their work. Despite their frequent criticism of the presence of an attorney during questioning, only 42 percent of the respondents specified that advising suspects of their right to counsel (either retained or appointed) posed more problems for the investigator than other warnings.[69] Moreover, 24 percent went as far as to say that this warning was *least* likely to interfere with the investigation. It should be emphasized, however, that 46 percent of the officers were unable or unwilling to designate any of the warnings as "least likely" to hamper their investigations. Two-thirds of those with less than a high school education designated the right to counsel as the warning most likely to interfere, while only 37.5 percent of those with at least one year of college expressed this view. Differences were also apparent from one jurisdiction to another. For example, the right to remain silent was specified by 69 percent of the Macon officers

69 See Table 8, *infra.*, p. 194.

Table 5.
RESPONDENTS PERCEIVING NEGATIVE EFFECTS IN *Miranda*
(BY AGE AND EXPERIENCE)

Age	Percentage	Number
29–32	40	2 of 5
33–36	50	3 of 6
37–40	50	3 of 6
41–44	71	5 of 7
45–48	45	5 of 11
49–52	100	4 of 4
53–56	75	3 of 4
57 +	80	4 of 5
		29 of 50

Years of Experience		
1–9	57	8 of 14
10–18	47	7 of 15
19–27	77	10 of 13
28–45	67	4 of 6
N–48		29 of 48

as most likely to interfere with investigations, while this figure for Knoxville was only 18 percent.

Failure to accord overriding importance to any single *Miranda* warning, as revealed in Table 8, suggests that the officers' basic opposition to the ruling was less bitter and inflexible than their generalized criticisms seemed to indicate. This view receives further support from information reported in Table 9. Despite their disapproval of *Miranda*, a majority of those interviewed acknowledged that this and related decisions nevertheless left room for traditional forms of interrogation. Those with more than a high school education were evenly divided on this question, while officers with a high school diploma or less gave a decided edge (56 percent) to the affirmative view. The two extremes on the education scale, those with four or more years of college and those with less than a high school diploma, gave overwhelming support to this position, thus underscoring the problematic relation between police attitudes and formal schooling. A jurisdictional comparison shows that the Macon detectives stood in sharp contrast with

Table 6.
POLICE VIEWS ON THE NECESSITY OF INTERROGATION

Is Interrogation Essential to Police Work?	Percentage	Number
Yes	96	48
Cannot say	4	2
	100	50

Reasons for Regarding Interrogation as Essential		
Filling "information gaps"	50	25
Lack of physical evidence	18	9
Implication of other suspects	4	2
Protection of innocent persons	4	2
Solution of crimes	4	2
Recovery of property	2	1
Did not explain	12	6
No response	6	3
	100	50

their counterparts in Bibb County, Knox County, and Knoxville. This result emphasizes the greater intensity of anti-Court sentiment apparent among most of the Macon officers.

Just over two-thirds of all officers agreed that the presence of an attorney made interrogation of the suspect impossible. But 60 percent stated that most suspects waived their right to the assistance of counsel during questioning. On the latter point, however, figures for Macon once more conflict with those from the other three jurisdictions. Only 38 percent of the Macon sample agreed that most suspects waived their right to counsel, while the corresponding figures for Knoxville, Bibb County, and Knox County were 64 percent, 72 percent, and 75 percent, respectively.

As previously noted, the *Miranda* decision requires that, even after rights are waived and questioning begins, a suspect is entitled to change his mind and call a halt to the interrogation. A majority of the respondents (58 percent) indicated that if the suspect exercised this option, they immediately stopped their questioning. Table 10 suggests that officers under forty years of age and those with one or two years of college were more persistent than other detectives in attempting to obtain statements from suspects. The

Table 7.
RELIANCE ON CONFESSIONS[1]

	Percentage	Number
About the same	20	10
Not as much	74	37
More than 5 years ago	4	2
No opinion	2	1
	100	50

By Education	About the Same as 5 Years Ago	Not as Much as 5 Years Ago	More than 5 Years Ago	No Opinion	Number
	Percentage				Number
Less than high school	67	33	0	0	6
High school diploma	21	68	7	4	28
College 1–7 years	0	100	0	0	16
					50
By Jurisdiction					
Knoxville	18	68	9	5	22
Knox County	38	62	0	0	8
Macon	15	85	0	0	13
Bibb County	14	86	0	0	7
					50

[1] Questions: Are confessions relied on as much today as, say, 5 years ago? About the same as 5 years ago? Not as much as 5 years ago? More than 5 years ago?

widespread impression that older officers and those with more limited formal education are less inclined to comply with the full *Miranda* requirements is thus unsupported by these responses.

Beyond the findings summarized in the foregoing tables, further understanding of the officers' perceptions of *Miranda* and its impact on interrogation may be conveyed through some of their individual comments. The range and variety of police reaction is suggested by a few illustrations. Some officers said, in effect, that *Miranda* had produced an ambiguous relationship between themselves and the suspects they wished to question. One detective saw

Table 8.
EFFECT OF PREINTERROGATION WARNINGS

Does Advising of Rights Hamper Investigation?	Percentage	Number
Yes	74	37
No	20	10
Cannot say	6	3
	100	50

	Warnings Least Likely to Interfere		Warnings Most Likely to Interfere	
	%	No.	%	No.
Right to remain silent	16	8	34	17
Suspect's statement may be used against him	8	4	10	5
Right to retained or appointed counsel during interrogation	24	12	42	21
Invoking of rights after initial waiver	6	3	6	3
Cannot say	46	23	8	4
	100	50	100	50

himself as "practically in the position of apologizing" to the suspect "before [asking] him his name." According to another officer: "When you stand up there and beg him [the suspect] to take a lawyer, a lot of times he thinks you're a fool." By contrast, some maintained that, in advising a suspect of his rights, it was possible to "build a confidence that you won't take advantage of him."

Many detectives apparently did not recognize the broad objectives of the *Miranda* decision. Whether this resulted from the Court's failure to communicate its goals in clearly understood language, or whether it simply reflected disapproval of these goals remains unclear. Perhaps both factors help to shape the attitudes of most of the officers. One detective ironically observed that the interrogating officer "has become more or less a con man in order to question effectively within legal bounds." Another remarked that in order to comply with *Miranda* it was often necessary to "stop" a suspect from talking until after advising him of his rights. This comment reflected unawareness of the Court's specific rec-

Table 9.
RELATION OF COURT DECISIONS TO TRADITIONAL
FORMS OF INTERROGATION[1]

Education	Yes	No	Cannot Say	Number
		Percentage		
Less than high school	83	17	0	6
High school diploma	50	39	11	28
Some college	27	73	0	11
Bachelor's degree and above	100	0	0	5
				50

Jurisdiction				
Knoxville	59	27	14	22
Knox County	63	37	0	8
Macon	39	61	0	13
Bibb County	57	43	0	7
				50

[1] Question: Do you think that Court decisions in this area leave room for traditional forms of interrogation? Yes, no, explain.

ognition of the admissibility of statements spontaneously "volunteered" to the police in the absence of warnings and waiver.[70] Most of the detectives stressed the importance of private interrogation and insisted that, whatever might have been the practice thirty or forty years ago, suspects are no longer subjected to undue pressure in the interrogation room. Several of the officers indicated that at one time, "years back," the use of physical force in obtaining statements from suspects was not uncommon. As one detective put it, "when I was first an officer, and even when I was first promoted to this department, if you was talking to somebody and they was just a little bit slow about telling you something, you could use just a little bit of force and they'd open up and tell you." There was overwhelming agreement, however, that such practices no longer occurred. Forty-six of the fifty respondents gave a nega-

[70] "There is no requirement that police stop a person who enters a police station and states that he wishes to confess to a crime, or a person who calls the police to offer a confession or any other statement he desires to make. Volunteered statements of any kind are not barred by the Fifth Amendment and their admissibility is not affected by our holding . . . ." 384 U. S., at 478.

Table 10.

PERCENTAGE AND NUMBER OF OFFICERS ATTEMPTING TO
CONTINUE QUESTIONING AFTER SUSPECT INVOKES
RIGHT TO REMAIN SILENT[1]

Age	Percentage	Number
29–32	60	3 of 5
33–36	50	3 of 6
37–40	50	4 of 8
41–44	29	2 of 7
45–48	45	5 of 11
49–52	25	1 of 4
53–56	0	0 of 4
57 +	0	0 of 5
		18 of 50

Education		
Less than high school	0	0 of 6
High school diploma	39	11 of 28
Some college	64	7 of 64
College 4–7 years	0	0 of 5
		18 of 50

[1] Question: Suppose a suspect waives his right to have counsel present during interrogation and later, after questioning begins, changes his mind and refuses to answer. What do you do in this situation?

tive answer to the following question: "Are there any circumstances in which the police are justified in using physical force to obtain a confession?" The remaining four officers answered with qualified affirmative statements, one of which is quoted in full: "Well, I don't know whether you're justified or not, but if you have a strong suspect in a rape case or in a murder case, or something where some child has been molested or mistreated—or some old person—I may be a little blunt—I think if you have to, you ought to be able to get up out of the chair and warp him over the head two or three times if you think that'll bring it out of him— which it will." Far more representative of the sample are the following excerpts: "of course physical force is out, and threats are out . . . ." "I don't think we have any right to use any physical force just for interrogation . . . I'm strictly against that." "No . . . a confession obtained this way is unreliable." We asked the officers to rank, in order of importance, the methods that they believed they should be free to use in trying to obtain confessions. A total of 46 percent indicated that "disclosure of incriminating evidence to the suspect" was the most important. Forty-four percent gave priority to a broad category designated "psychological persuasion, trickery, and deception." Seventy-eight percent of the sample ranked this category as either first or second in importance, while 66 percent listed the disclosure of incriminating evidence as first or second in importance. Nevertheless, they were opposed to Chief Justice Warren's assertion that "the very fact of custodial interrogation exacts a heavy toll on individual liberty and trades on the weakness of individuals." Above all, the Court sought to "dispel" what it described as "the compulsion inherent in custodial surroundings . . . ."[71] Because this image of the interrogation process assailed the professional integrity and even the self-respect of many officers, it is hardly surprising that they reacted defensively in flatly denying its validity. While emphasizing the utility of interrogation, some officers acknowledged its limitations as an investigative technique. Recognizing that "it would be easier to simply interrogate," one detective pointed to the greater reliability and value of "physical evidence."

As previously indicated, most of the detectives insisted that the presence of a lawyer during questioning usually prevented completion of the interrogation process. But a few officers drew distinctions between the roles of court-appointed and privately retained counsel in this situation. In rare instances an attorney might "allow" his client "to give . . . worthwhile information," but only "to bargain." In such a situation a court-appointed lawyer "will work with you," as one detective put it, "but when a suspect has his own attorney, you get nothing." This alleged difference between the services of retained and assigned counsel simply suggests another of the many qualitative problems left unresolved by the *Miranda* decision.[72]

[71] 384 U. S., at 455, 458.
[72] For an indication of the Court's subsequent reluctance to give meaning to the

With respect to formal education, amount of training, and experience, the four detective forces were very much alike. Yet, as previously noted, the Macon officers expressed decidedly greater disapproval of *Miranda* than did the other three groups. This apparent deviation is particularly baffling when it is recalled that one of the latter, Bibb County, exercised jurisdiction in the same urban area as Macon and dealt with many identical local crime problems. The difference might have resulted in part simply from the relatively smaller proportion of Macon officers interviewed (37.1 percent of the total by comparison with 59.9 percent for Knoxville and even larger proportions for the two county jurisdictions).[73] Apart from the discrepancy on this point, most officers in each jurisdiction continued to express strong misgivings about the *Miranda* procedure long after it had become a routine part of their work. They seemed to view the decision as a "stumbling block" to investigation—not so much because of any particular effect on the questioning process per se, but because, as one officer remarked, it required them "to go through the ritual and paper work and legal technicalities." They resented the alleged inconvenience and, to an even greater extent, the perceived affront implicit in the requirement of advising suspects prior to interrogation. Most of them were further annoyed by their belief that the justices who fashioned the *Miranda* rules had little understanding or appreciation of the difficulties and hazards of police work.[74] Many responses to our questions were, in short, reminiscent of the attacks leveled at the Supreme Court by its most vocal law enforcement critics. We noted, however, that the negative responses of most detectives were less extreme, less embittered, and less direct than the public condemnations that typically greeted *Miranda*.

Officers had received information about the *Miranda* requirements almost entirely through departmental channels, either in

concept of "effective counsel," see *Parker* v. *North Carolina*, 397 U. S. 790 (1970). Cf. *Anders* v. *California*, 386 U. S. 738 (1967).

[73] Suggested qualitative differences in professionalization within the departments could also have contributed to the disparity. Our data, however, provided no basis for systematic analysis of professionalization. For an inquiry into possible relationships between professionalization and the impact of *Miranda*, see Milner, *The Court and Local Law Enforcement*, esp. 74–75, 79, 201–03, 244 ff.

[74] Cf. "Interrogations in New Haven," at 1610.

the form of written memoranda or through oral presentations at training sessions. Presumably, the departments had obtained their information initially from higher sources within the law enforcement system, but through no uniform process of dissemination. Apparently each department relied on the FBI, in greater or lesser degree, for such information. Local prosecutors took a nominal part in providing the officers with an explanation of the meaning of the interrogation requirements. Accordingly, the perceptions expressed in answer to our questions gave an impression of the restricted and largely internalized communication process within these local police agencies.[75] Obviously, the acquisition of information in this manner can be colored by the evaluations of controversial requirements on the part of highly placed law enforcement officials. Implications for the shaping of commonly held police attitudes are clear. Nevertheless, we discerned sufficient diversity in the responses of those interviewed to suggest the absence of any effective effort at indoctrination.

Like several earlier post-*Miranda* studies, this survey indicated the existence of a high level of adherence to the letter of the decision but very limited compliance with its policy objectives. It revealed little suggestion of change in routine procedures characterizing the questioning of suspects. In general, those interviewed displayed an attitude of ambivalence in attempting to assess the importance of *Miranda*. A wide gap thus existed between their generalized negative reactions to the decision and their simultaneous acknowledgment that things continued to go on pretty much as usual. Part of the difficulty no doubt arose from the sharp disparity between the fundamental organizational goals of appellate courts and law enforcement agencies.[76] Internal contradictions apparent in the views of many officers also emphasize the practical limitations of rules of evidence when used as the basis of a major effort at law enforcement reform.

Despite its sweeping language, *Miranda* comes into operation only when the prosecution seeks to introduce evidence obtained

[75] Cf. Milner, *The Court and Local Law Enforcement*, at 95–97, 179.
[76] Reiss and Black, "Interrogation and the Criminal Process," at 48.

through police interrogation and when the admissibility of that evidence is brought into question. Since most criminal cases are decided on the basis of guilty pleas, not formal trials of the accused, the practical result is to discourage the raising of *Miranda* issues. The Supreme Court, unlike a legislature or an administrative agency, is limited to the negative requirements of an exclusionary rule. In dealing with real or potential law enforcement abuses, it has been unable to formulate a set of specific procedures that must be followed in all cases. All that the justices have done— and it is admittedly no insignificant achievement—is to say, in effect, that if certain procedures are not followed, certain kinds of evidence may not subsequently be introduced. Since the police interrogate suspects for a variety of reasons in addition to that of obtaining confessions and other statements that might subsequently be used as evidence, the limited efficacy of the *Miranda* requirements is further revealed.[77]

If the impact of *Miranda* is assessed strictly from the standpoint of its tangible effect on the interrogation process, the decision may thus be regarded as an act of judicial futility. If, on the other hand, its impact is seen largely in terms of the educational purposes served by many Supreme Court rulings, *Miranda* can be accorded great importance. Regardless of his estimate of the decision, each officer whom we interviewed displayed at least rudimentary knowledge of the Fifth Amendment requirements outlined in *Miranda*. Such knowledge, irrespective of competing policy considerations, could be an indispensable prerequisite to the recognition of fundamental rights and the constitutional performance of professional duties in this area. The educational dimension of police reform should be carefully considered in current reassessments of the exclusionary rules as applied not only to police interrogation but also to the complex area of search and seizure.

[77] Similar questions have been raised in connection with the Exclusionary Rule designed to implement search-and-seizure provisions of the Fourth Amendment. See, e.g., Chief Justice Burger, dissenting in *Bivens* v. *Six Unknown Named Agents*, 403 U. S. 388, 411, 415 (1971).

8

Conclusion

SHARP INTERNAL CONFLICT has plagued Supreme Court decision-making in the confession field continually since the 1940s and shows no clear sign of abating in the 1970s. Although usually expressed in the formal terms of doctrinal debate over the meaning of constitutional provisions, this conflict involves far more than abstract discourse on the meaning of language and precedent. At issue is the more immediate question of the proper scope of one of the Court's many roles—that of policy formulator in the criminal justice field. Should this role be confined to examination of courtroom proceedings and the ideal of fairness that they purportedly represent, or should the Court assume that the work of police officers is inseparable from the judicial process and therefore equally subject to supervision? Should the Court attempt some balancing of these dimensions on a case-by-case basis, or should it lay down broad rules applicable to routine trial court and police department operation? These and related questions, of course, have bearing on many activities other than that of police interrogation and go far toward accounting for intra-Court cleavages in such matters as the issuance of search warrants, electronic surveillance, search incident to arrest, lineup identification, and the presence of counsel at a preliminary hearing.[1] Like many of their fellow citizens, the justices have clashed repeatedly in propounding their own strongly held views of what the Court, as a coordinate branch of the national government and as the nation's highest appellate tribunal, is *constitutionally required* to do, and what, as a major political institution, it is *actually capable* of doing. Inevitably, disclaimers notwithstanding, these disputes over

[1] Recent decisions indicating disagreement among the justices in each of these areas respectively include: *Coolidge* v. *New Hampshire*, 403 U. S. 443 (1971); *United States* v. *White*, 401 U. S. 745 (1971); *United States* v. *Wade*, 388 U. S. 218 (1967); *Coleman* v. *Alabama*, 399 U. S. 1 (1970).

judicial function have been inextricably bound to personal moral judgments as to what the Supreme Court ought to do—the values for which it should stand and the methods by which it should seek to promote such values.

Like other American tribunals, the Supreme Court initially limited the examination of involuntary confessions to the English common-law rule that banned such evidence simply because of its unreliability.[2] But it soon became clear that far more basic considerations were at stake—that behind the narrow question of "untrustworthy" evidence were values of human decency and fair play, reflected in the right against self-incrimination and more broadly encompassed by the concept of due process of law. Once the Supreme Court moved beyond the old common-law rationale, whether on the basis of self-incrimination or due process standards,[3] it could not avoid direct evaluation of the interrogation process in terms of basic constitutional principles and values. At the federal level it postponed this direct confrontation—after some abortive early advances[4]—by confining its review of confession admissibility to extraconstitutional standards, relying exclusively on its authority to supervise the administration of justice in federal courts.[5] In reviewing the far larger number of state convictions, however, the Supreme Court could not avoid the assessment of police behavior in the context of broad constitutional requirements covered by the Due Process Clause of the Fourteenth Amendment.

By the mid-1940s two divergent policy objectives had begun to dominate Supreme Court activity in the confession field. With various embellishments and refinements these goals have continued to divide the justices ever since. The first is grounded in the "fair trial" doctrine of the Fourteenth Amendment, arising chiefly out of extreme police brutality, both physical and psychological.

[2] See *Hopt* v. *Utah Territory*, 110 U.S. 574 (1884); *Sparf and Hansen* v. *United States*, 156 U.S. 51 (1895); *Pierce* v. *United States*, 160 U.S. 355 (1896); and *Wilson* v. *United States*, 162 U.S. 613 (1896).

[3] Cf. *Bram* v. *United States*, 168 U.S. 532 (1897) and *Chambers* v. *Florida*, 309 U.S. 227 (1940).

[4] See, for example, *Bram* v. *United States*, 168 U.S. 532 (1897) and *Ziang Sung Wan* v. *United States*, 266 U.S. 1 (1924).

[5] See *McNabb* v. *United States*, 318 U.S. 332 (1943).

Early cases dating from the 1930s typically involved review of murder or rape convictions of uninfluential, uneducated, and otherwise vulnerable defendants, usually poverty-stricken Negroes in rural southern communities.[6] While police methods disclosed by such cases received the sharp condemnation of an aroused Supreme Court, primary attention was limited to the protection of individual defendants through the maintenance of elemental procedural standards at the trial level. A modern counterpart of this early emphasis is seen in the line of cases beginning with *Jackson* v. *Denno* in 1964, in which the Court has specified the relative constitutional responsibilities of trial judge and jury in determining the voluntariness of confessions.[7] The minimal fairness objective was also the controlling factor in some, but by no means all, of the cases decided in accordance with the due process, "totality of circumstances" approach during the fifties and early sixties.[8]

The second and far more ambitious judicial goal focuses directly on those law enforcement methods that many of the justices have deemed most likely to produce involuntary confessions. Its origins are found both in Fourteenth Amendment interpretations[9] and in the *McNabb-Mallory* line of federal decisions resting on extra-constitutional grounds.[10] Through application of an exclusionary rule of evidence, the Court ultimately developed an elaborate set of interrogation requirements focusing on routine police conduct rather than on isolated examples of coercion. Most fully developed in *Miranda* v. *Arizona*,[11] this rationale is predicated on the assumption that, in the absence of effective legislative or administrative alternatives, the Court is obligated to spell out interroga-

[6] See *Brown* v. *Mississippi*, 297 U. S. 278 (1936); *Chambers* v. *Florida*, 309 U. S. 227 (1940); *Ward* v. *Texas*, 316 U. S. 547 (1942).

[7] 378 U. S. 368. Cf. *Lego* v. *Twomey*, 30 L. Ed. 2d 618 (1972).

[8] See, for example, *Payne* v. *Arkansas*, 356 U. S. 560 (1958) and *Reck* v. *Pate*, 367 U. S. 435 (1961).

[9] See Justice Black's majority opinion in *Ashcraft* v. *Tennessee*, 322 U. S. 143, 154 (1944).

[10] *McNabb* v. *United States*, 318 U. S. 332 (1943); *United States* v. *Mitchell*, 322 U. S. 65 (1944); *Upshaw* v. *United States*, 335 U. S. 410 (1948); *Mallory* v. *United States*, 354 U. S. 449 (1957). See generally Hogan and Snee, "The McNabb-Mallory Rule," 1–46.

[11] 384 U. S. 436 (1966).

tion guidelines as a means of safeguarding basic constitutional values. Although expressed in terms of immunity against self-incrimination and right to counsel, these values represent far more than the commitment to formal trial court standards traditionally identified with such provisions. They embody principles of human dignity and primacy of the individual inherent in the accusatorial theory of criminal justice and in the adversary system through which that theory is presumably implemented. The *Miranda* majority seemed to take it for granted that these values and principles could be shielded against police abuse by simply applying a few components of the adversary system to custodial interrogation.

Ironically, the police themselves were entrusted with implementing the very procedure by which the compulsion of private questioning was supposed to be reduced. By merely informing a suspect of certain constitutional rights and obtaining a voluntary waiver of their exercise, officers could formally satisfy the Court's detailed requirements and at the same time retain intact the familiar routine of private interrogation. In keeping with several earlier decisions,[12] the *Miranda* ruling played down the importance of confessions as a form of evidence and questioned the key role accorded interrogation. Undoubtedly, the majority anticipated a substantial departure from established practices in this regard, apparently assuming that once suspects were advised of their rights, they would exercise them intelligently and, in most instances, insist on the presence of a lawyer during questioning. As it turned out, of course, this faith in the power of reasoned choice was badly misplaced. Available information indicates that only a small fraction of suspects refuse to sign waiver forms or request the presence of counsel during questioning, even when a systematic effort is made to assure the ready availability of attorneys for this purpose.[13] Moreover, the Court's interrogation guidelines are, as a practical matter, inapplicable to the vast majority of criminal cases. While precise nationwide figures are nonexistent, it is clear

[12] See especially *Haynes* v. *Washington*, 373 U. S. 503 (1963) and *Escobedo* v. *Illinois*, 378 U. S. 478 (1964).

[13] See Medalie, Zeitz, and Alexander, "Custodial Police Interrogation in Our Nation's Capital," 1347–1422.

that far more prosecutions result in pleas of guilty than in full-scale criminal trials.[14] Once the trial judge accepts a guilty plea, the admissibility of a confession or other evidence that might have encouraged that plea becomes an academic question—unless it can be shown that the plea itself was made under compulsion. In view of the Court's reluctance to disturb guilty pleas, this possibility is remote.[15]

The goal of interrogation reform via Supreme Court decision thus appears to have been seriously frustrated, if not totally undermined. Even though police departments have formally implemented the *Miranda* requirements on a widespread basis, the procedure has had little discernible effect on private questioning as an integral part of the law enforcement system. As time passes and the Court shows, if anything, an inclination to limit the scope of its effort to "police the police," the decision's nominal impact becomes more ephemeral. Probably nothing short of a blanket requirement that no suspect be questioned except in the presence of his attorney could be expected to remove the elements of psychological coercion to which the Court has so long objected. And this innovation (a bold step even for the most reform-minded Court) would not assure solution of the problem.

Notwithstanding its limited effect on interrogation practices, the Court's intermittent effort to upgrade police methods in this area aroused bitter public controversy. As we have seen, sharp congressional reaction to this effort can be traced to the aftermath of the *McNabb* decision.[16] Anti-*Miranda* legislation enacted in 1968 was simply an updated version of the sporadic attempt to curb a Court that, in the words of one critic, was showing "excessive and visionary solicitude for the accused" by inventing "new rules to turn loose on society self-confessed criminals."[17] A combination of factors made the Court a vulnerable and thus highly appealing target in the presidential election year of 1968. In addi-

---

[14] See *The Challenge of Crime in a Free Society*, 134–37.

[15] For an illustration of the Court's approach in this area, see *North Carolina* v. *Alford*, 400 U. S. 25 (1970).

[16] See U. S., Congress, House, Hearings before Subcommittee Number 2 of the Committee on the Judiciary on H. R. 3690. For discussion, see Ch. 6, *supra* 6–11.

[17] 112 *Cong. Rec.* 21040 (remarks of Senator Sam Ervin, Aug. 29, 1966).

tion to its support of legislation undercutting several criminal procedure decisions, including *Miranda*,[18] the United States Senate refused to confirm President Johnson's nomination of Abe Fortas as chief justice. Regardless of the extent to which this refusal might have been influenced by hostility to the President or to Fortas' unofficial role as his close adviser, it underscored the intensity of feeling that many political leaders held in opposition to "activist-libertarian" decisions of the Warren Court.[19] None of these decisions arouse more immediate negative response than the rulings aimed at criminal justice reform in general and at police investigation in particular.[20] Against the background of urban violence and growing clamor for "law and order," the Supreme Court's attempt to close the gap between theory and practice in the enforcement of law fell easy prey to simplistic attacks that somehow equated the reversal of a conviction with lack of concern about crime.

The interrogation rules were made still more vulnerable to attack because of the judicial rationale concerning their nonretroactivity. *Miranda*'s "self-inflicted wound," as Fred P. Graham has called it, resulted from the Court's application of the requirements to *trials* beginning after the date of the decision, rather than to *interrogations* beginning after that date.[21] The result was to render confessions and other statements obtained during interrogation inadmissible even though they might have been secured in full compliance with the law as it existed when the interrogation occurred. Although the number of cases thus affected was relatively small, this decision on retroactivity needlessly exposed the Court to charges that *Miranda* led to the release of confessed criminals whose guilt was not in doubt. Since *Miranda*'s central

[18] Pub. L. No. 90–351, Title II, Sec. 3501 (June 19, 1968), 82 Stat. 210.

[19] See, for example, U. S., Congress, Senate, *Nominations of Abe Fortas and Homer Thornberry: Hearings Before the Committee on the Judiciary, United States Senate*, 90 Cong., 2d sess., July 11–23, Sept. 13–16, 1968, pp. 107–25, 130–47, 149–63, 190–91, 1308–10, 1364–68.

[20] Graham, *The Self-Inflicted Wound*, Ch. 8.

[21] The Warren Court was unable to develop a uniform standard governing the question of retroactive application of its major criminal procedure decisions. For a criticism of its performance in this area, see Bickel, *The Supreme Court and the Idea of Progress*, 54–58.

objective was the removal of undue pressure during questioning, it would have been logical to specify the date of interrogation rather than the trial date in determining nonretroactivity.

Public criticism did not bring an immediate or dramatic reversal in the Court's stance on police interrogation. It did figure prominently, however, in influencing personnel changes, beginning with the appointment of Chief Justice Burger in 1969 and continuing through the appointments of Justices Harry A. Blackmun, Lewis Powell, and William Rehnquist. Burger wrote the majority opinion in the 1971 decision of *Harris* v. *New York*,[22] representing the first clear, if limited, break with the *Miranda* approach. In early 1972 the Court seemed to be on the verge of reconsidering at least the retroactivity question as applied to *Miranda* but withdrew its own grant of certiorari from the Pennsylvania case in which this issue was raised.[23] Despite speculation that anti-*Miranda* legislation would be put to an early constitutional test, the Court showed no ready inclination to review this question. On the other hand it was clear as early as 1970 that the changing Court majority was concerned with criminal justice priorities different from those of police reform in the name of procedural fairness.[24] Efficient operation of the system came to be identified more frequently with the goal of justice for all, and the Court seemed to have reached a point at which it would not attempt additional large-scale policy innovation on behalf of individual rights in the field of law enforcement.[25]

[22] 401 U. S. 222.

[23] *Pennsylvania* v. *Ware*, 284 A. 2d 700 (1971), petition for certiorari granted 31 L. Ed. 2d 453 (1972), order granting certiorari vacated 40 L. W. 3512 (1972).

[24] See, for example, *Parker* v. *North Carolina*, 397 U. S. 790 (1970); *McMann* v. *Richardson*, 397 U. S. 759 (1970); and *Brady* v. *United States*, 397 U. S. 742 (1970).

[25] It appears that a similar change of mood has been taking place in England with respect to the Judges' Rules. As previously indicated, Chief Justice Warren, in his *Miranda* opinion, referred with approval to the English practice of "cautioning" a suspect of his right to remain silent during police interrogation. Although judges have discretion to admit evidence obtained in violation of this guideline as well as of other procedures enumerated in the English Judges' Rules, the "caution" has been an object of increasing criticism. Its formal abolition was recently recommended by the Criminal Law Revision Committee. See *The Criminal Law Revision Committee, Eleventh Report, Evidence (General)* (London: Her Majesty's Stationery Office, 1972). For indication of a similar trend of judicial thinking in Canada, where the Judges' Rules have long been recognized, see A. F. Sheppard,

While criminal justice commitments of the Warren era had given way in part to new judicial priorities by the early 1970s, it remained unclear whether a serious effort would be made to overturn major policy decisions of the 1960s. Basic changes in constitutional interpretation and in the accompanying choice among competing policy objectives can, of course, be accomplished without overruling precedent. Strong doubts about the impact of constitutional requirements on police methods underscore the difficulties of achieving positive law enforcement reform through the negative application of exclusionary rules. Perhaps the Court's frustrated effort at interrogation reform has been most effective in revealing fundamental differences between criminal investigations and criminal trials in the United States. It might have been incorrect, after all, to assume that procedures which seemed to work well at the trial stage could be readily applied to custodial interrogation. On the other hand, Supreme Court decisions have frequently served to direct national attention to serious problems of government and politics that might otherwise go unattended. If its controversial attempt to upgrade interrogation practices has increased public and professional awareness of a weak point in the system, the Court's effort will not have been altogether pointless. Current emphasis on the greater professionalization of law enforcement may, in fact, owe much to Supreme Court involvement in the confession field. Whatever policy alternatives they choose in the future, the justices can be expected to continue grappling with many unresolved questions of confession admissibility. It seems likely, however, that the Court will defer to other agencies of government in the formulation of additional guidelines for police interrogation.

"Restricting the Discretion to Exclude Admissible Evidence; an Examination of *Regina* v. *Wray*," *Criminal Law Quarterly* 14 (June 1972), 334–52.

Appendix

TABLE OF CASES

REFERENCE IS MADE to chapters and footnotes in which the individual cases are cited rather than to pages of the text on which they are discussed.

Frazier v. *Cupp*, 394 U. S. 731 (1969). Ch. 6:100–101.

Frazier v. *United States*, 419 F. 2d 1161 (1969). Ch. 6:137.

Gallegos v. *Colorado*, 370 U. S. 49 (1962). Ch. 2:50; Ch. 5:61, 64–65.

Gallegos v. *Nebraska*, 342 U. S. 55 (1951). Ch. 5:12, 24, 34, 37, 107, 109, 117, and 120.

Gallegos v. *State* (Neb.), 43 N. W. 2d 1 (1950). Ch. 5:27.

Garrity v. *New Jersey*, 385 U. S. 493 (1967). Ch. 6:99.

Gideon v. *Wainwright*, 372 U. S. 335 (1963). Ch. 1:11; Ch. 6:7, 16.

Gilbert v. *California*, 388 U. S. 263 (1967). Ch. 6:71, 106.

Greenwald v. *Wisconsin*, 390 U. S. 519 (1968). Ch. 6:99.

Griffin v. *California*, 380 U. S. 609 (1965). Ch. 6:96.

Guinn v. *United States*, 238 U. S. 347 (1915). Ch. 3:20.

Haley v. *Ohio*, 332 U. S. 596 (1948). Ch. 3:69; Ch. 5:1, 13, 19, 37.

Hamilton v. *Alabama*, 368 U. S. 52 (1961). Ch. 6:16.

Hardy v. *United States*, 186 U. S. 224 (1902). Ch. 2:48.

Harris v. *New York*, 401 U. S. 222 (1971). Ch. 6:103, 129; Ch. 7:6–7, 60; Ch. 8:22.

Harris v. *South Carolina*, 338 U. S. 68 (1949). Ch. 5:13, 17; Ch. 6:91.

Haynes v. *Washington*, 373 U. S. 503 (1963). Ch. 5:61, 66; Ch. 6:6, 14; Ch. 8:12.

Hebert v. *Louisiana*, 272 U. S. 312 (1926). Ch. 3:13.

Hopt v. *Utah Territory*, 110 U. S. 574 (1884). Ch. 2:40, Ch. 8:2.

Hurtado v. *California*, 110 U. S. 516 (1884). Ch. 2:39, Ch. 3:12.

Jackson v. *Denno*, 378 U. S. 368 (1964). Ch. 3:46, Ch. 5:51, Ch. 8:7.

Jenkins v. *Delaware*, 395 U. S. 213 (1969). Ch. 6:82.

Johnson v. *New Jersey*, 384 U. S. 719 (1966). Ch. 6:52.

Katzenbach v. *Morgan*, 384 U. S. 641 (1966). Ch. 6:66, 69, 145.

Kent v. *Porto Rico*, 207 U. S. 113 (1907). Ch. 2:48.

Ker v. *California*, 374 U. S. 23 (1963). Ch. 6:126.

The King v. *Warickshall*, 1 Leach 263–64, 168 Eng. Rep. 234–35 (K. B. 1783). Ch. 2:27.

Kunz v. *New York*, 340 U. S. 290 (1951). Ch. 2:59.

Lang v. *State* (Wis.), 189 N. W. 558 (1922). Ch. 3:24.

Nardone v. *United States,* 308 U. S. 338 (1939). Ch. 4:4.

North Carolina v. *Alford,* 400 U. S. 25 (1970). Ch. 6:120–21, Ch. 8:15.

Norris v. *Alabama,* 294 U. S. 587 (1935). Ch. 2:58, Ch. 3:66.

Olmstead v. *United States,* 277 U. S. 438 (1928). Ch. 2:57.

Orozco v. *Texas,* 394 U. S. 324 (1969). Ch. 2:16, 33; Ch. 4:69; Ch. 6:80–81; Ch. 7:46.

Palko v. *Connecticut,* 302 U. S. 319 (1937). Ch. 3:56.

Parker v. *North Carolina,* 397 U. S. 790 (1970). Ch. 6:113, 117, 121, 123; Ch. 7:72; Ch. 8:24.

Patterson v. *Alabama,* 294 U. S. 600 (1935). Ch. 2:58.

Payne v. *Arkansas,* 356 U. S. 560 (1958). Ch. 5:49, 57; Ch. 6:91; Ch. 8:8.

Pennsylvania v. *Ware,* 284 A. 2d 700 (1971). Ch. 8:23.

People v. *Berardi* (Ill.), 151 N. E. 555 (1926). Ch. 3:24.

People v. *Cooper, et al* (N. Y.), 104 N. E. 2d 917 (1952). Ch. 5:42.

People v. *Dorn* (N. Y.), 159 A. 379 (1927). Ch. 3:24.

People v. *Lipsczinska* (Mich.), 180 N. W. 617 (1920). Ch. 3:24.

People v. *Lisenba* (Calif.), 89 P. 2d 39 (1939). Ch. 3:75–76.

People v. *Lisenba* (Calif.), 94 P. 2d 569 (1939). Ch. 3:76.

People v. *Stroble* (Calif.), 226 P. 2d 330 (1951). Ch. 5:33.

People v. *Weiner* (N. Y.), 161 N. E. 441 (1928). Ch. 3:24.

Pierce v. *United States,* 160 U. S. 355 (1896). Ch. 2:41, Ch. 8:2.

Pierre v. *Louisiana,* 306 U. S. 354 (1939). Ch. 3:66.

Powell v. *Alabama,* 287 U. S. 45 (1932). Ch. 1:3; Ch. 2:58; Ch. 3:43; Ch. 6:124.

Powers v. *United States,* 223 U. S. 303 (1912). Ch. 2:48.

Quicksall v. *Michigan,* 339 U. S. 660 (1950). Ch. 6:143.

Reck v. *Pate,* 367 U. S. 433 (1961). Ch. 3:4, Ch. 5:61, Ch. 6:4, Ch. 8:8.

Reece v. *Georgia,* 350 U. S. 85 (1955). Ch. 5:54.

Rochin v. *California,* 342 U. S. 165 (1952). Ch. 6:128.

Rogers v. *Richmond,* 365 U. S. 534 (1961). Ch. 2:18; Ch. 5:49, 61–62.

Rollins v. *State* (Ala.), 92 So. 35 (1922). Ch. 3:26.

Rowe v. *State* (Fla.), 123 So. 523 (1929). Ch. 3:26.

United States v. *White*, 401 U. S. 745 (1971). Ch. 8:1.

Vernon v. *Alabama*, 313 U. S. 547 (1941). Ch. 3:19, 71.

Walder v. *United States*, 347 U. S. 62 (1954). Ch. 6:132.

Waley v. *Johnston*, 316 U. S. 101 (1942). Ch. 2:56.

Ward v. *Texas*, 316 U. S. 547 (1942). Ch. 2:12; Ch. 3:19, 72–73; Ch. 8:6.

Watts v. *Indiana*, 338 U. S. 49 (1949). Ch. 5:1, 13–14, 17, 20, 24.

Weeks v. *United States*, 232 U. S. 383 (1914). Ch. 1:1, Ch. 2:57, Ch. 4:9, Ch. 6:126.

Whip v. *State* (Miss.), 109 So. 697 (1926). Ch. 3:26.

White v. *Maryland*, 373 U. S. 59 (1963). Ch. 6:16.

White v. *Texas*, 309 U. S. 631 (1940). Ch. 3:19, 71.

White v. *Texas*, 310 U. S. 530 (1940). Ch. 3:71.

Williams v. *Florida*, 399 U. S. 78 (1970). Ch. 6:125.

Williams v. *State* (Tex.), 225 S. W. 177 (1920). Ch. 3:26.

Williams v. *United States*, 341 U. S. 97 (1951). Ch. 2:4.

Wilson v. *United States*, 162 U. S. 613 (1896). Ch. 2:41–42, Ch. 8:2.

Wong Sun v. *United States*, 371 U. S. 471 (1963). Ch. 2:11.

Ziang Sung Wan v. *United States*, 266 U. S. 1 (1924). Ch. 2:28, 55; Ch. 4:3; Ch. 8:4.

Selected *Bibliography*

MOST OF THE PRIMARY SOURCE MATERIAL for this book is drawn
from the United States Supreme Court Reports and is cited in the
appendix. The following bibliography is restricted to the additional records and documents, as well as books, articles, and other
secondary materials deemed most important to the completion
of this study.

OFFICIAL RECORDS AND REPORTS

The Challenge of Crime in a Free Society. A Report by the President's Commission on Law Enforcement and Administration
of Justice, 1967.

Congressional Record. Vols. 103–108, 112, 114.

*The Criminal Law Revision Committee, Eleventh Report, Ev-
idence (General)*. London: Her Majesty's Stationery Office,
1972.

F. B. I. Uniform Crime Reports. Washington, D. C.: United
States Government Printing Office, 1969.

The Judges' Rules and Administrative Directions to the Police.
Home Office Circular No. 31 (1964). [Reprinted in *Criminal
Law Review* (Mar. 1964).]

National Commission on Law Observance and Enforcement. *Report on Lawlessness in Law Enforcement*. Washington, D. C.:
United States Government Printing Office, 1931.

————. *Report on Police*. Washington, D. C.: United States
Government Printing Office, 1931.

United States Commission on Civil Rights. Bk. Five. *Justice*.
Washington, D. C.: United States Government Printing Office, 1961.

U. S., Congress, House, *Admission of Evidence in Certain Cases.* Hearings before Subcommittee Number 2 of the Committee on the Judiciary, 78 Cong., 1 sess., Nov. 24–Dec. 10, 1943.

———, *Supreme Court Decisions.* Hearings before the Special Subcommittee to Study Decisions of the Supreme Court of the United States of the Committee on the Judiciary, 85 Cong., 2 sess., 1958.

———, Senate, *Admission of Evidence (Mallory Rule).* Hearings before a Subcommittee of the Committee on the Judiciary, 85 Cong., 2 sess., 1958.

———, *Controlling Crime Through More Effective Law Enforcement.* Hearings before the Subcommittee on Criminal Laws and Procedures of the Committee on the Judiciary, 90 Cong., 1 sess., 1967.

———, *Nominations of Abe Fortas and Homer Thornberry.* Hearings before the Committee on the Judiciary, 90 Cong., 2 sess., July 11–23, Sept. 13–16, 1968.

———, *Report 1097*, 90 Cong., 2 sess., 1968.

Books

Abernathy, M. Glenn. *Civil Liberties Under the Constitution.* 2d ed. New York: Dodd, 1972.

Abraham, Henry J. *Freedom and the Court.* 2d ed. New York: Oxford Univ. Press, 1972.

Backstrom, Charles H., and Gerold D. Hursh. *Survey Research.* Evanston: Northwestern Univ. Press, 1963.

Barth, Alan. *The Price of Liberty.* New York: Viking, 1961.

Beaney, William M. *The Right to Counsel in American Courts.* Ann Arbor: Univ. of Michigan Press, 1955.

Becker, Theodore L., ed. *The Impact of Supreme Court Decisions.* New York: Oxford Univ. Press, 1969.

Beisel, Albert R., Jr. *Control Over Illegal Enforcement of the Criminal Law: Role of the Supreme Court.* Gaspar P. Bacon Lectures on the Constitution of the United States. Boston: Boston Univ. Press, 1955.

Bickel, Alexander M. *The Supreme Court and the Idea of Progress.* New York: Harper, 1970.

Blumberg, Abraham S. *Criminal Justice.* Chicago: Quadrangle Books, 1967.

Borchard, Edwin M. *Convicting the Innocent.* New Haven: Yale Univ. Press, 1932.

Breckenridge, Adam Carlyle. *Congress Against the Court.* Lincoln: Univ. of Nebraska Press, 1970.

Carter, Dan T. *Scottsboro, A Tragedy of the American South.* Baton Rouge: Louisiana State Univ. Press, 1969.

Cleary, Edward W. *McCormick's Handbook of the Law of Evidence.* 2d ed. St. Paul: West Publishing Company, 1972.

Cook, Joseph G. *Constitutional Rights of the Accused—Pretrial Rights.* Rochester, N. Y.: Lawyers Cooperative Publishing Company, 1972.

Cortner, Richard C., and Clifford M. Lytle. *Modern Constitutional Law.* New York: The Free Press, 1971.

Cray, Ed. *Big Blue Line: Police Power vs. Human Rights.* New York: Coward-McCann, 1967.

Crime and Justice in America. 2d ed. Washington, D. C.: Congressional Quarterly Service, Dec. 1968.

Devlin, Patrick. *The Criminal Prosecution in England.* New Haven: Yale Univ. Press, 1958.

Easton, David. *A Systems Analysis of Political Life.* New York: Wiley, 1965.

Fellman, David. *The Defendant's Rights.* New York: Rinehart, 1958.

Fenton, John H. *Politics in the Border States.* New Orleans: Hauser Press, 1957.

Frank, Jerome, and Barbara Frank. *Not Guilty.* Garden City, N. Y.: Doubleday, 1957.

Frank, John P. *Mr. Justice Black—The Man and His Opinions.* New York: Knopf, 1949.

Frankfurter, Felix. *The Case of Sacco and Vanzetti: A Critical Analysis for Lawyers and Laymen.* Boston: Little, 1927; Universal Library Ed., 1962.

George, B. James, ed. *A New Look at Confessions: Escobedo—the Second Round.* Ann Arbor: Institute of Continuing Legal Education, 1967.

Graham, Fred P. *The Self-Inflicted Wound.* New York: Macmillan, 1970.

Hopkins, Ernest J. *Our Lawless Police.* New York: Viking, 1931.

Howard, J. Woodford, Jr. *Mr. Justice Murphy: A Political Biography.* Princeton: Univ. Press, 1968.

Karlen, Delmar *et al. Anglo-American Criminal Justice.* New York: Oxford Univ. Press, 1967.

Krislov, Samuel. *The Supreme Court in the Political Process.* New York: Macmillan, 1965.

Kurland, Philip B. *Politics, the Constitution, and the Warren Court.* Chicago: Univ. of Chicago Press, 1970.

Landynski, Jacob W. *Search and Seizure and the Supreme Court: A Study in Constitutional Interpretation.* Baltimore: Johns Hopkins, 1966.

Lavine, Emanuel H. *The "Third Degree," A Detailed and Appalling Exposé of Police Brutality.* New York: Vanguard Press, 1930.

Levy, Leonard. *Origins of the Fifth Amendment.* New York: Oxford Univ. Press, 1968.

Lewis, Anthony. *Gideon's Trumpet.* New York: Random, 1964.

Lytle, Clifford M. *The Warren Court and Its Critics.* Tucson: Univ. of Arizona Press, 1968.

McCormick, Charles T. *Handbook of the Law of Evidence.* 1st ed. St. Paul: West Publishing Company, 1954.

Mayers, Lewis. *The American Legal System.* 2d ed. New York: Harper, 1964.

Medalie, Richard. *From Escobedo to Miranda: The Anatomy of a Supreme Court Decision.* Washington, D. C.: Lerner Law Book Company, 1966.

Mendelson, Wallace. *Justices Black and Frankfurter: Conflict in the Court.* 2d ed. Chicago: Univ. of Chicago Press, 1966.

Milner, Neal A. *The Court and Local Law Enforcement: The Impact of Miranda.* Beverly Hills: Sage Publication, 1971.

Murphy, Walter F. *Wiretapping on Trial: A Case Study in the Judicial Process*. New York: Random, 1965.

Nagel, Stuart S. *The Legal Process from a Behavioral Perspective*. Homewood, Ill.: Dorsey Press, 1969.

Newman, Donald J. *Conviction: The Determination of Guilt or Innocence Without Trial*. Boston: Little, 1966.

Ovington, Mary White. *The Walls Came Tumbling Down*. New York: Henry Holt, 1948.

Pound, Roscoe. *Criminal Justice in America*. New York: Henry Holt, 1930.

Pritchett, C. Herman. *Congress versus the Supreme Court, 1957–1960*. Minneapolis: Univ. of Minnesota Press, 1961.

————. *The Roosevelt Court*. New York: Macmillan, 1948.

Radzinowicz, Leon. *A History of English Criminal Law*. New York: Macmillan, 1948.

Schaefer, Walter V. *The Suspect and Society: Criminal Procedure and Converging Constitutional Doctrines*. 1966 Rosenthal Lectures, Northwestern Univ. School of Law. Evanston: Northwestern Univ. Press, 1967.

Selltiz, Claire *et al. Research Methods in Social Relations*. Rev. ed. New York: Holt, 1959.

Silverstein, Lee. *Defense of the Poor in Criminal Cases in State Courts*. Chicago: American Bar Foundation, 1965.

Skolnick, Jerome H. *Justice Without Trial: Law Enforcement in Democratic Society*. New York: Wiley, 1966.

Sobel, Nathan R. *The New Confession Standards: Miranda v. Arizona, a Legal Perspective, a Practical Perspective*. New York: Gould Publications, 1966.

Spicer, George W. *The Supreme Court and Fundamental Freedoms*. 2d ed. New York: Appleton, 1967.

Swisher, Carl Brent. *The Supreme Court in Modern Role*. 2d ed. New York: New York Univ. Press, 1965.

Thomas, Helen Shirley. *Felix Frankfurter: Scholar on the Bench*. Baltimore: Johns Hopkins, 1960.

Vose, Clement E. *Caucasians Only*. Berkeley: Univ. of California Press, 1959.

Wasby, Stephen L. *The Impact of the United States Supreme Court—Some Perspectives.* Homewood, Ill.: Dorsey Press, 1970.

————. *Political Science: The Discipline and Its Dimensions.* New York: Scribners, 1970.

Way, H. Frank, Jr. *Liberty in the Balance: Current Issues in Civil Liberties.* New York: McGraw Hill, 1964.

Wigmore, John H. A *Treatise on the Anglo-American System of Evidence in Trials at Common Law.* 3d ed. Vols. 3 and 7. Boston: Little, 1940.

Wilson, James Q. *Varieties of Police Behavior; the Management of Law and Order in Eight Communities.* Cambridge, Mass.: Harvard Univ. Press, 1968.

Ziegler, Benjamin M. *Desegregation and the Supreme Court.* New York: Heath, 1953.

ARTICLES

Bader, Samuel. "Coerced Confessions and the Due Process Clause," *Brooklyn Law Review* 15 (Dec. 1948), 51–71.

Barth, Thomas. "Perceptions and Acceptance of Supreme Court Decisions at the State and Local Level," *Journal of Public Law* 17, no. 2 (1968), 308–50.

Boskey, Bennett, and John H. Pickering. "Federal Restrictions on State Criminal Procedure," *University of Chicago Law Review* 13 (Apr. 1946), 266–99.

Burt, Robert A. "*Miranda* and Title II: A Morganatic Marriage." In Philip B. Kurland, ed., *Supreme Court Review* (1969), 81–134.

Cohn, Edmond L. "Federal Constitutional Limitations on the Use of Coerced Confessions in the State Courts," *Journal of Criminal Law, Criminology and Police Science* 50 (Sept.–Oct. 1959), 265–73.

Cook, Joseph G. "Probable Cause to Arrest," *Vanderbilt Law Review* 24 (Mar. 1971), 317–39.

————. "Subjective Attitudes of Arrestee and Arrestor as Affecting Occurrence of Arrest," *Kansas Law Review* 19 (Winter 1971), 173–83.

Dershowitz, Alan M., and John Hart Ely. Comment, *"Harris v. New York*: Some Anxious Observations on the Candor and Logic of the Emerging Nixon Majority," *Yale Law Journal* 80 (May 1971), 1198–1227.

Donnelly, Richard C. "Police Authority and Practices," *Annals of the Academy of Political and Social Science* 339 (Jan. 1962), 90–110.

Elsen, Sheldon H., and Arthur Rosett. "Protections for the Suspect under *Miranda v. Arizona*," *Columbia Law Review* 67 (Apr. 1967), 645–70.

Enker, Arnold N., and Sheldon H. Elsen. "Counsel for the Suspect: *Massiah v. United States* and *Escobedo v. Illinois*," *Minnesota Law Review* 49 (1964), 47–91.

Graham, Fred P. "Congress Still Battling the Court," *New York Times*, May 26, 1968, E–15.

Green, John Raeburn. "The Bill of Rights, the Fourteenth Amendment and the Supreme Court," *Michigan Law Review* 46 (May 1948), 869–910.

Griffith, John, and Richard E. Ayres. "A Post-script to the *Miranda* Project: Interrogation of Draft Protesters," *Yale Law Journal* 77 (Dec. 1967), 300–19.

Hall, Jerome. "Police and Law in a Democratic Society," *Indiana Law Journal* 28 (Winter 1953), 133–77.

Harno, Albert J. "Proposed Rules of Criminal Procedure: Final Draft," *Michigan Law Review* 42 (Feb. 1944), 623–30.

Herman, Lawrence. "The Supreme Court and Restrictions on Police Interrogation," *Ohio State Law Journal* 25 (Fall 1964), 449–500.

Hogan, James E., and Joseph M. Snee. "The *McNabb-Mallory* Rule: Its Rise, Rationale and Rescue," *Georgetown Law Journal* 47 (Fall 1958), 1–46.

Hoover, J. Edgar. "Civil Liberties and Law Enforcement: The Role of the F. B. I.," *Iowa Law Review* 37 (Winter 1951), 175–95.

Inbau, Fred E. "The Confession Dilemma in the United States Supreme Court," *Illinois Law Review* 43 (Sept.–Oct. 1948), 442–63.

———. "Law Enforcement, the Courts, and Individual Liberties." In *Criminal Justice in Our Time*, ed. by A. E. Howard. Charlottesville: Univ. of Virginia Press, 1965.

———. "Police Interrogation: A Practical Necessity." In *Police Power and Individual Freedom: The Quest for Balance*, ed. by Claude R. Sowle. Chicago: Aldine Publishing Company, 1962.

"Interrogations in New Haven: The Impact of *Miranda*," *Yale Law Journal* 76 (July 1967), 1521–1648.

"Interrogations of Criminal Defendants—Some Views on *Miranda* v. *Arizona*," *Fordham Law Review* 35 (Dec. 1966), 169–262.

Kamisar, Yale. "Equal Justice in the Gatehouses and Mansions of American Criminal Procedure." In *Criminal Justice in Our Time*, ed. by A. E. Howard. Charlottesville: Univ. of Virginia Press, 1965.

Keedy, Edwin R. "The Third Degree and Legal Interrogation of Suspects," *University of Pennsylvania Law Review* 85 (June 1937), 761–77.

King, Donald B. "Developing a Future Constitutional Standard for Confessions," *Wayne Law Review* 8 (Summer 1962), 481–96.

Leiken, Lawrence S. "Police Interrogation in Colorado: The Implementation of *Miranda*," *Denver Law Journal* 47, no. 1 (1970), 1–53.

Levine, James P. "Methodological Concerns in Studying Supreme Court Efficacy," *Law and Society Review* 4 (1970), 583–611.

Lowell, A. Lawrence. "The Judicial Use of Torture," *Harvard Law Review* 11 (Nov. and Dec. 1897), 220–31.

McCormick, Charles T. "Some Problems and Developments in the Admissibility of Confessions," *Texas Law Review* 24 (Apr. 1946), 239–78.

———. "The Scope of Privilege in the Law of Evidence," *Texas Law Review* 16 (June 1938), 447–70.

Medalie, Richard J., Leonard Zeitz, and Paul Alexander. "Custodial Police Interrogation in Our Nation's Capital: The Attempt to Implement *Miranda*," *Michigan Law Review* 66 (May 1968), 1347–1422.

Meltzer, Bernard D. "Involuntary Confessions: The Allocation of Responsibility between Judge and Jury," *University of Chicago Law Review* 21 (Spring 1954), 317–54.

Milner, Neal A. "Comparative Analysis of Patterns of Compliance with Supreme Court Decisions: *Miranda* and the Police in Four Communities," *Law and Society Review* 5 (Aug. 1970), 119–34.

Moesley, Clement Charlton. "The Case of Leo M. Frank, 1913–1915," *Georgia Historical Quarterly* 51 (Mar. 1967), 42–62.

Morgan, E. M. "The Privilege Against Self-Incrimination," *Minnesota Law Review* 34 (Dec. 1949), 1–45.

Oaks, Dallin H. "Studying the Exclusionary Rule in Search and Seizure," *University of Chicago Law Review* 37 (Summer 1970), 665–757.

Orfield, Lester B. "The Federal Rules of Criminal Procedure," *Nebraska Law Review* 26 (May 1947), 570–627.

Paulsen, Monrad G. "The Fourteenth Amendment and the 'Third Degree,' " *Stanford Law Review* 6 (May 1954), 411–37.

Pittman, R. Carter. "The Colonial and Constitutional History of the Privilege Against Self-Incrimination in America." *Virginia Law Review* 21 (May 1935), 763–89.

Reiss, Albert J., Jr., and Donald J. Black. "Interrogation and the Criminal Process," *Annals of the American Academy of Political and Social Science* 374 (Nov. 1967), 47–58.

Ritz, Wilfred J. "Twenty-five Years of State Criminal Confession Cases in the United States Supreme Court," *Washington and Lee Law Review* 19 (Spring 1962), 35–70.

Robinson, Cyril D. "Police and Prosecutor Practices and Attitudes Relating to Interrogation as Revealed by Pre- and Post-*Miranda* Questionnaires: A Construct of Police Capacity to Comply," *Duke Law Journal* (June 1968), 425–524.

Rosett, Arthur. "The Negotiated Guilty Plea," *Annals of the*

American Academy of Political and Social Science 374 (Nov. 1967), 70–82.

Schaefer, R. C. "Patrolman Perspectives on *Miranda*," *Law and the Social Order* (1971), 81–101.

Seeburger, Richard H., and R. Stanton Wettick, Jr. "*Miranda* in Pittsburgh—A Statistical Study," *University of Pittsburgh Law Review* 29 (Oct. 1967), 1–26.

Sheppard, A. F. "Restricting the Discretion to Exclude Admissible Evidence: an Examination of *Regina* v. *Wray*," *Criminal Law Quarterly* 14 (June 1972), 334–52.

Spanogle, J. A. "The Use of Coerced Confessions in State Courts," *Vanderbilt Law Review* 17 (Mar. 1964), 421–61.

Spring, Raymond L. "The Nebulous Nexus: *Escobedo, Miranda* and the New Fifth Amendment," *Washburn Law Journal* 6 (Spring 1967), 428–47.

Stephens, Otis H., Jr. "The Assistance of Counsel and the Warren Court: Post-*Gideon* Developments in Perspective," *Dickinson Law Review* 74 (Winter 1970), 193–217.

———. "The Burger Court: New Dimensions in Criminal Justice," *Georgetown Law Journal* 60 (Nov. 1971), 249–78.

———. "The Fourteenth Amendment and Confessions of Guilt: Role of the Supreme Court," *Mercer Law Review* 15 (Spring 1964), 309–34.

———. "Police Interrogation and the Supreme Court: an Inquiry into the Limits of Judicial Policy-Making," *Journal of Public Law* 17, no. 2 (1968), 241–57.

———, Robert L. Flanders, and J. Lewis Cannon. "Law Enforcement and the Supreme Court: Police Perceptions of the *Miranda* Requirements," *Tennessee Law Review* 39 (Spring 1972), 407–31.

Sterling, David I. "Police Interrogation and the Psychology of Confession," *Journal of Public Law* 14, no. 1 (1965), 25–65.

Sutherland, Arthur E. "Crime and Confession," *Harvard Law Review* 79 (Nov. 1965), 21–41.

Swanson, Warren L., and Roger W. Eichmeier. "The Role of Judge and Jury in Determining a Confession's Voluntariness,"

Journal of Criminal Law, Criminology and Police Science 48 (May–June 1957), 59–65.

Swisher, Carl Brent. "The Supreme Court and 'The Moment of Truth,'" *American Political Science Review* 54 (Dec. 1960), 879–86.

Tigar, Michael E. "Waiver of Constitutional Rights: Disquiet in the Citadel," foreword to "The Supreme Court, 1969 Term," *Harvard Law Review* 84 (Nov. 1970), 1–29.

Waite, John Barker. "Police Regulation by Rules of Evidence," *Michigan Law Review* 42 (Feb. 1944), 679–93.

Way, H. Frank, Jr. "The Supreme Court and State Coerced Confessions," *Journal of Public Law* 12, no. 1 (1963), 53–67.

Wicker, William. "Some Developments in the Law Concerning Confessions," *Vanderbilt Law Review* 5 (Apr. 1952), 507–22.

Wickersham, Cornelius W., Jr. "The Supreme Court and Federal Criminal Procedure," *Cornell Law Quarterly* 44 (Fall 1958), 14–31.

Younger, Evelle J. "Results of a Survey Conducted in the District Attorney's Office of Los Angeles County Regarding the Effect of the *Miranda* Decision upon the Prosecution of Felony Cases," *American Criminal Law Quarterly* 5 (Fall 1966), 32–39.

COMMENTS AND NOTES IN LEGAL PERIODICALS

"Case and Comment," *Criminal Law Review* (Jan. 1972), 31–34.

Comment, "The Decade of Change Since the Ashcraft Case," *Texas Law Review* 32 (Apr. 1954), 429–40.

"Comment," *Iowa Law Review* 30 (Nov. 1944), 102–107.

"Comment," *Journal of Criminal Law and Criminology* 38 (July–Aug. 1947), 136–38.

"Comment," *Yale Law Journal* 73 (May 1964), 1000–57.

"Note," *American Journal of Police Science* 36 (Sept.–Oct. 1945), 222–26.

"Note," *Boston University Law Review* 29 (Apr. 1949), 250–53.

"Note," *Cornell Law Quarterly* 32 (June 1947), 594–600.

"Note," *Dickinson Law Review* 53 (Mar. 1949), 206–209.

Note, "Effect of *Mapp* v. *Ohio* on Police Search and Seizure Practices in Narcotics Cases," *Columbia Journal of Law and Social Problems* 4 (Mar. 1968), 87–104.

"Note," *Kentucky Law Journal* 43 (Spring 1955), 392–407.

"Note," *North Carolina Law Review* 27 (June 1949), 552–58.

"Note," *Utah Law Review* 1 (1949), 82–89.

"Note," *Wisconsin Law Review* (Jan. 1945), 105–11.

Notes, "Coerced Confessions," *Virginia Law Review* 8 (May 1922), 527–30.

Notes, "Third Degree," *Harvard Law Review* 43 (Feb. 1930), 617–23.

Report of Committee on Lawless Enforcement of Law. Section of Criminal Law and Criminology of the American Bar Association. *American Journal of Police Science* 1 (1930), 575, 593.

Index

due process (*cont.*)
confessions cases; Due Process Clause, of Fourteenth Amendment

Eastland bill. *See* United States Congress, Eastland bill
educational role, of Supreme Court, 15–16, 161, 184, 200, 208
Eighteenth Amendment, 39
Eighth Amendment, 121
empirical studies: and education and professionalization of police, 175–76, 178; of impact of *Miranda v. Arizona*, 8, 164, 165–68, 169–79. *See also* Knoxville-Macon study
England: Act of 1848, 21; criminal confessions in medieval period, 18; use of torture in, 18–19. *See also* English common law; Judges' Rules, of England
English common law: evidentiary rules originating in, 14; Roman law influence minimized by, 18–19; unreliable evidence from confessions in, 17–24, 26, 27, 28, 29. *See also* involuntary confessions rule
Equal Protection Clause, of Fourteenth Amendment, 33
Ervin, Sam J., Jr., 86, 88, 140–41, 144
Europe, criminal confessions in medieval period, 18
exclusionary rule: comparison of with Judges' Rules, 21–23, 133–34; limitations of, 157–58, 199–200, 208; *Miranda v. Arizona*, 129–39, 203–204. *See also* McNabb-Mallory Rule; Weeks Exclusionary Rule

fact, finding of, 14; in *Chambers v. Florida*, 53–54; and congressional reaction to *Miranda v. Arizona*, 142–43; in *Lisenba v. California*, 60; in *Lyons v. Oklahoma*, 95
"fair trial" standard, 4, 26–28, 31–36, 92–93, 102, 202–203; and *Brown v. Mississippi*, 31, 42–50; and *Chambers v. Florida* and related cases, 50–56; and ending of exclusive reliance on, 62; and extra-legal factors, 36–42; and Justice Frankfurter, 62; and *Lisenba v. California*, 56–61; and *Lyons v. Oklahoma*, 93–97; and *Stein v. New York*, 108–12

Federal Bureau of Investigation, 67, 133, 171, 187–88n, 199
federal cases: and concept of due process, 27–28, 31, 63–64; and involuntary confessions rule, 23–24; merging of, with state standards, 7–8; and Self-incrimination Clause, of Fifth Amendment, 24–25, 31. *See also* Due Process Clause, of Fifth Amendment; McNabb-Mallory Rule
federalism: and autonomy of state courts, 65, 92, 101, 106–107, 108–12, 118–19; and deference to state court finding of fact, 60; and *Miranda v. Arizona*, 129
Federal Kidnapping Act, 154
Federal Rules of Criminal Procedure, Rule 5 (a) of, 72, 75, 77, 79, 80, 82, 84, 86
"field interrogation," 85, 177–78
Fifth Amendment, 148. *See also* Due Process Clause of; Self-incrimination Clause of
First Amendment, 101. *See also* freedom of expression
Act of 1965
Fortas, Abe: appointment of, 130n; and *Miranda v. Arizona*, 140; opposition to nomination of for chief justiceship and resignation of, 153, 205–206
Fourteenth Amendment, 23, 128. *See also* Due Process Clause of; Equal Protection Clause of; Voting Rights
Fourth Amendment, 157. *See also* search and seizure, unreasonable; "probable cause," requirement of
France, use of torture in, 18–19
Frankfurter, Felix: dissents of, 92, 107, 112; and due process, 62, 98–99, 101–102, 117n, 123, 163; and federal confessions, 63, 64–67, 70, 73–74, 79, 85, 92; and Fourth Amendment, 160–61, 163; Frankfurter-Douglas-Black "block," 101; and self-incrimination, 117–18; and trustworthiness, 117–18
freedom of expression, 29–30, 121–22
free legal assistance, 171–72
Fuller, Melville, majority opinion by in *Wilson v. U.S.*, 24

Gasch, Oliver, 83
George, B. James, 12n
Georgetown University Law Center,

THE UNIVERSITY OF TENNESSEE PRESS
Knoxville, Tennessee

DATE DUE